CRICKET-A WAY OF LIFE

£2~50

G

0317

CRICKET-A WAY OF LIFE

CRICKET-A WAY OF LIFE

The Cricketer Illustrated History of Cricket

Christopher Martin-Jenkins

Photographs by Adrian Murrell

C

Century Publishing, London

The Cricketer

Founded by Sir Pelham Warner in 1921, *The Cricketer* is not only the oldest but also the largest selling cricket magazine in the world. Its popularity rests on its reputation for a fair, interesting and authoritative coverage of events in world cricket, and its interest in the game at all its levels including schools, clubs and villages. An estimated 200,000 people round the world read *The Cricketer* every month.

First published in Great Britain by
Century Publishing Co Ltd
Portland House, 12–13 Greek Street, London W1V 5LE

Copyright © in text Christopher Martin-Jenkins 1984

Martin-Jenkins, Christopher
Cricket–a way of life
1. Cricket–History
I. Title
796.35'8'09 GV913

ISBN 0 7126 0939 3

Made by Lennard Books
Mackerye End
Harpenden, Herts AL5 5DR

Editor Michael Leitch
Designed by David Pocknell's Co Ltd
Production Reynolds Clark Associates Ltd
Printed and bound in Spain by TONSA, San Sebastian

Jacket photographs
Front
Top left Alfred Mynn, the Lion of Kent.
Top centre Ian Botham shakes hands with Sir Gary Sobers after taking his wicket in a charity match at The Oval, 1982.
Top right Ground assistant at Calcutta
Bottom A collection of cricket gear from the turn of the century –including the bag, gloves, boots and cap of J.R. Mason (Kent and England) with which he toured Australia in 1897–98. The bat belonged to W.G. Grace and was presented by him to Lord Sheffield during the 1891–92 tour of Australia after W.G. had scored a century with it against Victoria. The I Zingari blazer belonged to Lord Dalmeny who played for Surrey, and the slatted pads are typical of those worn by many players at that time.

Back Worldwide enthusiasm for a great game.

CONTENTS

THE EARLY YEARS TO 1895

Cricket did not begin at Hambledon, but it was through Hambledon in Hampshire that the game became elevated and celebrated. Never, indeed, has cricket been better celebrated than in the vibrant reminiscences of John Nyren, son of Richard, the landlord of the Bat and Ball Inn on Broad-Halfpenny Down, the first of Hambledon's two grounds.

It is a bleak stretch of Hampshire heath, sheltered to some extent by bare-topped downs and an undulating sweep of ancient beech trees, with the blue hills of the Isle of Wight away in the distance. From 1782, on the advice of one of the great aristocratic patrons, the Duke of Dorset, who thought the old ground too bleak, the club pitched wickets instead on Windmill Down, slightly less exposed to the elements and nearer the village.

The Bat and Ball Inn at Broad-Halfpenny Down. This watercolour by G.F. Gale was painted in 1978, though little had changed since Richard Nyren was landlord in the club's halcyon days in the 1770s and '90s. His son John remembered that the inn was the scene not just of cricket talk but also of 'fine music and witty conversation'.

That this otherwise unexceptional village should have become prominent in cricket between about 1760 and 1785, and the undisputed centre of the game throughout the 1770s, is one of the more delightful accidents of English social history. It happened that there were many good cricketers in the area, a few keen patrons, and in Richard Nyren a man with a passion for cricket and an administrative flair which enabled him to draw players together to form elevens capable of taking on and beating the best team that 'All England' could muster. Indeed at Moulsey Hurst in 1772 Hambledon beat not XI but XXII of England; and again at Sevenoaks Vine five years later they thrashed what may justly be called a representative England side by an innings and 168 runs, James Aylward batting from five o'clock on Wednesday afternoon until after three on Friday for 167, defying all this time the formidably accurate bowling of

'Lumpy' Stevens, until finally bowled by the fast underarm bowler William Bullen.

Aylward, a left-handed opening batsman renowned for his sterling defensive qualities, was soon afterwards lured away from Hambledon by another of the game's great patrons, Sir Horace Mann, who employed him as his bailiff, and, of course, as a cricketer. Nyren recalls how Mann called Aylward to the side of the ground during one match and, in effect, signed him on during a short, business-like conversation. So close did patron and professional become in later years that, according to Fred Lillywhite, Aylward named his son Horace and the great man became his godfather. (Nyren relates that another Hambledon player, Noah Mann, also called his son Horace, though he was no relation of Sir Horace, so Lillywhite may have muddled the story.)

The 'signing' of Aylward is one of many extraordinarily vivid scenes depicted by John Nyren and also by another of the great Hambledon names, William Beldham, the silver-haired Billy who lived to the age of ninety and recalled many of the club's great players in an interview with the Rev. James Pycroft which reinforced the character and romance of Hambledon cricket. Here was a village, miles from anywhere of importance, attracting huge crowds for its great occasions. Nyren's description makes it possible to see and hear them still:

'Oh! it was a heart-stirring sight to witness the multitude forming a complete and dense circle round that noble green. Half the county would be present, and all their hearts are with us – Little Hambledon, pitted against All England was a proud thought for the Hampshire men. How those fine, brawn-faced fellows of farmers drink to our success! ... There would this company, consisting most likely of some thousands, remain patiently and anxiously watching every turn of fate in the game, as if the event had been the meeting of two armies to decide their liberty.'

One can imagine the roar, both rustic and aristocratic, for all sorts were drawn to the great contests, when a Hambledon batsman succeeded in clubbing the ball away through the ring of opposing fielders. Though there was certainly a rosy tint to Nyren's memoirs, one cannot doubt that the Hambledon matches were played in the manful, chivalrous tradition in which all had learned the game.

Amongst the stalwarts of the famed 'old' team were Richard Nyren himself, the cunning left-arm bowler and the club's 'head and right arm', a good 'face-to-face', unflinching, uncompromising, independent man and a hard-hitting batsman whose skill had been handed down to him by his celebrated uncle, Richard Newland of Slindon in Sussex. His partner was Thomas Brett, the first of Hambledon's fast bowlers, who believed in bowling as fast and as straight as he was able; then came the reliable change-bowlers, Barber and Hogsflesh; the well-made and talented John Small, speedy as a hare, who loved to steal short singles and who would entertain the teams afterwards by playing on the violin given to him by the Duke of Dorset; the fearless wicket-keeper and bold front-foot batsman Tom Sueter, and his colleague George Lear, a specialist long-stop in the days when wicket-keepers had little or no equipment.

Players from further afield joined as the club's reputation grew. Noah Mann came from North Chapel, near Petworth, a nimble little man, fine horseman and dextrous fieldsman, who once hit a ball so hard down the slope on Windmill Down that he and John Nyren ran ten; from Thursley in Surrey came the rustic Walker brothers, notably Tom with his rigid limbs and skin like the rind of an old oak, so cool a stonewaller that he drove the best of the aristocratic cricketers, Lord Frederick Beauclerk, to distracted fury; and a cunning bowler, who having been banned from bowling roundarm ahead of his time by a Committee of Hambledon Cricketers, instead became the first really to flight the ball. From Farnham came honest John Wells and the Beldham brothers, George and the brilliant batsman William; and from Odiham the potter David Harris, who bowled fast, lifting deliveries with a vigorous underarm action: 'His balls were very little beholden to the ground when pitched; it was but a touch and up again; and woe be to the man who did not get in to block them, for they had such a peculiar curl, that they would grind his fingers against the bat.'

We have William Beldham's word for the fact that these men would have taken the field in velvet caps, silk shirts, many of them frilled, knee-breeches, stockings and buckled shoes. Off the field they wore over their shirts their famous distinguishing badge: sky-blue coats with black velvet collars and buttons with 'CC' engraved on them. Smart, proud, happy men, who, by competition more regular than had been the case while the game was developing into an organized sport during the earlier part of the eighteenth century, did much to advance its technique to a more sophisticated level; to accelerate changes in the laws such as the addition of a third stump, and in equipment, for example the straight-bladed bat to combat airborne bowling, replacing the glorified hockey-stick which had sufficed for a delivery bowled along the ground; and, not least, to enhance its status as the 'glorious, manly game', unique in the demands it makes on the brains and bodies of those who want to play it successfully.

Above *A 1797 scorecard*

Left *'Lumpy' Stevens, a deadly fast bowler of shooters, who is said to have been responsible for the addition of the third stump.*

It is not in the nature of villages to be for long the centre of great institutions: sooner or later the village becomes a city or the institution itself moves to the city. In the case of cricket, Hambledon, though forever ennobled by its twenty-five years or so of prominence in the game, reverted to its former rural anonymity while the wealthy men without which 'great', as opposed to merely recreational, matches could not be played, found it more convenient to play their matches in London.

One such patron was the Earl of Winchilsea, who had learned his cricket at Eton, or so one assumes, and had taken a keen interest in Hambledon matches without actually playing in them. It remains a mystery why his first appearance in a recorded 'great match' was at the age of thirty-two in 1785, when he appeared as opening batsman for the White Conduit

The future Marylebone Cricket Club playing in Marylebone Fields (now Regent's Park) in the middle of the eighteenth century.

Club against Gentlemen of Kent in White Conduit Fields at Islington. It seems likely that the records of whatever team he had played for before the formation of the White Conduit Club, were either lost or never made. But it may have been that in the prime of his youth the Earl felt that wider duties came before cricket, for he had formed his own regiment at a cost of £20,000 to fight for King George III and country in what became known as the War of American Independence. At any rate it was Winchilsea who effectively formed the Marylebone Cricket Club in conjunction with his great friend, the adventurous Hon. Col. Charles Lennox, who was a fine all-round sportsman, fought a duel with the Duke of York on Wimbledon Common (both survived to play cricket against each other a year later), succeeded to the title of Duke of Richmond in 1806 and died of rabies when Governor General of Canada. Such was his love of cricket that he organized matches for the troops in

Brussels shortly before the Battle of Waterloo and later in Canada on the Heights of Abraham.

Lennox and Winchilsea were members of a select little band of brothers from London high society who used to meet at the Star and Garter in Pall Mall. Their club was called the 'Je ne sais quoi' and the cricketing enthusiasts amongst them began after 1780 to organize games near White Conduit House. They were not all happy, however, with the venue and Lennox and Winchilsea, looking for an alternative, approached an enterprising and engaging entrepreneur named Thomas Lord, whose father, a well-established Yorkshire yeoman, had been forced to migrate to Norfolk for espousing too honestly the cause of the Catholic Stuarts. Thomas Lord was therefore bred to fight back when things did not go his way. He himself had moved from Norfolk to London, where he later established a successful wine business and he eagerly accepted the suggestion that he should seek and open a private cricket ground, especially as the two noblemen guaranteed him against any losses.

Lord's first ground was on the land where Dorset Square now stands. In the first match Middlesex beat Essex by 93 runs and in 1788 MCC, formed the previous year, played its first game at Lord's, defeating the club from which it had emanated, White Conduit, by 83 runs. Lord's did not, of course, assume its present importance overnight. For a time it was just one ground where some important cricket matches were played. But in a remarkably short time the club which grew around it established an authority in the game which at least in one important respect has never been challenged, namely the control of the laws of the game. The club had been in existence only a year when it published a revision of the second known code of laws, which had been resolved by a committee of 'Noblemen and Gentlemen of Kent, Hampshire, Surrey, Sussex, Middlesex and London', meeting at the Star and Garter in 1774.

Though it was almost a hundred years before MCC became fully conscious of its national, even by then global, role, the most famous of all cricket clubs was already established as a 'private club with a public function'. By the turn of the century it was accepted as the leading club, different in character to the egalitarian Hambledon, with all the leading amateur players of the day proud to be members. Only MCC would at this time take the field for a great match without the aid of a few professionals, and a certain social cachet was starting to attach itself to those who were members. By 1800 two further revisions of the laws had been made by MCC committees, and they were accepted by all cricketers as having the ring of true authority. MCC and Lord's were already hallowed names.

The first Lord's in Dorset Fields, Marylebone, where the White Conduit Club played several matches in 1787, the year of MCC's foundation. The second MCC ground was rented by Thomas Lord from the St John's Wood Estate.

Two of the great early 'gentlemen players'. Left: Lord Frederick Beauclerk, in old age an autocrat at Lord's, in his youth the best bowler in the Cambridge XI but later better known as a graceful and prolific batsman. He once forced 'Squire' George Osbaldeston, right, to go ahead with a double-wicket match despite Osbaldeston's illness. The Squire was a brilliant all-round sportsman, whose cricket career came to an abrupt end when he resigned from MCC in 1818 after losing a single-wicket match.

Cricket was played at Thomas Lord's first ground for only twenty-two years. London was growing apace and the whole country, though perhaps it did not know it at the time, was stirring, with an abundance of capital available for investment, its markets increased by improving transport and a native inventiveness which had been stimulated by the needs of the Napoleonic Wars and a shortage of labour in the north of England. The economy, in fact, was buoyant and the value of the land on which MCC played its cricket

Cricket was first played at the present Lord's in 1814. This was the tenth recorded match, excluding single- or double-wicket contests. Modern echoes include the marquee, to be sold or let, foreshadowing the boxes so eagerly sought for business entertainment today; and the 'good stabling on the ground': these days there is all too little room for parking cars. Historians will note that play was due to begin two days after the Battle of Waterloo.

lay in its potential for building. Lord's landlord asked for too high a rent and before his lease ran out, in 1810, Lord had found a second ground, renting two fields on the St John's Wood Estate for an eighty-year term for £54 a year, free of land tax. During the winter of 1810–11, the turf from the old ground was removed to the new. Lord may have felt he had got a good deal, but the MCC members did not. The club played only three matches on the new ground, all in 1813 and all lost, before, providentially perhaps, Parliament decided in the spirit of the time which was moving towards the full Industrial Revolution, to create the Regent Canal on a path cutting straight through Lord's.

Undaunted, Lord secured from the owners of the St John's Wood Estate, the Eyre family, another suitable piece of land, half a mile further north, moving his turf there for the second and last time in the winter of 1813–14.

This is the same Lord's that in 1984 was considered by such a distance the most important ground in England that it was originally planned to stage two Test matches there against Australia the following year rather than one. From the start it may have had a greater feel of permanence about it than the two earlier grounds, because Lord enclosed it almost immediately with a high fence and built a tavern – removed, alas, in the march of progress in the 1960s – and a wooden pavilion in 1814, the year that the first recorded game on the new ground was played. MCC soundly thrashed Hertfordshire by an innings, though the latter were strengthened by the addition of Henry Bentley, a professional employed by MCC, who carried his bat through the first innings for 33 not out, but was run out for nought in the second. Whose fault it was, we shall never know.

One of the MCC side that day was William Ward who, eleven years later, more or less saved the present Lord's ground. Lord himself had received permission from the Eyre family to develop part of the ground for building, limiting the playing area to 150 square yards. Ward, a fine batsman, a director of the Bank of England and later MP for the City of London, bought Lord's interest in the ground for £5,000 in 1825. Lord moved from his home in St John's Wood Road five years later, retiring to Hampshire where he died in 1832, aged seventy-four, though his tombstone at West Meon says seventy-six.

In 1835 Ward in turn sold his lease, for £2,000 plus an annual annuity of £425, to James Dark, once a ground-boy for MCC, who set up home on the ground where the new Tavern Stand is now sited, and watched over its development with suitable devotion. So, too, without doubt, did William Ward, who in 1820 at the age of thirty-three had developed an undying affection for the ground by scoring 278 for MCC against Norfolk, the highest score made there until Percy Holmes of Yorkshire hit the first triple hundred 105 years later.

In 1825, on the evening of the match between Winchester and Harrow, the old pavilion was completely destroyed in a disastrous fire which burnt away all the club's precious possessions, including the score-books. A new pavilion was built the following year and replaced by the present handsome red-stone and wrought-iron structure in 1890, two years after the last threat to the ground had been successfully rebuffed. The Great Central Railway had sponsored a bill in the Commons that they should acquire the ground in order to run a railway through it. But this was in the Victorian High Noon; cricket was the national game, a cornerstone of society, and Lord's, praise be, was inviolate.

The 'Mecca of Cricket', seen on this page at various stages in its development. On the left is the ground in 1851 with the old Real Tennis court on the left of the picture; this was replaced by the Mound Stand.

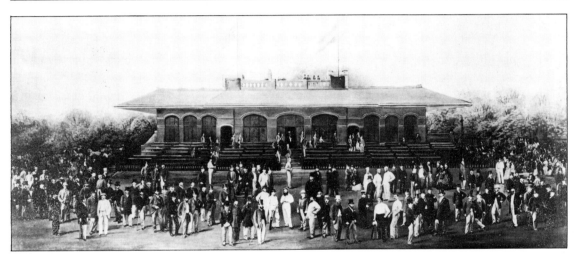

The old pavilion at Lord's, seen in 1874.

The old pavilion in 1889, after its enlargement and before its replacement in 1890.

All the early codes of cricket laws contain a significant clause along the following lines: 'Bets. If the notches of one player are laid against those of another player, the bets depend upon the first innings, unless otherwise specified.'

Gambling and cricket went hand in hand from the very start of the organized game, indeed the spread

THREE GRAND
CRICKET MATCHES,
For 1000 Sovereigns.

The First Match of the Three, between the Players of Sussex and the best of All England, commenced Playing on the New Ground, Darnall, on Whit-Monday Tuesday, and Wednesday, June 4th 5th, & 6th, 1827.

ALL ENGLAND.

	First Innings.			Second Innings.
1 — Flavell	0 bowled by Lillywhite	1	G. E. Dawson	15 bow. by J. Broadbridge
2 — Bowyer	0 hit wicket	2	— Jarvis	17 bowled by do.
3 J. Saunders	0 caught by Slater	3	W. Barber	1 do. by do.
4 W. Barber	1 caught by Dale	4	— Flavell	3 caught by Lillywhite
5 T. Marsden	0 hit wicket	5	F. Pilch	13 caught by Brown
6 G. E. Dawson	13 run out	6	— Jupp	20 caught by Lillywhite
7 F. Pilch	38 bowled by Lillywhite	7	T. Marsden	22 caught by Meads
8 — Matthews	2 ditto by ditto	8	J. Saunders	11 bow. by J. Broadbridge
9 — Beagley	17 ditto by ditto	9	— Beagley	5 not out
10 — Jarvis	9 c. by J. Broadbridge.	10	— Bowyer	0 bow. by J. Broadbridge
11 — Jupp	0 not out	11	— Matthews	1 bow. by Lillywhite
Byes 1 Total 81			Byes 4 Total 112	

SUSSEX

	First Innings.			Second Innings.
1 W. Slater	0 caught by Pilch	1	G. Brown	1 caught by Marsden
2 W. Lillywhite	14 stumped by Saunders	2	G. Meads	21 bowled by Pilch
3 Wm. Broadbridge	14 caught by Pilch	3	T. Pierpoint	23 bowled by Marsden
4 J. Twaites	0 caught by Jarvis	4	J. Twaites	37 not out
5 Jas. Broadbridge	0 stumped by Saunders	5	Jas. Broadbridge	15 not out
6 T. Pierpoint	3 caught by Marsden			
7 G. Brown	2 bowled by Matthews		Byes 6	Total 103
8 J. Dale	31 not out			
9 C. Duff.	0 caught by Marsden		Sussex won with 7 wickets to go down	
10 C. Pierpoint	1 bowled by Flavell			
11 G. Meads	26 bowled by Matthews.			
Total 91				

Umpire for Sussex, Mr. C. ROOTS, of Brighton.—Umpire for All England, Mr. JOSEPH DENNIS, of Nottingham.

NAMES OF THE GENTLEMEN BACKERS:—

H. TAMPLIN, Esq. on the part of Sussex; J. JENNER, Esq. on the part of All England.

☞ Every attention will be paid to render the Returns as correct as possible.

◀ T. ORTON, PRINTER, HIGH-STREET, SHEFFIELD. ▶

Evidence of the high stakes for which some cricket matches were played in the first half of the nineteenth century.

of big matches during the eighteenth century may be said to have depended on gambling for it was for a sporting wager between two noble or wealthy patrons that the original games were played. John Nyren mentions that all the Hambledon matches were played for a stake of £500 a side, a staggering purse when inflation is taken into account, one indeed which

dwarfs modern prize money even in the days of commercial sponsorship.

When Richard Newland of Slindon led three of England against three of Kent on the Artillery Field in London in 1743 before a crowd of 10,000, the purse was again £500. No doubt such a crowd made it a profitable exercise, even so, for the promoters of the match. Twopence a match was the average 'gate' money, but it tended to be raised for the big occasions.

One of the most zealous of the early patrons was the Earl of Sandwich (1718–92) to whom is dedicated James Love's famous epic poem about the Kent versus All England match at the Artillery Ground in 1744. Surrey's great patron was the Earl of Tankerville, one of the founding fathers of MCC, who employed at his estate at Mount Felix, near Walton-on-Thames, two notable players: as gardener, the redoubtable Lumpy Stevens, and as butler the county's leading all-rounder, William Bedster, quite possibly a forefather of Alec and Eric Bedser.

The greatest of what H.S. Altham called the 'feudal lords' of cricket were the Dukes of Dorset, the Sackville family, whose seat was at Knole Park in Sevenoaks. Two sons of the First Duke of Dorset were active sponsors of many of the early 'county' matches and one of them, Lord John Sackville, held a brilliant and crucial catch to dismiss Richard Newland in the Kent v All England match of 1744. His son, the Third Duke, was a good cricketer who employed three notable players of the time, Miller, Minshull and Bowra. The Third Duke's friend and contemporary was the same Sir Horace Mann who spirited away James Aylward from Hambledon to his own famous ground near Canterbury, Bishopsbourne Paddock.

Described as 'agreeable, gay and affable', Sir Horace also employed the Ring brothers, George and John. For some time John was the leading batsman of the Kent side; he died shortly after receiving, smack in the face, a ball bowled by his brother. Mann was well known, for all his affability, to be a gambler, and he was certainly not alone. The Earl of Sandwich's matches at Newmarket in 1751 were played for £1,500 between 'Old Etonians' and 'England' and a contemporary report said that 'near £20,000 is depending' in bets associated with these games.

A judge, summing up a lawsuit over a cricket debt in 1748, remarked: 'Cricket is, to be sure, a manly game and not bad in itself, but it is the ill-use that is made of it, by betting above £10 on it, that is bad and against the laws.' A man parted with his money is seldom very cheerful and it is hardly surprising that big matches were occasionally marked by crowd troubles not unrelated to modern 'hooliganism'.

That least reverent of famous clerics who have

INSTRUCTIONS AND RULES

FOR

PLAYING THE

NOBLE GAME OF CRICKET,

AS PRACTISED BY THE MOST EMINENT PLAYERS,

Containing a variety of directions little known to Players
in general.

ILLUSTRATED BY AN

Elegant Copper=Plate Engraving,

Exhibiting the Players in the Field,

TO WHICH ARE SUBJOINED

THE LAWS OF THE GAME,

WITH ADDITIONS AND CORRECTIONS.

BY WILLIAM LAMBERT.

SUSSEX PRESS, LEWES:

Printed and Published by J. Baxter, and sold in London by
Baldwin & Co Paternoster Row, and all Booksellers.

1816.

Left and far left William Lambert of Reigate and Surrey, a brilliant all-rounder, a 'most severe and resolute hitter'. His stance was wide, known as the 'Harrow straddle', his staple ball a slow, roundarm leg-break and his fielding excellent. His career reached both its height and its depth in 1817 when, after becoming the first man to score a hundred in each innings, he was banned from matches at Lord's having been accused of 'selling' the England v Nottinghamshire match. One year before his downfall, he lent his name to a volume of 'Instructions and Rules for Playing the Noble Game of Cricket'.

played 'first-class' cricket, Lord Frederick Beauclerk, an outstanding all-round cricketer, who in a long career never made a pair of noughts in a match and who was so confident of his own skill that he would put his gold watch on the bails and defy anyone to knock it off, was an active participant in the gambling which was a part of all eighteenth-century sport. He is said to have boasted that he made £600 a year from his wagering, though his most notorious bet ended in what might be called a just disaster.

With a speedy underarm bowler named Howard, he challenged another outstanding amateur, the famous Squire Osbaldeston and the gifted Surrey all-rounder William Lambert, to a two-a-side single-wicket match for fifty guineas. On the eve of the game Osbaldeston fell ill and sought a postponement but the noble cleric replied: 'No, Sir, play or pay.' Osbaldeston decided that Lambert should take on the other two more or less on his own, though by battling long enough to score one run, he sought at least to give Lambert a substitute fieldsman. This too was refused but it was Lambert who took the £100 after forcing Lord Beauclerk to lose his temper and give away his wicket. This he did by bowling wider and wider to him; wides did not then count against the bowler.

Lord Frederick became the first of the great autocrats of Lord's, and one of his firmest acts as an administrator there was to lead a crusade against the 'selling' of matches. He once presided over the dismissal from the club of two well-known players for exactly this form of corruption. Gradually the bookmakers, who had been familiar figures at the big

Cricket.

A MATCH WILL BE PLAYED,

IN THE

LONDON FIELDS, HACKNEY,

On THURSDAY, SEPTEMBER 14th, 1815,

Between eleven Gentlemen of

The Ratcliff Cricket Club,

AND ELEVEN GENTLEMEN OF THE

LONDON CRICKET CLUB,

FOR FIFTY GUINEAS A SIDE.

The Wickets to be pitched at Ten o' Clock.

Poster advertising a more moderately valued game in London Fields, Hackney.

matches, disappeared from cricket grounds in the nineteenth century, not to return until the middle of the twentieth, when they did so more discreetly.

'How the hop-men watch their hero,
massive, muscular and tall
As he mingled with the players, like a
king amongst them all;
'Till to some old Kent enthusiasts it
would almost seem a sin
To doubt their county's triumph when led on by
Alfred Mynn.' (W.J. Prowse)

The middle years of the nineteenth century
marked the beginning of the era of 'modern' first-class

Alfred Mynn, the first nationally famous cricket champion. Kind, manly, strong.

cricket, and produced in the six-foot-one-inch,
eighteen-stone hop merchant from Kent, Alfred
Mynn, the game's first truly national figure. Of all the
game's great individual champions of any era, he is the
one, except perhaps for Hobbs and Sobers, with the
most unblemished reputation.

Mynn was born at Goudhurst in 1807, the son
of a gentleman farmer, and followed his career at a
time when the game was being increasingly played,

watched and reported. Locally, village teams were
starting to organize themselves as proper clubs, and,
led by I Zingari, 'wandering' clubs began to be formed
as the opening up of the railways in the 1840s made it
possible to play against teams further afield. It was
partly thanks to the railways that some of Mynn's most
memorable matches, either as part of a team or at
single-wicket, were played against opposition from the
North of England. There, it was still some time before
soccer would gain a hold on affections, and cricket was
the chief athletic occupation of the workers who, after
the Factory Act of 1850, also had a free Saturday
afternoon to watch a big match if they did not wish to
play.

No-one was watched with more enjoyment than
the mighty Mynn. As a batsman he used his physical
advantages to the full, hitting the ball harder and
further than any contemporary, 'excelling especially in
the drive and leg hit'. Long before boundaries were
mentioned in the laws of the game, he would score at a
rate of thirty runs an hour, 'a celerity equalled by few'.
Everyone loves a hitter, though Mynn was no mere
blind swiper. What made him time and again the
champion in single-wicket encounters was his
fearsome, fast roundarm bowling. Haygarth described
it memorably in *Scores and Biographies:*
'As a bowler he was very destructive. His delivery was
noble, walking majestically up to the crease, though
when he first began he used to advance with a run. His
bowling was very fast and ripping, round-armed, and
of a good length; and though at first not very straight,
he afterwards became as steady as could be wished,
rarely delivering a wide. It was always considered one
of the grandest sights in cricket to see Mynn advance
and deliver the ball.'

From the age of eighteen he became well known
in Kent, playing for various clubs but in particular for
Lord Sondes at Lees Court near Maidstone. None of
the scores of these early games has survived, but in
1825 Mynn moved to Harrietsham, later to Thurnham
and eventually to London where he died more or less
penniless, his head for business being well inferior,
apparently, to his feeling for cricket.

At single-wicket he defeated three challengers
twice each: Thomas Hills in 1832, James Dearman of
Sheffield in 1838 and Nicholas Felix in 1846. Three
thousand people saw the first game against Felix at
Lord's, probably par for the course, and the
spectators who watched the Lion of Kent's victory
over Dearman at Sheffield saw Mynn score 46 runs off
46 hits. This was considered a phenomenal
achievement, for runs were only counted if they were
scored in front of the wicket and in one of these games
Felix defended his wicket for two hours without

scoring a single run; it was hardly gripping spectator sport by modern standards, but such feats give some indication of the intense interest in these men as individuals. In 1847 a special Kent v England match was arranged at Lord's in Mynn's honour (one assumes it was also for his financial benefit). He responded by scoring most runs, taking most wickets (ten), holding a couple of catches and hitting the winning runs.

The key to Mynn's lasting fame and popularity lay in two things: his good nature, which never, it seemed, failed him, and the verses by W.J. Prowse which were written in his memory after his death in 1861 and published in *Bell's Life*:

'With his tall and stately presence, with his nobly moulded form,

His broad hand was ever open, his brave heart was ever warm.

All were proud of him, all loved him...as the changing seasons pass,

Proudly, sadly we will name him – to forget him were a sin –

Lightly lie the turf upon thee, kind and manly Alfred Mynn.'

The courage and skill which inspired these lines are best summed up in perhaps his finest innings, in August 1836 when, playing for South v North at Leicester he followed a first innings of 21 not out with a heroic 125 not out. In the first innings he had gone in at number ten after being hit painfully on the ankle in a practice before the match. (It did not prevent his doing some bowling, though less than usual.) The South led by 55 on first innings, William Lillywhite taking five wickets, and on the third day, his ankle still badly swollen, Mynn walked out at number five to face the hostile fast bowling of Sam Redgate. 'The better I bowled,' said Redgate later, 'the harder he hit me away.' Mynn, batting with a runner, was time and again struck on his unprotected leg and when he showed it to his colleagues in the tent after his five hours at the crease, they were horrified by the red and black limb, grossly swollen. Lord Frederick Beauclerk insisted that he should leave the match at once and go straight to a doctor in London, but when the stagecoach arrived they could not fit his huge frame inside so instead he was strapped to the roof.

The agony of the journey of some one hundred miles over pot-holed roads can only dimly be imagined. Spending that night at the Angels Tavern in St Martin's Lane, he almost lost his leg, the surgeons deciding only at the last minute not to amputate. He recovered slowly, but missed all the 1837 season. During his absence, both his parents and his only son died. These misfortunes would have broken most men: not Mynn. He left a wife, five daughters, and a legend.

STATE OF THE MATCH OF CRICKET

PLAYED AT WEST MALLING, KENT.

The 29th and 30th of July, 1841,

Between

KENT & ENGLAND.

ENGLAND.	1st Innings	2nd Inn.
Box c A Mynn	5—	c Whittaker. 3
Sampson c A Mynn	14—	b Hillyer 1
Hawkins.. c W Mynn	0—	c Mills 7
Ward esq c Pilch	1—	c Mills 3
Redgate ....run out	8—	b Hillyer 3
Sewell b Hillyer	13—	c Mills 7
Guy, ... not out	42—	b Hillyer 22
Kynaston esq c Pilch	6—	b Hillyer 22
Lillywhite c Adams	7—	s Wenman 10
Cobbett b A Mynn	3—	s Wenman, 7
Thackeray esq. s Wenman	9—	not out 11
Byes 9 Wide 1 no b. 1 Total 119	Bys 10 W 2 n b 2 110	

KENT,		
R Mills .. s Box	10—	c Sampson. 0
W Mynn esq not out	26—	s Box 0
E. Wenman, b Cobbett	27—	c Kynaston. 6
Pilch .. c Cobbet	3—	c Sewell 16
Hillyer .. b Redgate	9—	leg b wicket 0
A. Mynn esq. c Cobbett	48—	b Redgate 29
Adams, .. b Redgate	1—	b Redgate 0
C. Whittaker esq s Box	0—	b Redgate. 9
Baker esq ..run out	12—	not out 7
W. Dorrinton, c Redgate	0—	not out 6
Martingale, c Guy	4—	
Byes 7 Wide 3 Total 150	Byes 4 Wide 3 80	

Windsor, Printer, Cricket Ground, MALLING

Umpires—Messrs. Dean & Bailey.

A Dinner on the Ground at Three o'Clock.

A match played at Fuller Pilch's renowned ground at West Malling in Kent. Unusually, William Lillywhite, the 'nonpareil' bowler, took not a single wicket. A dinner on the ground at three o'clock suggests either a very late lunch or a very early supper! Walter Mynn was Alfred's elder brother, a six-footer, a steady batsman and a brave long-stop to his brother's 'tremendous fast bowling'.

A ticket to the special testimonial match held at Lord's in 1847 to help bale out Mynn from his financial difficulties.

Admission

TO THE TESTIMONIAL IN HONOR OF

A. MYNN, Esq.

AT LORDS, JULY 26th & 27th, 1847,

Patronized by

THE MARYLEBONE CLUB.

A. Mynn

Match—Between Two Select ELEVENS of all England.

The North versus South fixtures, matches between Gentlemen and Players and various matches between sides representing counties, though not as yet organized into regular county clubs, made up the majority of the 'grand matches' played during the first half of the nineteenth century. The name 'England' was frequently used, and William Clarke, a shrewd and far-sighted professional cricketer from Nottingham, saw the potential profits of flying the flag by forming a group of the best players to tour the country and take on local teams of up to twenty-two players.

Clarke first played for Nottinghamshire in 1816 at the age of seventeen and was still playing in first-class matches forty years later. A slow underarm bowler in a period when roundarm was generally taking over, he was a prodigious wicket-taker, using the air skilfully, having perfect control of length and turning his leg-breaks sharply. It was years before he was recognized for the canny cricketer he was – 'crafty and fox-headed' is Haygarth's description – and he was an effective batsman too, despite losing the sight of his right eye when playing fives, a game at which he also excelled. The Surrey player William Caffyn left a vivid description of Clarke's passion for fives which tells something also of his perseverance as a character: 'He would play the game for hours together and made such hard work of it that when he leaned exhausted against the wall of the fives-court, he often left a sort of silhouette of himself in perspiration on the wall.'

Clarke's first claim to undying cricket fame lies in his acquisition, as a licensed victualler, of the Trent Bridge Inn, which still stands beside the Nottinghamshire ground. He opened the Trent Bridge ground in 1837 and dogmatically charged entrance fees for matches there, much to the annoyance of the Nottingham public. How soon after that he formed the idea of his touring England eleven we do not know, but he seems to have sold the scheme to his fellow professionals, not to mention 'amateurs' like the Kent stalwarts Felix and Mynn, during the MCC v North match at Trent Bridge in 1845.

A year later he collected a squad of fifteen men to play in his own benefit match at Southwell. In the same month of August 1846, the 'All England' eleven played their first match, against 'XX of Sheffield' at Hyde Park in Sheffield. 'England' were a strong team: William Hillyer of Kent took 17 wickets in the match with his fluent action and nippy medium-paced deliveries which tended to cut sharply from leg to off. He had able support from 'The Ploughboy', Jemmy Dean of Sussex, a strongly built fast roundarm bowler with endless stamina, who took 14 wickets in that first game. But, to South Yorkshire delight, it was the local

team who won. If defeat in the first match was a setback for Clarke, it probably did much to gain publicity for his 'troupe' of touring star cricketers. In any case the second match was won by an innings over three days against XVIII of Manchester, with Hillyer taking 18 wickets and Fuller Pilch making 62.

In 1848 Clarke sailed full steam ahead with his enterprise, the All England Eleven playing sixteen matches and being watched, and competed against, with much enthusiasm. There was no doubt that his team fully deserved its grand title. Most of the best players in the country were under his charge including, partly no doubt for respectability, two who were, indeed, respected amateurs: Alfred Mynn, by now past his peak and in financial difficulties, and the urbane and witty artist and schoolmaster Nicholas Felix, whose real name was Wanostracht. Although it was Clarke who planned the fixtures and negotiated terms, including a guarantee of £70 a match as insurance against rain, and free meals and entertainment for his men, it was Felix who usually made the speeches. Clarke used him as what we would call now the public relations man. He was also a skilful left-handed batsman with a searing cut-stroke. With Pilch, the commanding front-foot player who had been lured from his native Norfolk to play for Kent for £100 a year (and who later kept a pub in Canterbury), and supported by the redoubtable leg-side hitter George Parr (who peppered a tree at Trent Bridge on the mid-wicket boundary so regularly that it is known as 'Parr's Tree') plus the reliable Sussex wicket-keeper Thomas Box, who had turned himself also into an outstanding batsman, and the elegant Nottinghamshire player Joseph Guy, there were usually plenty of runs for Clarke's team. The bowling was even stronger, with a choice of Clarke himself, who seemed to improve with age, Mynn, Hillyer, Dean, and the Sussex pair John Wisden, small but very fast and hostile (he took all ten wickets, and all bowled too, for North v South in 1859), and William Lillywhite, known as the 'nonpareil' bowler because of his unfailing accuracy and personal integrity. Roundarm slow, he was, says Haygarth, 'like a piece of machinery, and in his old age wanted only a little oiling'.

No-one prospered more from the whole enterprise than Clarke himself. In addition to guaranteeing his men their board and lodging, he paid them, it is estimated, about £4 a match. The two amateurs, Felix and Mynn, both for many years stalwarts of the Gentlemen (i.e. amateurs) against the Players (professionals) probably got a little more for each match than the professionals. But no-one got as much as Clarke; one of the players, Tom Sherman, later told the historian F. S. Ashley-Cooper:

Lithograph by Nicholas Wanostracht (Felix) of William Clarke, demon slow bowler, founder of the All England Eleven and the inspiration of cricket at Trent Bridge.

'The cricketers went up to him one after the other for their money, and as I was the last in the row I was able to take in all that transpired. Clarke had a heap of gold and silver in front of him, and during the paying-out process you would hear something like this: "Four pounds for you, fifty shillings for you, three pounds for you," the amounts varying according to a player's fame and what he had done in the match. When I approached him he looked up, saying "Fifty shillings for you" and then, shovelling the balance into his trouser pockets, and giving a most satisfied smile, added "and thirty-seven pounds for me!"'

By 1850 there were signs that MCC were getting anxious about the growing status of the All England Eleven matches. A note in *Scores and Biographies* concerning the Kent versus England match at Cranbrook states: 'This was one of the All England matches got up by W. Clarke; the other two, at Lord's and Canterbury, were managed (as usual) by the Marylebone Club.' Incidentally, it was not until this period, when Clarke was in his late forties, that he started playing with any regularity in 'great matches' at Lord's. Possibly MCC now preferred him as a friend rather than as a rival.

In 1854 an inevitable fixture-clash occurred. The All England Eleven were committed to play XVIII of Maidstone on the same day as the Gentlemen v Players match at Lord's. Parr, Julius Caesar of Surrey and William Caffyn were all invited to play for the Players but Clarke, apparently piqued that at the age of fifty-five he had not himself been asked (!) refused to release them. Lillywhite reported in his *Guide* that Clarke's name was expunged from the books forthwith.

He had other rivals, mainly because he was considered too strict a disciplinarian and too greedy. He was succeeded as secretary and captain of the Eleven by George Parr and the team took on a new identity as 'Parr's Cracks'. In 1852 Dean and Wisden launched a rival enterprise, the 'United All England Eleven' which included other defectors from Clarke's circle, and they pointedly made it plain that their matches would not interfere with important county matches, which were starting at this time to become more significant from all viewpoints.

In all there were seven different touring 'elevens' of varying strength before the idea perished in 1881 with the breaking-up of George Freeman and Roger Iddison's United North of England Eleven. The novelty of a side of stars playing against town and village teams inevitably wore off. Usually the matches were too one-sided, no matter how many lined up against the Cracks. But the touring teams did much to spread the gospel, not just of cricket itself but of how it should be played. Batting techniques were becoming

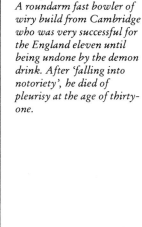

George 'Tear'em' Tarrant. A roundarm fast bowler of wiry build from Cambridge who was very successful for the England eleven until being undone by the demon drink. After 'falling into notoriety', he died of pleurisy at the age of thirty-one.

Richard Daft of Nottinghamshire, an urbane and gentlemanly character, graceful batsman and outstanding leg-side fielder. Originally an amateur, he joined the touring professionals, representing both the Gentlemen and the Players, but playing the game because he loved it, not, as Haygarth sternly remarked, 'as some do, entirely for profit'.

Far right H.H. Stephenson of Surrey, captain of the first touring team to Australia in 1861-62 and one of those Englishmen instrumental in coaching the Australians with such skill that within a generation they were outplaying the best players from the Mother Country. A tall, commanding batsman, he was also an outstanding wicket-keeper and a bowler of prodigious leg-breaks.

George Parr, who took on the management of the touring England eleven from Clarke and became one of Trent Bridge's most famous sons. The tree he used to pepper with powerful blows to mid-wicket became known as 'Parr's Tree'. For years the 'crack' batsman in England, he was highly regarded and given a benefit match at Lord's by MCC in 1858.

The United South of England XI who played XX of Lewes at Lewes on 7-8-9 September 1865. The match was for the benefit of the Sussex batsman C.H. Ellis who had lately become 'Mine Host' of the Royal Oak at Lewes. He was unable to play having cut his hand severely whilst 'attending to the Victualling Department'. Back, standing, left to right: Pooley, Mortlock, two 'attendants', Hearne, Willsher, Sewell, Griffith (sitting on back of table), John Neaves ('waiter'), small boy, Jupp. Seated: James Lillywhite, John Lillywhite (on end of bench), Julius Caesar, Lockyer (elbow on table), Humphrey.

Far left John Lillywhite, the son of the great bowler, William. Like his father, John was small and stocky and although he started as a quick bowler he turned with success to 'slow twisters'. He became coach at both Rugby and Harrow Schools and opened a successful family business, manufacturing cricket gear in conjunction with his father and his brothers, James and Fred.

Roger Iddison, co-founder with George Freeman of the United North of England Eleven in 1869. Yorkshire-born, and settling eventually in York, he played for both the Red and White Roses and held professional playing and coaching engagements at a wide variety of clubs and public schools.

Scorecard of a typical All England match, though XVIII of Broughton (Manchester) gave Parr's team a tougher fight than many opposing sides, losing by only four wickets. Haygarth's Scores and Biographies gives some of the Broughton side differently, including Bleackley for Davies and Middlemost for Brown; hence the corrections.

more sophisticated and the last great change in bowling styles, from roundarm ('legalized' by MCC in 1828) to overarm (fully legalized in 1864) had taken place.

Much is therefore owed to the first of these cricket tourists. They were relatively well rewarded but one only has to consider what mid-nineteenth-century travel was like to appreciate the toughness of the life they led. The railways were by no means always able to get them to all of their twenty-five or thirty fixtures a year. At other times it was a matter of hours on end in a bumpy coach, or a tiring journey through the night, and Richard Daft in his *Kings of Cricket* left a vivid picture of how George Parr and his men nearly ended their days in a thunderstorm on a bleak moorland road in Cornwall.

BROUGHTON CRICKET CLUB.

ALL ENGLAND ELEVEN v. BROUGHTON EIGHTEEN

Thursday, Friday, & Saturday, June 18, 19, & 20, 1863.

ENGLAND	FIRST INNINGS.		SECOND INNINGS.	
E. Stephenson c. Rowley b Payne	...	1	c & b McIntyre	5
J. Rowbotham c Armitage b McIntyre	21		b Greenwood	2
G. Anderson run out	0		b McIntyre	4
T. Hayward run out	2		not out	3
R. Carpenter c Crankshaw b Payne	24		not out	2
G. Parr b. McIntyre	16			
G. Tarrant c H. Whittington b Payne	13		c & b Greenwood	15
A. Clarke, c McIntyre b Payne	10			
E. Wilsher l b w b Payne	32		c H. Whittington	10
R. C. Tinley, c Crook b Payne	3			
J. Jackson, not out	2		c Greenwood b McIntyre	4
Byes, &c	7		w. 5 n. b 2	7
	Total......	131	Total......	52

BROUGHTON	FIRST INNINGS.		SECOND INNINGS.	
Mr. J. S. Whittington b. Willsher	0		c Hayward b Jackson...	0
„ J. B. Payne b. Jackson	26		b Willsher	0
„ R. Crankshaw c. Rowbotham	0		c Tinley b Tarrant	0
„ Greenwood c.Carpenter b.Willsher	7		c Parr b Jackson	0
Bleakley „ D. Davies c.Rowbotham b Tinley	3		b Willsher	3
„ H. W. Barber run out	3		c Stephenson b Willsher	0
„ E. J. Beasfield c Rowbotham	16		b Jackson	7
„ E. Dawson c. Willsher b. Jackson	17		c Hayward b Jackson...	4
„ E. B. Rowley b. Tarrant	3		c Hayward b Willsher	21
„ F. Higgins c. & b. Jackson	0		b Jackson	0
„ V Armitage b Tarrant	1		c Willsher b Jackson	3
„ J. Wheatley b. Jackson	0		c Parr b Jackson	0
„ H. Whittington b. Jackson	7		c Rowbotham b Willsher	3
„ McIntyre c. Willsher b. Jackson	2		c Rowbotham b Jackson	18
„ F. Rutter c Parr b Jackson	4		b Tarrant	12
„ T. Crook c Willsher b Jackson	1		not out	4
„ J. McCartney not out	0		l b w, b Jackson	0
Middlemost „ J. Brown b. Willsher	5		Absent	0
	b. 5, l. b. 2, w. 1	8	l. b	2
	Total......	105	Total......	77

BY ORDER, ARTHUR BURGESS, PRINTER.

William Clarke and his followers had proved that touring was a profitable and, for all the hardships of travel, also an enjoyable exercise. As the British Empire grew, it was really no more than a step forward in the mind to extend the idea of touring to countries overseas. The first to adventure abroad went not to Australia but to Canada and the United States – these two having played their first fixture against each other as early as 1844.

The course of cricket history might have been different had the Third Duke of Dorset, Britain's ambassador in France, not been forced to abandon his idea of 'educating' the French in 1789. He had arranged an exhibition match in Paris and gathered

The English team that toured America, 1859. Back, left to right: R. Carpenter, W. Caffyn, T. Lockyer (looking away). Seated and middle: J. Wisden, H.H. Stephenson, G. Parr, J. Grundy, J. Caesar, T. Hayward, J. Jackson (with ball). Front: A. Diver, John Lillywhite.

together some of the best players of the day, but the breaking-out of a 'little local difficulty' (the Revolution) forced him to meet the team at Dover and advise them to return to their homes.

The first tour of America, in the autumn of 1859, was organized by the Montreal club, then very much Canada's 'MCC', and the Cambridge blue, W. P. Pickering. A merchant named Waller from New York put up £500 for two matches in the United States and the Montreal club guaranteed Pickering £50 for each of the English team of twelve, plus all expenses. In his account of the tour, William Caffyn says that he actually came home with £90.

It was a more representative England team than

many which have toured since. The differences between the rival 'England Elevens' had more or less been buried with the death of Clarke in 1856, and a Cricketers' Fund, which later developed into the Cricketers' Friendly Society, had already been set up to help the professionals towards the end of their careers. The first overseas touring team contained players from both North and South.

George Parr was captain, with two other Notts men, Jemmy Grundy and the fierce fast bowler John 'Foghorn' Jackson, who had a habit of blowing his nose loudly after each wicket he took; Jackson's bowling terrorized local sides, and he got his fair share of runs too. Cambridgeshire provided two outstanding batsmen, Tom Hayward and Robert Carpenter, and a versatile all-rounder in A.J. 'Ducky' Diver. From the South were four of the powerful Surrey team, Caffyn, a remarkably consistent all-rounder, the dashing little batsman Julius Caesar, the polished wicket-keepers H.H. Stephenson and Tom Lockyer – it is interesting that they should have taken two specialist 'keepers. Sussex provided John Lillywhite, the batsman son of the 'nonpareil' bowler, and John Wisden. Fred Lillywhite, who in 1848 had introduced a portable printing press to manufacture scorecards wherever a great match was being played, travelled with Parr's team as scorer and reporter, later producing a full account of the tour.

On 7 September 1859, they set sail on the *Nova Scotia*, many of the men suffering badly from seasickness, and arrived in Canada fifteen days later. The first match, against Montreal, was easily won, though more by the gentle lobs of George Parr than the pace of Jackson or Grundy; the captain took 16 wickets. A three-day match against XXII of New Jersey was even more comfortably won, with 25,000 people in all watching England's victory by an innings and, on a poor pitch, Caffyn's useful return of 16 for 25. The touring team were triumphant again at Philadelphia, which was to remain the chief centre of American cricket and a place frequently visited by both amateur and professional teams from England. The Philadelphians also made two tours to England in the 1880s and a particularly successful one in 1897, when Sussex and Warwickshire were defeated and Bart King established himself as one of the great bowlers of the time, hustling out Sussex with waspish inswingers that earned him 7 for 13 on a good wicket at Brighton.

The 1859 visit might have had the same inspirational effect in other American cities – matches were also played at Hamilton and Rochester, where snow stopped play – had it not been for the advent of the Civil War in 1861. One of its unfortunate side-effects was to prevent the maintenance of cricket grounds and

The impressive Philadelphians' ground in 1891, as grand as anything in England or Australia at the time.

the free flow of equipment; consequently baseball, much less reliant on proper facilities and gear, took a popular hold on the troops of both sides as a recreational activity which cricket never again matched.

Instead, it was Australia which became the fashionable country to tour, and within a remarkably short time cricket developed there to a standard which enabled the Colonials to take on and defeat the Mother Country both at home and abroad. Within sixteen years of the first English visit in 1861, the combined strength of Victoria and New South Wales was to prove too much for England's touring team in what became recognized as the first Test match.

The game was already much more solidly established in Australia than it was in America when the catering firm Spiers and Pond, originally planning a lecture tour by Charles Dickens, agreed instead to underwrite a visit by a cricket team based on six of the best Surrey players. H.H. Stephenson was captain, with Caffyn again a willing and successful companion. When they landed at Melbourne on Christmas Eve they were met by a crowd of some 10,000 and taken by coach and four to an official reception. The English players were impressed by the Melbourne Cricket Ground, where 15,000 saw them win the first of twelve matches on the tour. The MCG, developed from a paddock in 1841, was already more advanced than Lord's in its seating capacity.

The first tour of Australia was a success from every point of view. The English team lost only two games, both against XXIIs rather than XIs, and the sponsors made a profit estimated at £11,000 – and thereafter, until the arrival of Mr Packer in 1977, all tours were guaranteed, and all profits taken, by cricketing rather than commercial interests. One of the tourists, Surrey's Charles Lawrence, stayed behind to coach in Sydney and, after the second tour by a side under Parr's captaincy two years later – also a great success – William Caffyn was engaged to coach in

Melbourne. He moved on to Sydney and in all spent seven years teaching the essential techniques of the game and a proper attention to etiquette and excellence in the field.

The independence of the Australian spirit soon surfaced as the cricket bigwigs of Victoria and New South Wales vied for the position of major host on subsequent tours. The two states had first played each other in 1856 and the game quickly became popular in other centres where British soldiers and sailors had visited. Inter-state rivalry is nicely illustrated by a story told of the eleven Australians who in 1878 made the first tour of England (other than the visit of the Aboriginals in 1868). They played games in Australia itself at the start of the tour and it took them six months of arduous travel even to get to England via America. Early on in the voyage they were caught in a fearful storm and Fred Spofforth is reputed to have asked Charles Bannerman, an excellent swimmer, what he would do if they were wrecked. 'First,' said Bannerman, 'I'll save my brother Alec, then Murdoch, then you.' 'What about the Victorians?' asked Spofforth, to which Bannerman retorted: 'Let them drown.'

Any doubts about the cricketing significance of Anglo-Australian tours ended when W.G. Grace himself took out the third English team in 1873–74. He was personally paid a very large sum to make the tour, accompanied by his new wife, but like all tours and especialy these early ones, it was no cakewalk. The team set sail in October, played fifteen matches between 1 January and 28 March, all against odds and with much difficult travelling in between, and did not land back in Britain until 18 May. Ten of the fifteen games were won and Grace pronounced the tour a 'conspicuous success', but his brother Fred reported that 'from a cricketing point of view we were met in a bad spirit as if contending cricketers were enemies'.

Bad pitches and umpiring irritated 'The

The first team to bring back the Ashes, 1882–83. Back, left to right: W. Barnes, F. Morley, C.T. Studd, G.F. Vernon, C.F.H. Leslie. Seated: G.B. Studd, E.F.S. Tylecote, Hon. Ivo Bligh (capt.), A.G. Steel, W.W. Read. Front: R.G. Barlow, W. Bates.

Champion' throughout the trip, social success though it was, and his own competitive nature did not go down well if an Australian newspaper report is accurate: 'We did not take kindly to W.G. For a big man he is surprisingly tenacious on very small points.'

Grace himself was the side's most successful batsman, without enjoying one of his more purple periods, but he was sufficiently impressed by many of the bowlers he played against to predict their success in England. Within a few years he had been proved right.

The fourth English tour of Australia was made in 1876–77 by an all-professional side under the captaincy of James Lillywhite of Sussex. Towards the end of the tour, weary from a rough passage across the Tasman Sea, England were defeated at Melbourne in the first match against a combined Australian eleven, or the first Test match as it later became known.

Above right and right Alfred Shaw, Nottinghamshire and England, a shrewd slow bowler and enterprising professional. The letter was written by Shaw to Sydney H. Pardon (editor of Wisden); it refers to Shaw's 'master' Lord Sheffield and reveals frailities of spelling and grammar which suggest that his writings on cricket were 'ghosted'.

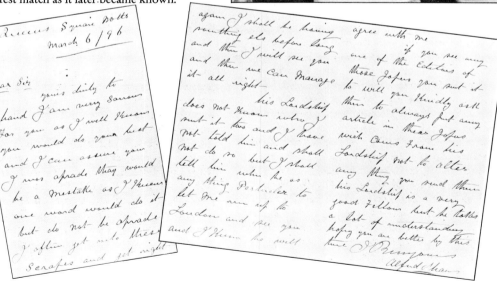

SHAW AND SHREWSBURY'S TEAM OF 1884-5.

1. M. Read.   5. Joe Hunter.   10. J. Lillywhite.
2. G. Ulyett.   6. W. Attewell.   11. W. Flowers.
3. W. Scotton.   7. A. Shrewsbury.   12. J. Briggs.
4. R. Peel.   8. Alfred Shaw (capt.). 13. W. Bates.
                      9. W. Barnes.

(All from Photos by J. Bentley, Sydney.)

Charles Bannerman scored his immortal 165 to inspire the Australians' victory by 45 runs; this was avenged a fortnight later.

The excitement of these first Tests and of the whole adventure are vividly documented in the reminiscences of the great Nottinghamshire bowler Alfred Shaw. He tells the full story of how the team's wicket-keeper, Ted Pooley of Surrey, came to miss the first Test match because he was fretting in a New Zealand gaol, committed for trial for 'maliciously injuring property above the value of £5' during a fight over the non-payment of a gambling debt. He tells too of perhaps the most frightening of all the travelling mishaps which beset the early touring teams. On a journey from Hokitika to Christchurch the coach in which Shaw was travelling got stuck in torrential rain at midnight in the middle of Otira Gorge. Normally the road crossed a shallow ford but the level of the water had risen to the extent that the horses could not battle their way through. Jumping out of the coach and immediately up to their waists in water, the cricketers unyoked the horses and pulled them to the bank, then waded back in to pull the coach out as well. Tom Armitage of Yorkshire carried the only female passenger to safety. They spent the night on the floor of a shoddy hotel lounge at Otira, drying out naked in front of the fire, their change of clothes having gone ahead to Christchurch by boat.

Next day they were prevented from going more than a mile by a landslip and returned to spend the day at a hotel which had no food left. A roadman saved the day by disappearing into the bush and returning with a dead lamb which was promptly roasted. They set out again at five o'clock on Sunday morning in a highly uncomfortable coach: 'The seats were cross planks of wood, and if you had a side seat you had to be constantly on guard lest you received a rousing knock on the head against the wooden supports, or were pitched unceremoniously into the bush ... the loose couplings and the apparently slovenly way in which the coach was driven made your hair lift at the thought of impending disaster.'

They arrived to play XVII of Christchurch at eleven-thirty for a twelve-thirty start!

Top *The Madras eleven who played Calcutta in a nineteenth-century fixture. Not a native Indian in sight!*

Above *China XI (v Japan) at Kobe, 1893. Back, left to right: Heffer (Shanghai), McGregor (Shanghai), C.S. Barff (Hong Kong), A.J. Abbot (Shanghai), ?, L.V. Stride (Hong Kong). Seated: Firth (Hong Kong), J. Mann (Shanghai), Captain Dumbleton (Hong Kong), A.P. Wood (Shanghai), Lt E.D. Markham (Hong Kong), Another Hong Kong player.*

25

The establishment of inter-county cricket as the staple diet of the English cricket season at first-class level came about by accident and evolution. The first known county cricket match took place at Dartford Brent between Kent and Surrey in 1709. In the modern sense it was not a county match at all, but a challenge match between groups of cricketers from those two counties. The era of organized county clubs was still more than a century away.

In the following twenty years other games were played by sides assuming the titles of 'Sussex', 'Hampshire', 'London' and 'Middlesex' and there was a notable increase of such fixtures in the 1730s, played under the patronage of men such as Edwin Stead and the Second Duke of Richmond, the early patrons of Kent and Sussex respectively. The next really marked increase in county matches came when cricket began to be played in earnest again after the Napoleonic Wars. By the 1830s Nottinghamshire had begun to rival the three strongest southern counties, Surrey (the unofficial champions of the Hambledon era), Sussex and Kent.

From time to time the newspapers made reference to a 'Championship', notably during the 1860s, and in 1862 the MCC defined qualification rules for the first time, namely that a player had either to be born in the county or to have been a *bona fide* resident there for two years. In 1872 and 1873 the leading nine county clubs, Surrey, Kent, Sussex, Middlesex, Gloucestershire, Nottinghamshire, Yorkshire, Lancashire and Derbyshire, met three times in London to discuss these qualification rules and came up with a repetition of the MCC dictates, plus a stipulation that no-one could play for more than one county in a season and that any dispute over residential qualification should be referred to the MCC committee.

There was a steady increase in the number of inter-county matches between the 1870s and the 1890s. Two of the most active clubs, Surrey and Yorkshire, for example, played only ten matches each in 1876 but in 1896 Yorkshire played 32 and Surrey 28. 'The Championship', though an intangible prize, had become established during this period as one of the focal points of any cricket season. By 1870 county

The Surrey XI, 1861. Left to right: W. Mortlock, T. Lockyer, H.H. Stephenson, W. Caffyn, G. Griffith, E. Dowson Esq, F.P. Miller Esq, C.G. Lane Esq, F. Burbidge Esq, J. Caesar, T. Sewell.

tables started to be published in the press, though there was as yet no definition of which counties were first-class and which not. Most counties, indeed, including many of the modern 'minor' counties and a good many in Scotland and Wales, had by this stage played at some time or other under a county title and in the 1860s the more formal organization of official clubs began in earnest. Surrey had been founded in 1845, based at Kennington Oval, but many of the other clubs were formed, fell apart and formed again.

As the matches of the various All England elevens began to lose their public appeal, and the demand grew for something more genuinely competitive than matches played by experts against local novices, the county clubs became the main employers of an increasing number of professional cricketers, whose match fees (never, in those days, a salary) were supplemented by bigger pay-days if they were invited to play in one of the prestige games of the season, North v South or Players v Gentlemen, or to represent MCC, or travel abroad in the winter. Many of the county professionals in the second half of the nineteenth century also took jobs as coaches at the public schools or as ground bowlers at Lord's or The Oval, working in the nets, helping with the ground upkeep and bowling in the matches. W.G. Grace, in his *Cricketing Reminiscences,* says that the last two years of the 1860s were the ones in which 'county cricket began to take a prominent place and to excite great interest'. Nottinghamshire, Yorkshire, Surrey, Lancashire, Kent, Sussex and Middlesex were the leading counties in 1870 but by 1876 the influence of the Grace family and W.G. in particular had pulled the then all-amateur Gloucestershire side to the top of the tree.

There was one great casualty amongst the first-class counties in this period: Cambridgeshire, who for most of the 1860s had a side capable of beating anyone. They possessed two great batsmen in Tom Hayward, whose nephew was to become the first man after W.G. to score a hundred hundreds, and Robert Carpenter; a brilliant all-rounder in 'Ducky' Diver, and two feared bowlers, 'Tear'em' Tarrant with his fierce pace and long run and the medium-paced leg-spinner Billy Buttress. But Hayward, Tarrant and Buttress all died young, the county suddenly faded and any future players of great skill from East Anglia gravitated towards the south-eastern clubs, notably Tom Hayward Junior and Jack Hobbs. Between 1873 and 1887, when Surrey started a period of supremacy, the 'Championship' was dominated by Nottinghamshire, Gloucestershire and Lancashire.

The legalizing of overarm bowling in 1864 (the year in which John Wisden's almanack made its first

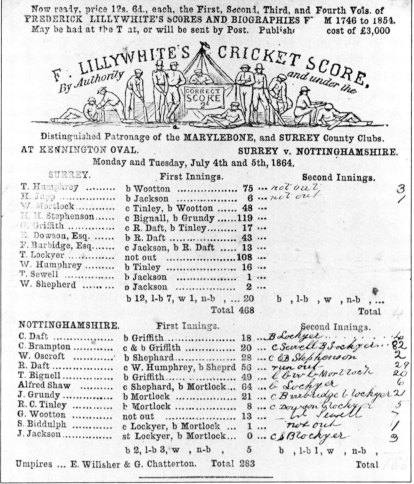

appearance and W.G. played his first major match, scoring 170 and 56 not out for South Wales Club against the Gentlemen of Sussex at the age of 16) was more than countered by a vast improvement in the preparation, mowing and rolling of pitches, and county scores steadily increased in size. Nottinghamshire had their share of prolific batsmen, with George Parr, fuelled on copious quantities of his favourite tipple, gin and water, very much to the fore with his leg-side hitting, and Richard Daft, one of the finest players in the land, later followed by four of the best batsmen of the early Test era, Arthur Shrewsbury, Billy Barnes, the stone-waller W.H. Scotton, and William, the first of the Gunn family to serve the county with distinction. To support them in the field they had the unfailingly accurate Alfred Shaw and later two fast left-arm bowlers in J.C. Shaw and Fred Morley.

Lancashire's Championship successes came in 1879, 1881 and 1882, though they had to share the

One of Fred Lillywhite's famous scorecards. His Scores and Biographies, *advertised here for 12s 6d, would now be worth over £50 a volume.*

27

Sussex County ❦ **Cricket Ground.**

2d.

AUTHORIZED CRICKET SCORE
ISSUED BY
H. CROWHURST,
Letter-Press, Lithographic, and Copper-Plate Printer,
15 and 50, Market Street, Brighton.

Gentlemen of Sussex v. Gentlemen of Hampshire.
Thursday, Friday, & Saturday, July 22nd, 23rd, & 24th, 1869.

Hampshire. First Innings. Second Innings.
A. H. Wood, Esq ...... c Wollaston b Blaker ......30 ... b Kelly 6
G. H. Butler, Esq ...... b Kelly ......36 ... b Winslow 3
C. Lucas, Esq ...... lbw b Winslow 92
E. L. Ede, Esq ...... b Onslow ......23 ... not out 16
J. Frederick, Esq ...... b Winslow ......25 ... not out 14
G. M. Ede, Esq...... c & b Cotterill ......7 ... c Wollaston b Kelly......12
O. B. Longcroft, Esq c Winslow b Blaker......0
Colonel Bathurst ...... run out 39
E. Hemsted, Esq ...... hit wicket b Blaker 11
Captain Austin ...... b Kelly ......10 ... run out 0
Captain Eccles .... not out ...... Total ...28 b. 1-b.3 w. n-b. Total 3
b. 20 l-b. 4 w. 4 n-b. Total ..321 Total ..53

Sussex. First Innings. Second Innings.
G. W. King, Esq...... b Hemsted ......9 ... b E. L. Ede 20
Major Scott ...... c Wood b E. L. Ede ......22 ... b Longcroft 6
H. B. Cotterill, Esq...... c Frederick b E. L. Ede......32 ... c Austin b Longcroft......8
O. E. Winslow, Esq...... c Substitute b Longcroft ......24 ... b Hemsted 46
W. B. Weighell, Esq b Longcroft......0 ... c Austin b ede......101
D. R. Onslow, Esq...... b Longcroft......0 ... c Frederick b Longcroft......1
H. C. Blaker, Esq...... c Hemsted b Longcroft......19 ... b ede......27
W. R. Gillespie, Esq.. not out ......2 ... b E. L. Ede 15
C. Wollaston, Esq.... b Longcroft......0 ... not out 6
W. W. Kelly, Esq ... c Lucas b Hemsted......0 ... run out 0
W. Napper, Esq ...... thrown out Lucas ......8 b. 9 l-b.5 w. 3 n-b. Total ...247
b.5 l-b. w.3 n-b Total...126

Umpires—Killick and Stubberfield.

TRUEFITT'S PERFUMED SHOWER,
After Cricket, or any long day in the sun, this refreshing and luxurious process removes lassitude, recruits the nervous system, and sets you up for the evening. In perfection only at

---

GENTLEMEN OF LANCASHIRE v. GENTLEMEN OF YORKSHIRE.
Played on the Old Trafford Cricket Ground, on Tuesday, Wednesday, & Thursday July 9th, 10th, and 11th, 1867.
W. WHITTAM'S CORRECT SCORE. 37, WEST BAR, SHEFFIELD.

LANCASHIRE. First Innings. Second Innings:
W. Watson, Esq. ....
J. Leese, Esq. .... c Savile, b Sale
E. B. Rowley, Esq. .... b Savile .. 18
. Johnson, Esq. .... c Roper b Sale .. 72
J. W. Barber, Esq. .... c Verelst, b Sale .. 219
Hardcastle, Esq. .... b Sale .. 29
Whittaker, Esq. .... c Sale b Savile .. 18
Grave. Esq. ...... not out 31
Rutter, Esq. ...... b Sale .. 146
D. Raven, Esq. ...... c Roper b Prest .. 9
W. Wright, Esq. .... l b w b Prest .. 5
...... b Sale .. 0
Wides,7 Bys 12, 1-b.6 n-b. 25 Wides byes 1-b1 n-b .. 23
Total.... 586 Total....

YORKSHIRE. First Innings. Second Innings.
..e, Esq. ...... b Rutter .. 56 c Hardcastle b Wright 35
..aud, Esq. ...... b Rutter .. 3
Verelst, Esq. ...... c Wright b Whittaker .. 4 c Johnson b Whittaker 29
.. Esq. ...... c Grave b Wright ..49 c Whitaker b Wright 28
..s, Esq. ...... c and b Wright ..48 not out 0
..on, Esq. ...... b Rutter .. 0 not out 4
..sq. ...... b Rutter .. 1 b Whittaker 0
..sq. ...... c Barber b Wright .. 15
..n, Esq. ...... not out .. 17 c Raven b Wright 10
..absent .. 0 b Johnson 29
wides4, bys9 1-b,5 n-b.1 19 Wides 4 bys 13 1 b 5 n b 22
Total.. 212 Total 157

Umpires, Messrs. Reynolds and Ferrand,
..nshaw, Printer and Stationer, 39, West Bar, Sheffield.
..age of Lancaster County and Manchester Cricket Clubs.
F. REYNOLDS
..men, Secretaries of Clubs, &c., that he has for disposal
..t of every article required in the game. Three year old
Bats warranted. Cricket Grounds and Bowling
..y laid during winter season.
Address—F. Reynolds, Manchester Cricket Ground, Stretford.

Above Early county scorecard. The Prince of Wales feathers are normally associated not with Sussex but with Surrey. Hampshire, with a notable batsman in C.F. Lucas, were too good for Sussex on this occasion, winning by five wickets.

Above right A gentlemanly Roses match! Seldom have Lancashire so dominated, even at Old Trafford.

honour with Notts in the first and last of these years. The spirited little amateur opening batsman 'Monkey' Hornby was captain, Dick Barlow his more sedate opening partner, A.G. Steel one of the best amateur all-rounders of his day, Dick Pilling a brilliant wicket-keeper and William McIntyre and Jack Crossland, whose action was suspect and caused one of the first of the overarm 'throwing' controversies, were effective opening bowlers. Middlesex, champions in 1866 and in some tables again in 1878, also had a happy blend of amateur and professional strength, based on the famous Walker family of Southgate, with other dashing amateur batsmen in A.J. Webbe, the Lytteltons, F.G.J. Ford, A.E. Stoddart and Sir Timothy O'Brien, augmented by professional bowlers of whom the best was the unfailingly reliable medium-fast man, J.T. Hearne.

By gradual degrees more and more counties took on separate identities and players became associated with their county – Mycroft of Derbyshire, Lillywhite of Sussex, W.H. Patterson of Kent, etc. In 1870 the regular fixtures between counties numbered only 22. By 1880 this number had more than doubled and in 1890, after a winter meeting, the counties themselves formally constituted a Championship, for the first time agreeing a method of deciding it. Until that time it had been an accolade awarded in the press and in the various cricket annuals, and they were not always unanimous. Finally, in 1894, the Championship was considerably extended when MCC decided to classify Derbyshire, Essex, Leicestershire and Warwickshire as first-class (Derbyshire having been demoted in the late '80s), and added Hampshire to the list at the end of the season.

RULES

OF THE
Cheltenham and County of Gloucester

CRICKET CLUB.

President—COLONEL BERKELEY, M.P.

Vice-Presidents:

CHARLES SCHREIBER, ESQ. | REV. G. BUTLER, M.A.
REV. A. BARRY, B.D. | REV. T. A. SOUTHWOOD, M.A.

Committee:

COLONEL HART, | MR. F. DOWLE, | MR. C. JESSOP,
CAPTAIN LAMBERT, | MR. J. J. ENGALL, Jun. | MR. F. JESSOP,
MR. E. ALDER, | MR. E. GRIFFITHS, | MR. J. LILLYWHITE,
MR. H. G. DAVIES, | MR. G. HODGE. | MR. E. S. MORRIS.

Treasurer—MR. C. ANDREWS.

Secretary—MR. F. P. FENNER.

Collector—SERJEANT-MAJOR HOLLAND.

1.—That the Club be called "THE CHELTENHAM AND COUNTY OF GLOUCESTER CRICKET CLUB."

2.—That the Officers of the Club consist of a President, Vice-Presidents, Treasurer, Secretary, and Committee of twelve, to be elected annually from the Members of the Club.

3.—That the Annual Subscription of Members be One Guinea, but that Playing Members be admitted at half a guinea, subject to the discretion of the Committee.—No Subscriber of less than a guinea to be entitled to vote in the affairs of the Club.

4.—That all Subscribers of One Guinea be privileged to the use of Ground for Cricket, Archery, Bowls, Quoits, &c.—the implements for the practice of which, excepting Bows and Arrows, to be provided from the general fund of the Club.

5.—That persons wishing to become Members be proposed at a Meeting of the Committee, at which the votes of two-thirds of the Members present be necessary to elect.

6.—That the Subscriptions be payable in advance on the 1st of March in each year.

7.—That Members be held responsible for the payment of their Annual Subscriptions until a written notice of their intention to withdraw from the Club be sent to the Treasurer or Secretary.

8.—That there be two General Meetings of the Club for business annually, viz :—in the months of March and October.

9.—That any Vice-President with five of the Committee, be empowered to call a Special General Meeting of the Club.

10.—That all Officers of the Club be *ex officio* Members of the Committee.

11.—That the Committee meet on the first Tuesday of each month for the election of Members and the transaction of general business.

12.—That the Secretary or any three Members of the Committee be empowered to call a Special Meeting of the Committee.

13.—That the Committee, not less than five being present, decide on all Matches, choose the Players, appoint the Captain, regulate the expenses, and manage the affairs of the Club generally.

14.—That any Member guilty of impropriety of conduct be amenable to the Committee, who shall have power to act in the matter, whether by expulsion or otherwise, as they may deem desirable for the interests of the Club.

15.—That the time for opening of Ground be decided by the Committee at their first Meeting in March, from which time there shall be two field days in each week during the Season—Mondays and Thursdays—play commencing at Three o'clock.

VISITORS.

That Visitors to Cheltenham be admitted Members of the Club, for a time not exceeding two months, and subject to the approval of the Committee, on payment of half a guinea.

BY ORDER OF THE COMMITTEE,

F. P. FENNER,
HON. SECRETARY.

Rules of the Cheltenham and County of Gloucester Club, founded on 3 November 1863 and wound up on 14 March 1871 when the new county club was established. Two Jessops were on the committee.

Gloucestershire County Cricket Club.

THORNBURY, GLOUCESTERSHIRE R.S.O.,
June, 1873.

DEAR SIR,

The following Matches are arranged to be played by the County this season :—

June 9, 10, 11 .. Gloucestershire *v.* Surrey, at the Oval.
" 12, 13, 14 .. " *v.* Sussex, at Brighton.
" 28, 29, 30 .. " *v.* Yorkshire, at Sheffield.
July 14, 15, 16 .. " " at Clifton.
August 25, 26, 27 .. " *v.* Surrey, at Clifton.
" 28, 29, 30 .. " *v.* Sussex, at Cheltenham.

These Matches are necessarily a great expense to the County Club, will you therefore kindly become a Subscriber to our funds? The following are the Committee for this season :—

President:
HIS GRACE THE DUKE OF BEAUFORT, K.G., Badminton, Chippenham.

Vice-President:
RIGHT HON. LORD FITZHARDINGE, Berkeley Castle, Gloucestershire.

Treasurer:
WILLIAM HENRY HARFORD, Lawrence Weston, Henbury.

Captain:
W. G. GRACE, Downend, near Bristol.

Secretary:
E. M. GRACE, Thornbury, Gloucestershire.

Committee:
ALLEN A. BATHURST, M.P., Cirencester, and 32 St. James's Place, London.
J. C. BENGOUGH, The Ridge, Wotton-under-Edge.
J. ARTHUR BUSH, 7 Rodney Place, Clifton.
Colonel BUSH, Clifton.
S. H. BROOKES, Cheltenham.
Rev. C. R. DAVY, Tracey Park, near Bath.
Rev. JOSEPH GREENE, Clifton.
Sir WM. V. GUISE, Bart., Elmore Court, near Gloucester.
HENRY GRACE, Kingswood Hill, near Bristol.
WILLIAM HENRY MILES, Ham Green, near Bristol.
R. FENTON MILES, Clifton.
T. G. MATTHEWS, Clifton.
Rev. C. H. RIDDING, Slymbridge Rectory, near Stonehouse.
F. TOWNSEND, Clifton.

Copy of Rule 6.

That an annual subscription of 10/- shall entitle a member to a ticket of admission to all matches played in the County, and a subscriber of £1 or upwards shall have a ticket to admit his family, and a subscriber preferred, and a donation of £5 5s. shall constitute a life member with the foregoing privileges.

We were very successful in 1872, only losing one Match and that by only one wicket, and to keep the Club in its present state of efficiency we require funds to bring forward any young players who are likely to become ornaments to the Eleven. Therefore I hope I may be allowed to place your name upon the list of Subscribers.

An early answer will much oblige,

Yours faithfully,

Edward Mills Grace
Secretary to the Gloucestershire County Cricket Club.

A letter asking for support for the relatively new county club in 1873. Gloucestershire were generally acknowledged to be joint champions this year with Nottinghamshire.

Australia's triumph at Melbourne in the first Test, in March 1877, emboldened cricketers at both ends of the world to consider for the first time a full-scale 'return' tour to England. The pioneering effort of 1868 by a team of Aboriginals from Victoria, led by the English cricketer Charles Lawrence and managed by the son of a respectable English settler at Edenhope, W.R. Hayman, had been a limited success and at least one of the 'blacks', Johnny Mullagh, had been a match for the best first-class cricketers, but no-one in England was fully prepared for the shock they got at Lord's on 27 May 1878.

The first representative Australian side – only twelve in number, six from New South Wales, five from Victoria and one from Tasmania – had lost their opening match at Trent Bridge, no doubt very tired after what had already been a long tour (starting round Australia and New Zealand) as well as being quite unfamiliar with the cold English summer. Then, against MCC at Lord's, 'The Demon' Fred Spofforth hustled out a strong side, led by W.G., for a first innings total of 33, with personal figures of 6 for 4. Alfred Shaw, right-arm slow-medium, used the wet wicket equally well, taking 5 for 10 as the Australians could better that score by only eight, and at four o'clock Grace and Hornby walked out to open MCC's second innings before a crowd now grown to 5,000 and fascinated by the battle in the middle.

Spofforth had Grace dropped first ball, but bowled him with the second and then knocked over the stumps of A.J. Webbe, another celebrated amateur, first ball. His partner Boyle also took two wickets in his first over and this time finished with the better figures, a remarkable analysis of 6 for 3, as MCC collapsed again and were bowled out for 19 in a humiliating 55 minutes. The Australians won by nine wickets at twenty past six. Haygarth records: 'The actual duration of play ... amounted to only four and a half hours, only 105 runs being scored for thirty-one wickets. The match was therefore doubly sensational, and will be pointed out to future generations of cricketers.' The periodical *Punch* was moved to parody Byron:
'The Australians came down like a wolf on a fold,
The Marylebone "cracks" for a trifle were bowled,
Our Grace, before dinner, was very soon done,
Our Grace, after dinner, did not get a run.'
No English team ever thereafter took an Australian cricket side lightly. This victory seized the public imagination and regular visits of Australian touring teams followed at two-yearly intervals through the 1880s.

English batting techniques were generally superior at this stage, for all the excellence of the Bannerman brothers and in particular of William Lloyd Murdoch, but J.M. Blackham was the finest wicket-keeper anyone had yet seen and the pace of Spofforth and Garrett, augmented by Boyle's medium-paced leg-spin and Allan's left-arm medium swing, amounted to a better attack. Spofforth alone took 326 wickets on his first trip to England, and during the long tour round Australasia, through North America and England, and back for a few more matches in Australia, he collected no fewer than 764 at an average of less then seven apiece.

Spofforth was absent through injury in 1880 when the first Test in England was played at The Oval,

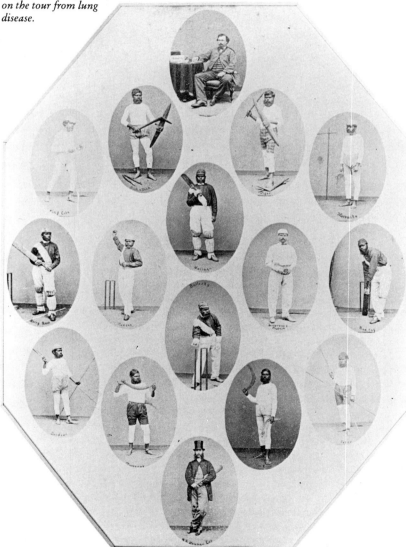

The Aboriginal touring team to England in 1868. They were captained by former Surrey professional Charles Lawrence (middle row, second right). King Cole (at 10 o'clock in outer ring) died in Guy's Hospital on the tour from lung disease.

Lord's Ground.

M.C.C. AND GROUND v. AUSTRALIANS.

MONDAY, MAY 27, 1878.

M.C.C.

	First Innings.		Second Innings.	
W. G. Grace, Esq.	c Midwinter, b Allan	4	b Spofforth	0
A. N. Hornby, Esq.	b Spofforth	19	b Boyle	1
C. Booth, Esq.	b Boyle	0	b Boyle	0
A. W. Ridley, Esq.	c A. Bannerman, b Boyle	7	b Boyle	0
A. J. Webbe, Esq.	b Spofforth	1	b Spofforth	0
Wild	b Boyle	0	b Spofforth	5
Flowers	c and b Spofforth	0	b Boyle	11
G. G. Hearne	b Spofforth	0	b Spofforth	0
Shaw	st Murdoch, b Spofforth	0	not out	2
G. F. Vernon, Esq.	st Murdoch, b Spofforth	0	b Spofforth	0
Morley	not out	1	c Horan, b Boyle	0
	B , l-b 1, w , n-b 1	1	B , l-b , w , n-b ,	
	Total	33	Total	19

AUSTRALIANS.

	First Innings.		Second Innings.	
C. Bannerman	c Hearne, b Morley	0	b Shaw	1
W. Midwinter	c Wild, b Shaw	10	not out	4
T. Horan	c Grace, b Morley	4	not out	7
A. Bannerman	c Booth, b Morley	0		
T. W. Garrett, Esq.	c Ridley, b Morley	6		
F. E. Spofforth, Esq.	b Shaw	1		
D. W. Gregory, Esq.	b Shaw	0		
H. F. Boyle, Esq.	c Wild, b Morley	2		
W. L. Murdoch, Esq.	b Shaw	9		
F. E. Allan, Esq.	c and b Shaw	6		
G. H. Bailey, Esq.	not out	3		
	B , l-b , w , n-b ,		B , l-b , w , n-b ,	
	Total	41	Total	12

Umpires—Rylott and Sherwin.   Scorers—W. Hearn and McCanlis.

BOWLING ANALYSIS.

	M.C.C.—First Innings.				Second Innings.			
	O.	M.	R.	W.	O.	M.	R.	W.
Boyle	14	7	14	3	8.1	6	3	5
Spofforth	5.3	3	4	6	9	2	16	5
Allan	9	4	14	1				

	Australians—First Innings.				Second Innings.			
Shaw	33.2	25	10	5	8	6	4	1
Morley	33	19	31	5	8	4	8	0

PRICE TWOPENCE.

SURREY COUNTY CRICKET CLUB,

KENNINGTON OVAL,

On MONDAY, SEPTEMBER 6th, 1880, and two following Days

ENGLAND v. AUSTRALIA

ENGLAND.

	1ST INNINGS.		2ND INNINGS.	
Dr. W. G. Grace	b Palmer	152 not out		9
Dr. E. M. Grace	c Alexander, b Bannerman	36	c Blackham, b Palmer	2
A. P. Lucas, Esq.	b Bannerman	55	c Blackham, b Palmer	2
Barnes	b Alexander	28	c Moule, b Boyle	5
Lord Harris	c Bonnor, b Alexander	52		
F. Penn, Esq.	b Bannerman	23	not out	27
A. G. Steel, Esq.	c Boyle, b Moule	42		
Hon. A. Lyttelton	not out	11	b Palmer	13
G. F. Grace, Esq.	c Bannerman, b Moule	0	b Palmer	0
Shaw	b Moule	0		
Morley	run out	2		
	B 8, l-b 11, w , n-b	19	B , l-b , w , n-b 1	1
	Total	420	Total	57

AUSTRALIA.

	1ST INNINGS.		2ND INNINGS.	
W. L. Murdoch	c Barnes, b Steel	0	not out	153
A. Bannerman	c Morley	32	c Lucas, b Shaw	8
T. U. Groube	b Steel	11	c Shaw, b Morley	0
P. S. McDonnell	c Barnes, b Morley	27	l b w, b W. G. Grace	43
J. Slight	c G. F. Grace, b Morley	11	c Harris, b W. G. Grace	0
J. M. Blackham	c and b Morley	0	c E. M. Grace, b Morley	19
G. J. Bonnor	c G. F. Grace, b Shaw	2	b Steel	16
H. F. Boyle	not out	36	run out	3
G. E. Palmer	b Morley	6	c and b Steel	4
G. Alexander	c W. G. Grace, b Steel	6	c Shaw, b Morley	33
W. H. Moule	c Morley, b W. G. Grace	6	b Barnes	34
	B 9, l-b 3, w , n-b	12	B 7, l-b 7, w , n-b	14
	Total	149	Total	327

UMPIRES—
Thoms & H. Stephenson.   Total   149   Total   327

Printed by JOHN SHAW & Co., 6, Pilgrim Street, Ludgate Hill, London, E.C.

---

and England based their victory on W.G.'s 152 in *his* first Test. But by 1882 another great bowler, George Palmer, a leg-spinner with subtle changes of pace and an easy action, had taken over from Allan, and George Giffen of South Australia had arrived as an all-round rival to W.G. At the end of August came the famous first Australian Test victory on English soil, at The Oval, when England, needing only 85 to win, were bowled out for 77 in one of those desperately tense, slowly evolving finishes which only cricket, and especially only Test cricket, can provide. At one stage twelve successive maiden overs were bowled by Spofforth and Boyle to Lyttelton and Lucas, who had come together for the fifth wicket after W.G. had fallen, caught at mid-off for 32 made out of 53. A deliberate misfield, at Spofforth's suggestion, allowed 'The Demon' to bowl instead at Lyttelton and a ball from that tall wiry fast bowler, coming out of the dark background of the Oval pavilion, duly accounted for England's wicket-keeper after four more maidens. Still England needed only 19 to win with five wickets left, but they could not do it. The Secretary of Surrey, C.W. Alcock, recorded: 'Men who were noted for their coolness at critical moments were trembling like a leaf; some were shivering with cold, some even fainted. At times there was an awful silence.'

Tom Horan, who batted at number five in that match and became one of the earliest player-writers, said that the excitement was so desperate that one spectator fell dead, another bit a chunk from his umbrella-handle, and one of the English batsmen could barely speak as he made his way to the wicket, his lips ash-grey. Perhaps it was the last man, C.T. Studd, most unwisely demoted by England's captain, Monkey Hornby, and according to one witness so overcome by nerves that he walked round the pavilion wrapped in a blanket. At any rate, Studd, after a first

Above Australians of 1878. *Back, left to right: J. McC. Blackham, T. Horan, G.H. Bailey, J. Conway, A.C. Bannerman, C. Bannerman, W.L. Murdoch. Seated: D.W. Gregory (capt.). Front: F.R. Spofforth, F. Allan, W.E. Midwinter, T.W. Garrett, H.F. Boyle.*

Above left 'The Australians came down like a wolf on the fold . . .' *Scorecard of the match which made everyone realize how good the Australians had become. Though the Notts pair, Alfred Shaw and Fred Morley, took all the Australian wickets, they were out-bowled by Spofforth and Boyle. On a wet pitch 31 wickets fell in four and a half hours of actual play.*

Left The scorecard of the first Test match in England. *W. G. gave Murdoch his gold watch for bettering his own score, but England won by five wickets despite second innings alarms. This was easily W. G's best match for England, though (despite his Indian Summer) he was past his best when the Test era started.*

The Great Northern Railway knew the attractions of the Australian cricketers!

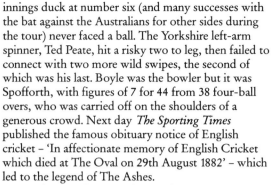

Australians of 1888. Back, left to right: J.J. Ferris, S.P. Jones, A.H. Jarvis, J. Worall, C. W. Beal (manager), J.J. Lyons, J. McC. Blackham, H.F. Boyle, J. Edwards. Front: G.J. Bonnor, C.T.B. Turner, P.S. McDonnell (captain). H. Trott, A. C. Bannerman.

innings duck at number six (and many successes with the bat against the Australians for other sides during the tour) never faced a ball. The Yorkshire left-arm spinner, Ted Peate, hit a risky two to leg, then failed to connect with two more wild swipes, the second of which was his last. Boyle was the bowler but it was Spofforth, with figures of 7 for 44 from 38 four-ball overs, who was carried off on the shoulders of a generous crowd. Next day *The Sporting Times* published the famous obituary notice of English cricket – 'In affectionate memory of English Cricket which died at The Oval on 29th August 1882' – which led to the legend of The Ashes.

This was the tour which really set the pattern for the future. The side of thirteen players had arrived at Plymouth on 3 May, after leaving Melbourne on the P&O steamer *Assam* on 16 March. Between 15 May at Oxford and 26 September at Harrogate, Murdoch's men played 38 fixtures, almost all over three days, winning 23, drawing 11 – usually because of rain – and losing only 4. They travelled the country by train, staying at good hotels and being received everywhere as more-than-welcome visitors – indeed as celebrities.

Their matches were fully reported in the newspapers and a book of the tour, written by C.F. Pardon, was published by the leading sports journal of the day, *Bell's Life In London*. Each game was reported in detail (though Pardon makes no mention of the gentleman dropping dead at the climax of the Test match) and Pardon was a fearless critic, suggesting, for example, that much of the umpiring was not good, that Hornby had no right to have been chosen captain of England, that W.G. Grace was guilty of discourtesy if not of sharp practice when running out young Jones when he strayed out of his ground after taking a single, and that Massie, the opening batsman who began the tour with a double century against Oxford and whose 55 in the second innings of the Test match was easily the highest score of the game, was, despite his 'splendid hitting ... likely to demoralise the field and change the aspect of the game ... a rash, impatient hitter who too often sacrifices safety for the sake of brilliancy.'

The success of the 1882 tourists established Australia as the most important of the early cricket countries to tour England. They were not, however, the only ones. Apart from the Aboriginals in 1868, tours were also made by a team of Indian Parsees in 1886 and again in 1888, when they won eight of a long programme of 31 games, the fast bowler Dr M.E. Pavri taking 170 wickets at less than 12 apiece. South African teams came in 1894, 1901 (despite the Boer War!) and 1904, by which time they were good enough to play England on equal terms, although no Tests were

Gentlemen of Philadelphia, 1889 (the second Philadelphian side to visit England, the first having toured in 1884). The team were amateurs, and their share of the gates went to the Cricketer's Fund. Back, left to right: R.D. Brown, N. Etting, E.W. Clark Junior, G.L. Warder (sec.). Seated: H.P. Baily, C.R. Palmer, D.S. Newhall (capt.), F.E. Brewster, D.P. Stoever, G.S. Patterson. Front: W.C. Morgan, W. Scott, A.G. Thomson.

The first touring Parsees, of 1886, photographed at the match v Lord Sheffield's XI, 24 May 1886 at Sheffield Park. Back, left to right: A.B. Patell, S. Bezonjee. Standing: G. Payne (umpire), M.P. Banajee, P.C. Major, S.N. Bhedwar, D.D. Khambatta, A.C. Major, D.J. Pochkhana. Seated: A.R. Libuwalla, P.D. Dastur, Dr D.H. Patell, M. Framjee, B.P. Balla. Front: J.M. Morenas, B.B. Baria, S.H. Harvar.

actually played until their next tour.

Not the least popular of the relatively minor visits, however, were those by the Philadelphians, who enjoyed some success against good club sides in 1884 and 1889, and then in 1897 did well during an entirely first-class programme, beating two counties, drawing against three and producing in J. Barton King a bowler of world renown. In 1903 and 1908, Philadelphian sides again held their own against the first-class county sides, but top-class cricket in the United States did not survive the First World War.

Cricket being always a more or less faithful mirror of society, it was not surprising that as the Industrial Revolution gained force in Britain, a greater awareness developed of the differences between those who played cricket as a pastime – the amateurs and 'Gentlemen' – and those who played it for a living – the professionals and 'Players'. The first official fixture between the Gents and the Players took place at Lord's in 1806.

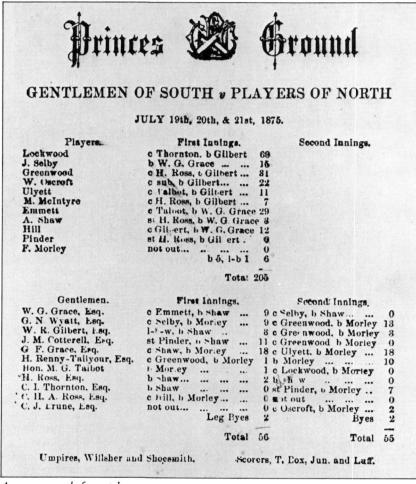

Princes Ground

GENTLEMEN OF SOUTH v PLAYERS OF NORTH

JULY 19th, 20th, & 21st, 1875.

Players.	First Innings.		Second Innings.
Lockwood	c Thornton. b Gilbert	69	
J. Selby	b W. G. Grace	15	
Greenwood	c H. Ross, b Gilbert	31	
W. Oscroft	c sub, b Gilbert	22	
Ulyett	c Talbot, b Gilbert	11	
M. McIntyre	c H. Ross, b Gilbert	7	
Emmett	c Talbot, b W. G. Grace	29	
A. Shaw	st H. Ross, b W. G. Grace	3	
Hill	c Gilbert, b W. G. Grace	12	
Pinder	st H. Ross, b Gilbert	0	
F. Morley	not out	0	
	b 5, l-b 1	6	
	Total 205		

Gentlemen.	First Innings.		Second Innings.	
W. G. Grace, Esq.	c Emmett, b Shaw	9	c Selby, b Shaw	0
G. N. Wyatt, Esq.	c Selby, b Morley	9	c Greenwood. b Morley	13
W. R. Gilbert, Esq.	l-b-w. b Shaw	8	c Greenwood, b Morley	3
J. M. Cotterell, Esq.	st Pinder, b Shaw	11	c Greenwood b Morley	0
G. F. Grace, Esq.	c Shaw, b Morley	18	c Ulyett. b Morley	18
H. Renny-Tailyour, Esq.	c Greenwood, b Morley	1	b Morley	10
Hon. M. G. Talbot	b Morley	1	c Lockwood, b Morley	0
H. Ross, Esq.	b Shaw	2	b Shaw	0
C. I. Thornton. Esq.	b Shaw	0	st Pinder, b Morley	7
C. H. A. Ross, Esq.	c Hill, b Morley	0	not out	0
C. J. Lrune, Esq.	not out	0	c Oscroft, b Morley	2
	Leg Byes	2	Byes	2
	Total 56		Total 55	

Umpires, Willsher and Shoesmith.   Scorers, T. Cox, Jun. and Luff.

A rare scorecard of a match at Prince's Ground in London, a venue for several big matches, including this one between Southern Gentlemen and the (much stronger) Northern Players.

Ninety years later, a Test match at The Oval between England and Australia was threatened when five of the 13 from whom the home team was to be selected demanded that their match fee, a standard £10, should be doubled. Between the middle years of the touring elevens, when the top professionals made a handsome living, and the end of the century, the financial status of the full-time cricketers had failed to grow in line with their value as entertainers and public personalities. Yet those who went on tours and earned

'benefits' could do well, and even the average professional cricketers made more than unskilled labourers of the time. Few who were good enough to play cricket professionally would turn down the opportunity – although, ironically, several amateurs, for example Reggie Spooner, were able to play little first-class cricket because they were obliged to make progress in military or business careers, in Spooner's case in both.

The five professionals who made their bold challenge to the Surrey committee in 1896 were Abel, Hayward, Lohmann and Richardson, all of Surrey, supported by Gunn of Nottinghamshire (Notts had had their own players' strike in 1881). Gunn and Lohmann refused to play in the Test match unless their ultimatum was met. The other three relented after promises that their pay would be reviewed and thereafter the match fee for professionals was, indeed, raised to £20. Allowing even for inflation, however, it was modest remuneration for the ultimate honour in the game.

This show of professional strength was accompanied by press suggestions that W.G. Grace, in common with other 'amateurs', was being paid more than his expenses for playing in the Test match. This prompted the Surrey committee to issue a strongly worded statement to the effect that whenever W.G. played at The Oval, be it for a Test match or a Gentleman v Players game, his only remuneration was £10 to cover his expenses of coming to London and staying for the three days of the game.

That W.G.'s career as a doctor sometimes became secondary, during the season at least, to his cricket would not have been doubted by the Surrey committee or anyone else. There was no secret made of the fact that in 1891–92 he was given the then huge sum of £3,000, plus expenses, to tour Australia for the second time under Lord Sheffield (it was perhaps one reason why his Lordship lost £2,000 of his own money on the venture, though he had undertaken it for reasons of altruism rather than profit). Alfred Shaw, who published these figures, did not mention what the professionals were paid but it would not have been much more than a tenth of what was paid to the captain. But then the Doctor was the Doctor. It should be remembered that the amateurs of this and later periods who took considerably more than legitimate expenses from the game, were obliged to do so to compensate for loss of income in other fields and in order to meet the considerably greater expenses demanded by the lifestyle of a 'gentleman'.

Those professionals who went on the early tours to Australia could return, according to Shaw, with £100 or £150 in their pockets 'with ordinary care'.

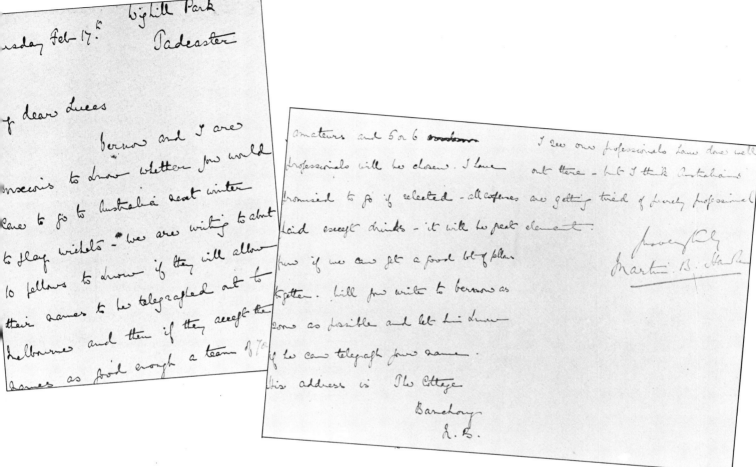

A letter from Lord Hawke to the prominent amateur A.P. Lucas, asking him to join G.F. Vernon's team to Australia in 1887-88. Lucas did not do so! Hawke says: '. . . all expenses paid, except drinks – it will be great fun if we can get a good lot of fellows together . . . I see our professionals have done very well out there – but I think Australians are getting tired of the purely professional element.'

A sum of £50 was always left behind with the players' wives, but Shaw added that in fact a good many professionals came home with very little profit because the 'hospitality of our colonial cousins knew no bounds' and expensive habits were easily acquired. Some, however, made the most of their bonanzas. The 1863-64 side made a profit of £475 a man, each took home 'enough jewellery to stock a small shop' and one of the team, the Notts all-rounder William Oscroft, had the foresight to take out a good deal of extra cricketing equipment which he sold at a profit!

As a manager of tours to Australia, Shaw, in partnership with Lillywhite and Shrewsbury, made a personal profit of £700 from the 1880-81 trip after paying the players £250 each and all expenses. Thereafter things went less well: the profit was cut to £150 per promoter in 1883-84 and Shaw's next two ventures were financial failures, especially that of 1887-88 when he and Shrewsbury each lost £1,200 because Lillywhite could not pay his share of the loss and also because the Melbourne club, jealous of its great rival, Sydney, had invited another English team, under G.F. Vernon. In fact the Melbourne tour had been hatched first, so the fault for the clash lay more with Shaw and his partners.

For those who stayed behind, to make a living from cricket in the summer only, wages stayed ahead of those available to factory or agricultural workers. Opportunities in county cricket steadily increased in step with the development of the county game, Lillywhite's *Cricketers' Annual* listing 79 professionals employed by 13 counties in 1872, these figures climbing to 154 players employed by 19 different counties in 1891 and 180 employed by 25 counties five years later. Apart from county cricket there were coaching opportunities at public schools, the universities, clubs and, increasingly, overseas in Australia, South Africa, the United States, New Zealand and India.

Match fees were raised only very slowly. In the 1860s the average was £3 a match with a £1 bonus for a win; a decade later the fee was £5 with a £1 bonus

Right and centre A letter from J. T. Brown to his parents in Driffield, sent during the 1894–95 tour to Australia led by A. E. Stoddart, just prior to the decisive last Test in which Brown was to be a hero, hitting 140 in 2 hours 25 minutes to win the series for England. He says in his letter: 'I am glad to say I get on very well with the amateurs and the managers. We have some rare fun.'

Another dutiful letter from Brown to his parents . . . 'I have been poorly lately and have had bad luck, so you must not think I have been out of form. I ought not to have played in two or three of the matches but Stoddart would like me to play in every match . . .'

and, in some instances, a travel allowance. According to T.P. Horan in 1889, the average income of the ordinary pro was £85 for a five-month season, double that for the top players. But by the end of the century the historian Rowland Bowen estimated the average professional income to be £275, compared with £95 for an unskilled labourer.

The lifestyle, moreover, was infinitely preferable, despite its insecurity. The trouble came on retirement. The luckier cricketers could expect a benefit–sometimes a very lucrative one: Bobby Peel made £2,000 from his in 1894. But like many other cricketers who had built up some income, he used it to take the lease of a pub and his career came to a sad end three years later when he took the field intoxicated and was dismissed on the spot by Lord Hawke.

Alcohol and the psychological blow, when retirement came, of descending into obscurity after having been a respected and well-known figure, were the undoing of many, though by no means all. The two most prominent aristocratic Victorian cricketers, Lord Harris of Kent and Lord Hawke of Yorkshire, did their best to protect the later years of the professionals. Hawke decreed that two-thirds of a player's benefit funds should be held back until his retirement and Harris put his formidable influence behind the Cricketers' Fund Friendly Society, originally set up by the All England and United elevens in 1862.

But the fund was insufficient. John 'Foghorn' Jackson, a hero of national fame twenty-five years before, was paid 5s 6d a week by the Society yet ended his days hovering near the Liverpool workhouse, in the words of A.W. Pullin 'a bent and grisly man of sixty-seven, having no permanent address'. Julius Caesar of Surrey, despite two benefits in the 1860s, died in 1878 'in the depths of poverty'. Many players died much younger. The Australian historian W.F. Mandle found a high number of deaths from consumption, three of cold and wet and one of rheumatism. For others the dangers were diseases of the liver and kidneys from too much drink. As Lord Harris observed, 'professional cricketers rarely make old bones'.

By the end of the nineteenth century things were looking up again. Writing in *Cricket* in 1903, R.H. Lyttelton observed that in the 1860s and '70s one had been able to tell a professional by his colourful, odd attire but that nowadays he was better paid, better educated and in better trim. Ranji pointed out that the professionals were noted for their 'respectfulness and respectability' and in 1885 George Freeman, the Yorkshire professional fast bowler, actually crossed the Rubicon by playing for the Gentlemen.

J.T. Brown.

Cricket tours in the 1980s tend to be hectic and obsessive. Their social purpose is minimal. A century ago, despite the fact that no-one organized a tour without careful consideration of its financial viability, players and organizers alike considered that what happened off the field was at least as important as the matches themselves and the profits – or losses – they made. Cricket could build bridges between nations. Visitors had to be looked after, entertained, wined and dined. None did better than the five Australian teams who between 1884 and 1896 opened their tour at Sheffield Park in Sussex, the Arundel of Victorian cricket.

Of all the private patrons of cricket, in any era, none was so passionate, and yet so disinterested in personal prestige, as Henry North Holroyd, the Third Earl of Sheffield. A lifelong enthusiast for cricket, he was no great player, though he once, as Lord Pevensey, played for the Gentlemen of Sussex against the Gentlemen of Kent. That was in 1856, when he was twenty-four and his private ground at Sheffield Park was already open, a ground of exceptional scenic grandeur, most beautifully maintained, at its best in early summer when the rhododendrons and azaleas were in bloom.

Surviving menus show something of the hospitality afforded to the visiting Australians, and in 1894 the South African tourists were also splendidly entertained at Sheffield Park. The public was never charged for entry to these matches against the touring teams, which were played very seriously – especially no doubt by Lord Sheffield's XI which often amounted almost to an England side – though in an atmosphere of 'cordial happiness'. The pitch was described as being 'good if a trifle fiery in dry weather and, like all wickets on infrequently used grounds, apt to crumble'.

The Australians enjoyed notable innings victories in 1884 and 1890, on both occasions despite the presence of W.G., who was one of an eleven bowled out for only 27 (Grace 20) by Turner and Ferris in 1890. The last first-class match at Sheffield Park, against the 1896 Australians, was marked by a brilliant 95 not out on a crumbling wicket by F.S. Jackson. Not many years afterwards the ground had become a hayfield.

The Australians had double reason to be grateful for Lord Sheffield's friendship. In the winter of 1891–92, entirely at his own expense, he took an England touring team to Australia, partly, it was said, to show W.G. Grace to a new generation of Australian spectators. The Doctor was now a real veteran, but he did not let anyone down and, despite an incident or two involving the umpires *(plus ça change)*, the team was popular in Australia, not least for losing the Test series 2–1! To commemorate the trip, Lord Sheffield presented the famous Shield for which the leading state sides have battled every peacetime season since.

Lord Sheffield was even more generous in his own county. President of Sussex from 1879 to 1897, he resigned after receiving a number of 'poison-pen' letters, but returned to the post in 1904, four years before his death. For ten years he employed Alfred Shaw of Notts and William Mycroft of Derbyshire to coach Sussex cricketers at a time when the county was struggling to hold its own. Three or four trial matches were held at Sheffield Park every year before the season opened – Shaw estimated that 'they cost his Lordship not less than £50 each' – and all through the summer Shaw would officiate at further trial matches round the county, seeking out new talent. Promising players were given special coaching, and Shaw himself received a generous salary. Amongst those thus spotted were Billy Newham, George Brann, Aubrey Smith, F.M. Lucas and A.E. Relf.

Shaw also accompanied the philanthropic Earl on trips 'combining cricket with pleasure' to France and Holland and on non-cricketing journeys up the Nile to Egypt, to the Holy Land, to the Crimea and to Norway. Presumably Shaw was invited on these trips to do the next best thing to playing cricket – talking it instead. But wherever Lord Sheffield went, a chance to play the game was never missed. As Shaw recalled, it was inevitably his idea to play a game at midnight on board the *Lusitania:*
'The scene of this novel match was the anchorage in the ice fiord at Spitzbergen, about forty miles up the fiord … we were nestling in the bosom of a peaceful fiord at midnight, with the Arctic sun at its lowest point lighting up the snow-clad mountains and the magnificent glaciers around us. The light was equal to noonday at an English cricket match; indeed it was much superior to the average light of one or two famous cricket grounds in the North of England that I wot of.

'It was Lord Sheffield who suggested a cricket match at this weird hour and amongst these eerie surroundings. Wickets were pitched, a ball improvised, and at a quarter to twelve on the night of August 12th, 1894, this strange game commenced. Of course I had to bowl and Lord Sheffield opened the batting. Between a quarter to twelve and half past twelve, I had bowled out practically all the gentlemen passengers and officers, certainly forty persons all told.'

The noble Earl and his fellow-passengers were in good company. Shaw is believed never to have bowled a wide and he bowled W.G. Grace on 20 occasions, more than any other man. That was another kind of Sheffield Park hospitality!

Cricket Match
between the
South African Eleven and the Earl of Sheffield's Eleven
in Sheffield Park.
on May 22nd & 23rd
Admit Mr. Sourest
to the Private Marquee.
Not Transferable.   No one will be admitted without this Card.
and Signature attached.
Sheffield
Signature of Bearer.

Lord Sheffield's coat of arms, from the front of an admission ticket to Sheffield Park. The admission to the private marquee (left) was for the 1894 match with the South African tourists.

Sheffield Park in the 1880s.

Lord Sheffield's XI v South Africa at Sheffield Park, 22–23 May 1894. Back, left to right: Carpenter (umpire), Humphreys, Bates (scorer), Bailey, Butt, Thoms (umpire). Seated: A.F. Somerset, G. Brann, W.L. Murdoch (capt.), A. Blackman, B.C.V. Wentworth, MP. Front: Briggs, W. Newham, Payne.

The South African team at Sheffield Park in 1894. Back, left to right: D.C. Davey, T. Routledge, C.O. Sewell, W.V. Simkins (manager), G. Rowe, G. Glover, C. Mills. Seated: G. Kempis, G. Cripps, H.H. Castens (capt.), C.L. Johnson, A.W. Seccull. Front: F. Hearne (from the famous Kent family of Hearnes), J. Middleton, E.A. Halliwell, D.C. Parkin.

HAMBLEDON, HANTS

THE CRADLE OF CRICKET.

A GRAND MATCH

WILL BE PLAYED ON

BROADHALFPENNY DOWN,

(the original Ground of the famous Hambledon Club of 1750),

On Sept. 10th, 11th, 12th.

HAMBLEDON
v.
ENGLAND

The following Members of the Hambledon Cricket Club have been selected to play against
MR. JESSOP'S ENGLAND ELEVEN:

E. Whalley-Tooker, Captain.	Captain W. White.	W. Langridge.	Llewellyn.
E. M. Sprott.	Captain E. G. Wynyard.	Mead.	Newman.
C. B. Fry.	A. J. Hill.	Stone.	

On the first day of the Match, during Luncheon interval,

A * GRANITE * MEMORIAL

which has been erected to mark the site of the original Cricket Ground of the celebrated Club
of 150 years ago, will be unveiled by DR. W. G. GRACE.

Admission to the Ground will be Free, except to Horses, Vehicles and Cycles. Seating accommodation will be fitted up in an enclosure, for which a charge of 1/- will be made. Tickets can be obtained at either entrance or of Members of the Committee. Refreshments and Luncheons will be supplied on the Ground at a tariff approved by the Committee.

Horses must be tethered at owner's risk, on that part of the Ground apportioned by the Committee, and with halters supplied for that purpose.

THE BAND OF THE TRAINING SHIP "MERCURY" has been engaged to play on the Ground during the Match.

The London and South-Western Railway Company will issue Cheap Tickets from London and various stations to West Meon, Droxford, Petersfield and Rowland's Castle, in connection with this Match. For particulars see Company's bills.

Any further particulars may be obtained from the Hon. Secretary, Mr. J. A. Bxst, Hambledon.

F. O. EDNEY, Printer, Hambledon.

Hambledon's fame has grown rather than diminished. This match in 1908 is one of many celebrations over the years of the cradle of cricket. Amongst Hambledon's many distinguished honorary members taking on Gilbert Jessop's England XI, the most influential was C.B. Fry who had allowed the band of the training ship Mercury (which Fry commanded) to play on the Ground during the game.

FAMOUS ENGLISH CRICKETERS. – 1880.

J. SELBY.   G. ULYETT.   W. R. GILBERT, ESQ.   A. N. HORNBY, ESQ.   A. P. LUCAS, ESQ.   W. OSCROFT.   R. DAFT.   A. J. WEBBE, ESQ.   E. LOCKWOOD.   F. MORLEY.
J. LILLYWHITE.   A. SHAW.   LORD HARRIS.   H. JUPP.   W. G. GRACE, ESQ.   THE LATE G. F. GRACE, ESQ.   A. G. STEEL, ESQ.   E. POOLEY.   T. EMMETT.   R. PILLING.
W. BATES.

Above *The great names of 1880.*

Right *George Parr of Nottinghamshire and All England, as depicted on a Staffordshire jug, c. 1850-70.*

Far right *A fan produced by Eugene Rimmel, one of many handed out to ladies attending the 1876 Eton v Harrow match: an indication both of the elegance of the occasion, and an early recognition that for a company to associate its name with cricket might be good for sales and public relations.*

The Centenary of the present ground in 1914 was marked by a rather disappointing match between the winter touring team, minus the injured Sydney Barnes, and The Rest. A dinner was held on the second evening of the game at the Hotel Cecil with speeches by, amongst others, W. G. Grace and Lord Harris.

Far left *A Centenary reproduction of the first match at the new Lord's ground. The MCC side included four of the best known early figures at Lord's – Beauclerk, Osbaldeston, Budd and Ward.*

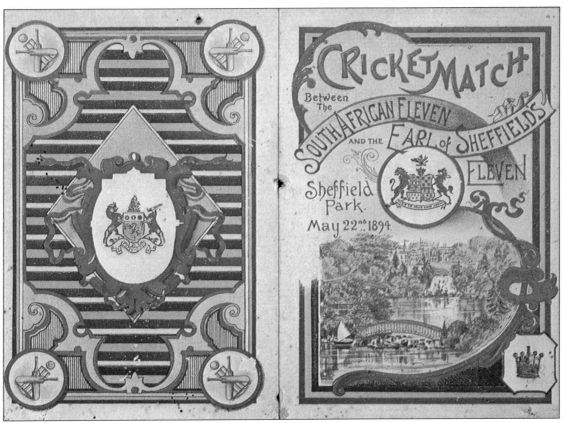

A beautifully produced menu, showing the house, ground and coat of arms of the Sheffield family of Sheffield Park in Sussex where, for some years, it was traditional for the touring team of the summer to play its opening match. This menu was for a dinner during the 1894 match against the South Africans which Lord Sheffield's team, despite having only six county players, won by ten wickets, the lob bowler Humphreys discomforting the visitors by taking eight wickets in the match. (Who knows if the combination of lobs and rich hospitality might not equally discomfort even hard-bitten modern touring teams!)

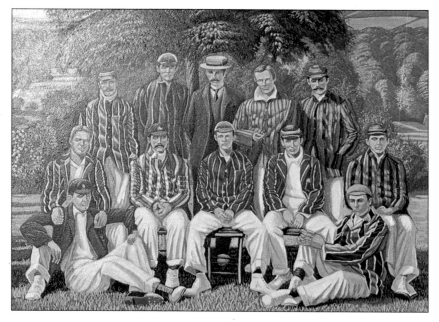

Above left *A painting commissioned by the Devonshire collector Roger Mann from the artist Gerry Wright. It depicts Plum Warner's touring team to the USA in 1897 but the commissioner and the artist have indulged their licence and fancy in depicting some of the players in blazers of their choice. (For original colours see photograph on page 45.)*

Above right *An autograph collector's gem. Eminent names adorn the back of a menu (the 1907-08 team to Australia). Amongst the easily recognizable signatures: S.F. Barnes and J.B. Hobbs.*

Far left *The MCC Centenary Dinner at Lord's.*

Below *A jug and one of two mugs in a set produced to commemorate the 150th anniversary of the MCC.*

One of the features of cricket, especially English cricket, in the late Victorian era, was the almost ritual significance accorded to the photographic team group. The first cricket photos were taken, almost certainly, in the 1850s. Parr's team to America in 1859 posed on board a ship (not the one in which they sailed) in the Liverpool docks, dressed in smart polka-dot shirts. One of their number, the wicket-keeper Tom Lockyer, used to play on cold days in a short white coat, like a waistcoat. It was not long before the amateurs, at least, would consider it taboo not to wear a blazer at a meal in a cricket pavilion, and certainly not to do so in any cricket photograph.

The term 'blazer' is first thought to have been used in connection with the rather garish 'scarlet coats' worn by the Lady Margaret boat crew at St John's College, Cambridge in 1862. The Oxford cricket eleven of the following year wore blue blazers, and during the 1870s county groups began to be photographed in their blazers and Spy's famous cartoon of 'The Demon' Fred Spofforth in 1878 shows him smartly attired in a blue and white striped coat. The first of the England teams managed by Shaw and

Shrewsbury, in 1881–82, did not wear blazers; their next two teams most certainly did. The 'uniforms' gave any team an appearance, at least, of smartness and unity of purpose.

Unconsciously, a sort of unwritten etiquette seems to have developed amongst amateur sides which dictated who should wear which blazers in which team. The I Zingari colours of black, red and gold – out of darkness, through fire or blood, into light – were well suited to the dashing, gypsy ethos of the club formed after a dinner by three enthusiasts in 1845. They took precedence over most. In the late 1860s, in fact, there was a minor row when loyal Zingaros complained about the adoption by MCC (in existence since 1787 without distinct colours) of two of the IZ colours, red and gold. Neither tie is likely to be worn by the fashion-conscious, and certainly not with anything other than a monochrome shirt. (This is not to claim that many members of these wandering clubs were or are fashion-conscious. On the contrary, though they will know at once from the sound of bat on ball if a particular stroke has been well timed or not, they may see nothing out of tune about a blue and white vertically striped shirt 'set off' by the green, red

The heraldry of cricket, manifested in the caps and blazers worn by Pelham Warner's all-amateur side that toured the USA in 1897. Back, left to right: Messrs G.L. Jessop (Crusaders), F.W. Stocks (?), A.D. Whatman (plain clothes), R.A. Bennett (Eton Ramblers), J.R. Head (Free Foresters). Seated: W. McG. Hemingway (?), J.N. Tonge (Free Foresters), P.F. Warner (Lord Hawke's), H.D.G. Leveson-Gower (Lord Hawke's blazer, I Zingari cap), H.B. Chinnery (I Zingari cap and blazer). Front: F.G. Bull (probably Essex cap and blazer), H.H. Marriott (Cambridge cap, blazer?).

Lord Sheffield's team to Australia, 1891-92, photographed in the Botanical Gardens, Adelaide. In the original caption, following convention, the professionals were listed without initials. Back left to right: Shaw, A.E. Stoddart, J.M. Read, H.P. Philipson, O.G. Radcliffe. Front: Abel, Lohmann, G. Macgregor, Briggs, Peel, W.G., Attewell, Bean, Sharpe.

Among the sober rig of Lord Hawke's mainly professional Yorkshire side, only three blazers are outstanding and only one can be identified with certainty – that of Hon. F.S. Jackson (seated, second left) which reveals that he also turned out for Lord Hawke's amateurs.

and white diagonals of the Free Foresters.)

Probably the most exotic blazer ever devised was the original design for the Butterflies, featuring a plain white flannel jacket on which members persuaded the ladies of their family to embroider butterflies according to taste. This was soon found, for various reasons, to be impracticable, and no surviving specimen is known. For other reasons, it became unfashionable to wear an MCC cap in a first-class match, and the last man to have done so is thought to have been Budge Firth, later a Winchester master and Master of the Temple, who wore his while playing for Notts at Lord's in 1919. He is also remembered for being the only man who ever ran after a Portuguese train and failed to catch it!

Victorian cricketers were not so much fashion-conscious as etiquette-conscious. IZ colours predominate in the *Vanity Fair* cartoons of the Victorian period, although W.G. himself preferred his

MCC cap and, a little later, L.C.H. Palairet reminded everyone of his Oxford background by continuing to wear the Harlequin colours, later associated with D.R. Jardine, when playing for Somerset. County caps and blazers were generally more sober and monochrome but the professionals had to be content with them because by the end of the nineteenth century the coloured, striped or spotted shirts which, a generation earlier, had been characteristic of the wandering elevens, had been replaced by the basic, sober white which was to remain standard cricket uniform until, in the late 1970s, Mr Kerry Packer, with one eye on William Clarke and the other on American baseball, brought back the bright colours to the cricket fields of Australia.

The blazers worn by Gregor Macgregor's Middlesex side, which he captained from 1899 to 1907, were more spectacular than the Yorkshiremen's. Back, left to right: J.T. Hearne (Lord Hawke's), Mr R.W. Nicholls, Mr B.J.T. Bosanquet (both Free Foresters), J.T. Rawlin (Middlesex ?). Seated: Mr L.J. Moon, Mr C.M. Wells (both Quidnuncs), Mr G. Macgregor, Mr P.F. Warner (both Free Foresters), Mr G.W. Beldam (?). Front: Mr J. Douglas (Quidnuncs), A.E. Trott (shirtsleeves), Mr E.A. Beldam (?). Some variations in the colours can be attributed to the light and to natural fading.

Who first decided to abandon the eighteenth-century method of scoring at cricket matches by cutting notches into a piece of wood to count the runs, we shall never know. The first surviving record of cricket scores in any number dates from 1790 when Samuel Britcher, 'a highly educated individual, who abandoned the old method for the pencil', and who was for many years employed by the MCC as their official scorer, published his *List* of all the 'Principal Matches of Cricket with a correct state of each innings'. He published a similar *List* every year for the next thirteen. It is likely that he had moved to London from his native Kent in 1783 (according to the researches of David Rayvern-Allen) but any earlier scores produced by him of matches played by MCC, after their foundation in 1787, have been lost.

Earlier scores do, however, exist in some form, giving an idea of how it became steadily more important throughout the eighteenth century for cricket devotees to have a record of their main matches. A reference in 1718 gives just a bare result: London beat Surrey. By 1730 we are given a little more information: London beat Surrey by six notches. In 1734 respective totals are given: 'So that the Londoners, with one hand, without going in the second time, beat the Kentishmen by 25.' In 1737 the first mention is made of how many wickets fell in a match between London and Chertsey. In 1751 there is a record of the total when the wickets fell in a match at the Artillery Ground in Finsbury Park. The ground was also the scene, in 1744, of the first fully recorded match, the famous encounter between Kent and All England for which even 'bye-runs' were written down.

A scoresheet of 1773 indicated who were the bowlers, wicket-keepers and long-stops, that position on the boundary behind the ill-protected 'keeper which in Hambledon days was one of the most important in the field. Modes of dismissal in some of these early scorecards were inventively described. Hit wicket was sometimes given as 'struck himself out' or 'beat down his own wicket', and during a match between Wadhurst and Mayfield in 1796 T. Cruttenden got himself out in a manner which has defied rational interpretation. He was recorded as 'shambled out'.

A mid-nineteenth century scoresheet. No bowlers' figures are given but there were wickets for the prominent amateur fast bowler, Sir Frederick Bathurst, who became MCC President in 1857.

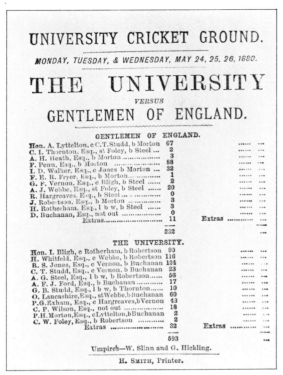

Far left *Cambridge University scorecard of 1880: a rich collection of names of men who were, or would become, the soul of English cricket between 1870 and 1900.*

Left *Lillywhite's scorecard of an important county match in 1863. Notts v Surrey was almost always a well-fought match between strong elevens.*

It was a long time before bowlers were given credit on scorecards for any wickets other than those taken by clean-bowling. The first instances of their being awarded credit for stumpings and catches date from 1836. As for information on the field, the first telegraphs at Lord's and The Oval began operation in 1846 and 1848, and spectators owed much after this time to Fred Lillywhite, who from 1848 began taking his own portable printing press round with him to big matches along with a portable booth in which to house it. He took both to North America on the famous first tour of 1859, often holding up the coach whilst his 'contraption' was placed on board. Lillywhite thus became the first of the many travelling cricket reporters who are now an integral part of every tour.

It took a long time, however, for cricket authorities to realize that if the game were to be properly covered, reporters needed proper facilities. As Sydney Pardon remarked in *Wisden* in 1893: 'Cricket can hardly be well reported if those who describe it are placed–as they often are–in the least favourable position for seeing the game.'

This criticism appeared in an introduction to a piece by Stewart Caine who observed that county grounds often placed their press tents or boxes in a hopeless position for judging the course of a game,

Fred Lillywhite in the scoring booth he took with him, not only round England but also to America in 1859.

usually in a windy spot far removed either from the scorers or the telegraph office (if there was one on the ground) or both. But things, he said, were improving at some grounds and 'the managers of cricket grounds are beginning to realize that cricket reporters are not so much necessary evils as men whose efforts do much to popularise the game'.

Writing in 1911, the Rev. R.S. Holmes reminisced that some fifty years before 'a few of us can remember the old scoring boxes at Lord's and The

As late as 1900 MCC showed their unconcern for the press by suddenly removing their box from the grandstand to the roof of the ground bowlers' house in the corner of the ground. Thunderously criticized for this by Pardon, MCC quickly provided a new box at the Nursery End, only for it to be blown down in a storm in 1906. The club then built a new box at the north-west corner of the pavilion which in 1958 was replaced by much more comfortable, though less favourably placed, facilities in the new Warner Stand.

Scorecard of the Australian first innings in the First Test at Sydney in the 1894–95 series. England eventually followed on after Giffen had inspired Australia to this tremendous start, yet won the match when Peel and Briggs bowled out Australia on a 'sticky dog' on the last day.

Oval–a small wooden structure on wheels–and a backless form in front of it, on which sat three or four reporters who made their notes on their knees and without protection from the sun'. In 1865 a combined scorers' and telegraph box was first utilized, and two years later special accommodation for the press was provided for the first time. It was in a glass-enclosed section of the old grandstand, messages being let down by a string from the front row to be telegraphed from the post-office below.

Thus, gradually, the cricket press gained a somewhat grudging acceptance, though to this day the number of press boxes placed looking down the wicket–the only place to judge lateral movement of the ball–are absurdly few.

THE CHAMPAGNE YEARS 1896-1914

It is doubtful if anyone in the history of sport has had quite such a popularizing influence as W.G. Grace. When, at the age of fifteen, he scored 170 and 56 not out in his second 'first-class' match, for South Wales Club against Gentlemen of Sussex at Brighton in 1864, cricket was a game steadily increasing in public affection as both a participant and spectator sport. In the next generation the game became a national institution, widely reported in the newspapers, a part of every boy's education. Its leading players became famous and W.G. himself was the most famous Englishman barring only the indomitable Mr Gladstone.

XXII of Lansdowne, Bath who played an All England XI at Bath on 28–30 May 1863. W.G. is fourth from right, seated. At the age of fourteen he began his first-class career in this match with two ducks, but a year later scored 170 and 56 not out.

centuries were rare and 1,000 runs in a season even more so, he dominated cricket for more than twenty years. He was the first man to do the double of 1,000 runs and 100 wickets, in 1873, and promptly repeated the achievement in each of the next five seasons. In 1876, in the space of just over a week, he hit 344 against Kent, 177 against Nottinghamshire and 318 not out against Yorkshire. And as late as 1895, when it had seemed his powers were waning as his eyes grew older and his weight increased (he retired from Test cricket four years later because, he said, 'The ground is getting too far away') he scored 1,000 runs in May. Spontaneously, four separate public testimonials were started for him.

His secrets were innate skill, the ability to see the ball early and judge its length, great powers of concentration allied to a powerful physique and exceptional stamina, and an orthodox batting method developed in his Gloucestershire youth. His mother, who played with him so often at Downend, said when her elder son Edward, a gifted, unorthodox player, was the best batsman in England, that young W.G. would supersede him because his defence was so much sounder. Later the Doctor kept a net and practice pitch outside his surgery at home, and from February on he would practise for the coming season.

Apart from just under 55,000 first-class runs and 126 catches, Grace took 2,876 wickets with bowling which began as roundarm fast and changed with age to subtle roundarm slow. During his career pitches greatly improved. Mowers only began to be used with any regularity from about 1850, though at Lord's they continued for many years to keep the grass down with sheep, and the heavy roller was first used at Lord's in 1870. Two years later came the first experiment in covering the pitch before the start of the match. Between them Grace's achievements and the improvement in wickets forced a sophistication in bowling techniques which was hastened by the Australians, notably by Spofforth. The all-out speed, which had been the main weapon on poor wickets, or sheer accuracy on the part of slow bowlers, now had to be augmented by swing, cut and spin if it was to get past the bat of 'The Champion'. W.G. thus paved the way for the Golden Age, the twenty years or so before the First World War, the hallmark of which was the beauty and brilliance of the batting and especially the amateur batting. Amateurs had been eclipsed before he came onto the scene but the quickest measure of his influence and genius is that in 1865, when he first played for the Gentlemen, the Players had won the last nineteen games between the two. When he last played in the match in 1906, the Gentlemen had lost only four more times.

Like Gladstone, Grace's undying fame rests partly on the longevity of his career. But the affection with which the British public, and all cricketers, regarded him was based not just on the length of his career, nor its outstanding success. It was his character, warm, unspoilt, brave, frank, which won so many hearts. He became the symbol of cricket, the focal point for the nation's passion for the game itself.

Very few cricketers change the game but Grace undoubtedly did. From the year 1871, when he scored 2,739 first-class runs at an average of 78 in an era when

The Grand Old Man in his MCC cap.

W. G. in action, his eyes locked on the ball.

W.G. captained England at bowls in the first match played at Crystal Palace in 1903, and continued to do so until 1908.

The Grace family and a few others representing 'West Gloucestershire' in July 1866. Back, left to right: Rev. H. W. Barber, H. M. Grace (father of W.G.), H. Gruning (bushy beard), Alfred Pocock (uncle). Middle: W.G., Henry Grace, Dr. E.M. Grace, Alfred Grace (all brothers). Front: F. Baker, W.J. Pocock, G.F. Grace (aged 15), R. Brotherhood.

A characteristically brief Grace letter, on London County notepaper.

W.G. batting at Crystal Palace, probably in 1903. He had founded London County in 1899 and was both its secretary and captain for the five years, 1900–04, in which the 'County' fulfilled a strong first-class fixture list. But W.G. was past his best and the club folded.

LONDON COUNTY CRICKET CLUB,
CRYSTAL PALACE.

Telegraphic Address:
"GRACE, SYDENHAM."

"ST. ANDREW'S,"
LAWRIE PARK ROAD,
SYDENHAM, S.E.

Dec 17th 190 3

Dear Madam

I thank you for your letter which I am handing to Mr Collins Levey C.M.G. of 20 Victoria Street, who is arranging the Exhibition no doubt he will send you all particulars

Yours truly
W. G. Grace

Surrey County Cricket Club.

KENNINGTON OVAL, APRIL 28, 29 & 30, 1902.

SURREY v. LONDON COUNTY C.C.

SURREY.	First Innings.		Second Innings.	
1 Abel	b Braund	... 18	not out	... 75
2 Brockwell	c Wood, b Braund ...	39	c Fry, b Llewellyn	... 5
3 Hayes	st Board, b Grace ...	50	c Walker, b Llewellpn	... 0
4 Mr. H. S. Bush ...	b Braund	9	c Fry, b Grace ...	30
5 Holland	b Braund	8	c Smith, b Braund ...	32
6 Mr. V. F. S. Crawford ...	c Fry, b Grace ...	97	c Lawton, b Grace ...	0
7 Nice	b Braund	10	b Grace	23
8 Lees	b L ewellyn	31	c & b Braund ...	8
9 Stedman	b Llewellyn ...	6	l-b-w, b Llewellyn	3
10 Mr. H. O. Dolbey ...	not out	18		
11 Smith	run out	0		
	B 6, l-b 5, w , n-b	,... 11	B 5, l-b 4, w , n-b	9
	Total	...297	Total ...	...185

1st Innings ... 1 for 56   2·75   3·105   4·129   5·131   6·160   7·205   8·241   9·293
2nd Innings ... 1 for 5   2·5   3·50   4·118   5·126   6·166   7·178   8·   9·

LONDON COUNTY C.C.	First Innings.		Second Innings.	
1 Mr. W. G. Grace ...	b Nice	61		
2 Mr. C. B. Fry ...	c Nice, b Dolbey ...	82		
4 Mr. C. J. B. Wood ...	c Bush, b Dolbey ...	59		
8 Mr. W. L. Murdoch ...	b Dolbey	23		
3 Mr. G. W. Beldam ...	b Smith	0		
9 Braund	c & b Nice ...	35		
5 Mr. W. Smith ...	c Dolbey, b Smith ...	15		
10 Llewellyn	not out	65		
7 Mr. A. E. Lawton ...	c Bush, b Nice ...	0		
6 Mr. L. Walker ...	b Dolbey	6		
11 Board	b Smith	31		
	B 21, l-b 7, w 1, n-b 1, ...	30	B , l-b , w , n-b , ...	
	Total ...	...407	Total ...	...

1st Innings ... 1 for 130   2·164   3·208   4·209   5·231   6·257   7·342   8·342   9·350
2nd Innings ... 1 for   2·   3·   4·   5·   6·   7·   8·   9·

Price 1d.

Printed on the Ground by *Merritt & Hatcher, Ltd.,*
168, *Upper Thames Street, E.C.*

Umpires—W. A. J. West and Titchmarsh.   Stumps Drawn 6 p.m.

Score of the last match in which the late Dr. W. G. Grace took part.

GROVE PARK v. ELTHAM.

PLAYED AT GROVE PARK,

SATURDAY, JULY 25th, 1914.

ELTHAM.	First Innings.		Second Innings.
1 C. B. Grace	c Lamb, b Hobrow	4	
2 R. E. Adams..	b Beavis	5	
3 F. S. Neame	c Lavender, b Beavis	10	
4 J. Cooper	l b w, b Hobrow	0	
5 J. R. S. Murphy	st Lamb, b Beavis	12	
6 Dr. W. G. Grace	not out	69	
7 G. T. Eagleton	c Beavis, b Lavender	13	
8 D. E. Henshall	not out	28	
9 J. R. Eagleton			
10 R. W. Hubbard	Innings closed.		
11 S. A. Thomas			
	Extras	14	Extras ...
	Total	155	Total ...

GROVE PARK.	First Innings.		Second Innings.
1 J. B. Concanon	b Cooper	20	
2 D. Lavender	b Cooper	0	
3 C. S. Gaskain	run out	11	
4 C. Luffman	l b w, b C. B. Grace	0	
5 E. F. Tyler	not out	30	
6 L. H. Hay	c Cooper, b C. B. Grace	9	
7 J. A. Beavis	b Thomas	0	
8 V. T. Cowley	c G. T. Eagleton, b C.B. Grace	8	
9 H. Croxford	c Neame, b C. B. Grace	5	
10 F. E. Lamb	not out	11	
11 E. J. B. Hobrow			
	Extras	5	Extras ...
	Total	99	Total ...

MATCH DRAWN.

London County v Cambridge University, on 16–17–18 June 1902. Cambridge won by 5 wickets.

Far left The first match of Surrey's 1902 season (second day scorecard): London County won by 9 wickets early on the third day. Surrey were missing Lockwood, Hayward, Jephson and Richardson. Fry had appeared for Southampton two days earlier in the FA Cup Final.

The final appearance.

By 1890 the County Championship was firmly established as the frame on which any English cricket season was hung. In some people's minds its importance exceeded even that of matches against visiting teams from overseas. In 1890, for example, A.E. Stoddart chose to play for Middlesex rather than in two Tests against Australia, and Lord Hawke responded by refusing to release two of his professionals, Ulyett and Peel, for the Second Test because it coincided with the game between Yorkshire and Middlesex.

Since 1872, when MCC had first formed qualification rules for county cricket (actually for a knockout cup which did not properly get off the

Kent, the 1906 County Champions. Back, left to right: C. Blythe, F.E. Woolley, W. Hearne (scorer), J. Seymour, A. Fielder, F.H. Huish. Seated: E.W. Dillon, J.R. Mason, C.H.B. Marsham (capt.), S.H. Day, K.L. Hutchings. Front: E. Humphreys, W.J. Fairservice.

ground for another 91 years), the main participants in the Championship had been Nottinghamshire, Yorkshire and Lancashire in the North, with Derbyshire amongst the élite before dropping out for a time; Surrey, Middlesex, Sussex and Kent from the South-East, and Gloucestershire, or the Grace family and supporting cast, from the West.

In 1887 a County Cricket Council was set up to help MCC in its running of the game and as many as twenty counties were given separate and equal representation, thanks to a powerful lobby from some of the then minor counties such as Hampshire, Warwickshire and Leicestershire. These three joined the first-class ranks in 1895 along with Essex and a re-elevated Derbyshire, preceded in 1891 by Somerset, who had emerged powerfully the previous season.

Worcestershire followed in 1899, Northamptonshire in 1905 and Glamorgan in 1921. Each earned a place following success in the Minor Counties Championship, officially started in 1895.

In December 1889 a meeting of some of the senior counties at Lord's agreed for the first time an official method of deciding the Championship: points were determined by the subtraction of losses from wins, a method very much simpler than many that have followed although not entirely fair because some counties played more games than others. Champions elected by common consent of the press prior to 1890 had usually earned their title on the basis of fewest matches lost.

At the end of 1890 the County Cricket Council dissolved itself and devised a scheme to divide the counties into three divisions with promotion and relegation by means of 'qualifying matches between teams at the top of one division and the bottom of another'. The idea was revived in the 1980s (and at various times previously) in order to prevent meaningless matches when halfway through the season it has become obvious who is in the running for the Championship and who is not. It may yet be put into effect but in 1890, despite the fact that it offered the 'second-class' counties a way forward, they opposed the idea. Dr Russell Bencraft of Hampshire was the most voluble opponent.

At the inaugural meeting of the Cricket Council the influential Surrey secretary, C.W. Alcock, had stated that 'the Council should have control over all matters concerned with county cricket, but none over the laws of the game itself'. When in 1903 the Council was effectively reconstituted in the form of the Advisory Cricket Council, this was the effective distinction between the two bodies although MCC officials continued to have an influence in the affairs of the county game.

The two decades before the First World War saw some of the most entertaining county cricket ever played, with big crowds, big scores and larger-than-life cricketers. The 1890s were dominated by Surrey almost as completely as were the 1950s. They won the title seven times outright between 1887 and 1895, mainly under the captaincy of the popular John Shuter. The outstanding individuals were Walter Read, the dashing amateur, Bobby Abel, the deft little professional opener, and George Lohmann, an Adonis of a figure, splendid batsman and the best medium-paced bowler of his time. In his wake came one of the outstanding county fast-bowling attacks of all time, Bill Lockwood, ex-Nottinghamshire, and Tom Richardson, tall dark and strong with the looks of a gypsy and the heart of a lion.

COUNTY CRICKET

CHAMPIONSHIP, 1906.

BANQUET

TO

THE CHAMPION TEAM,

CORN EXCHANGE,

MAIDSTONE,

10th October, 1906.

HIS WORSHIP THE MAYOR
IN THE CHAIR.

·K·C·C·C·
1906

This is the Kent club's banquet to its own XI: there was a presentation by Lady Harris of 'souvenirs' in the form of gold inscribed cuff-links (see page 80).

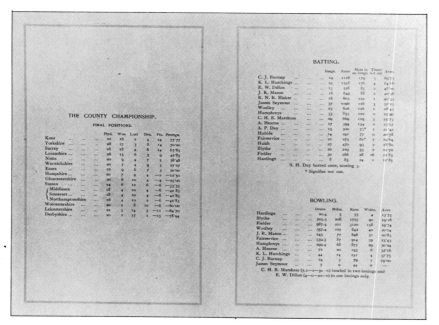

The statistics of Kent's triumphant season of 1906.

Cricket at Canterbury. The support for Kent remains to this day more devoted than in any other county other than Yorkshire.

Kent amateurs, 1906. Back, left to right: K.L. Hutchings, E.W. Dillon, R.N.R. Blaker. Front: C.J. Burnup, F. Marchant, G. Marsham, C.H.B. Marsham, J.R. Mason.

Far right *This dinner was for the Kent amateurs only (most of whom worked in London). The 6th Earl of Dartmouth was President of MCC in 1893.*

Jack Hobbs played his first match at The Oval in 1903, and in 1906 the boy wonder J.N. Crawford did the double at the age of nineteen. His brilliant career foundered on a mixture of his own pride and committee stubbornness when he became involved in a row over the make-up of the Surrey team to play the Australians in 1909. Against the combined might of the Surrey President, no less a man than the Lord Chief Justice, Lord Alverstone, and Surrey's official captain of that year, later to be knighted, 'Shrimp' Leveson-Gower, Crawford was bound to lose, as do almost all cricketers who fight the establishment.

The second outstanding county team of the period belonged to Yorkshire. They were a formidable and characterful side under the benevolent dictatorship of Lord Hawke. The batting was based on a great opening pair, Brown and Tunnicliffe, who put on 554 for the first wicket against Derbyshire at Chesterfield in 1898. Then came the brilliant David Denton, the great all-round amateur F.S. Jackson and another fine amateur bat, T.L. Taylor, and the all-rounders Wainwright, Hirst and Rhodes. Rhodes began his

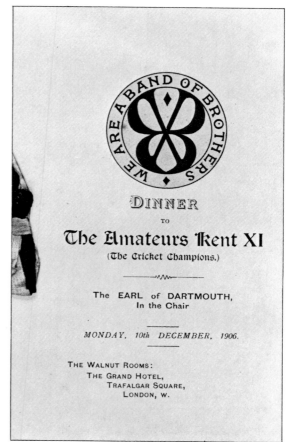

prolific career with 154 wickets in 1898 and in the ensuing years worked his way doggedly up the batting order from number eleven to number one.

It was in 1906 that George Hirst achieved the monumental double-double: 2,385 runs in the season and 208 wickets. Despite his performances Yorkshire, with 17 victories in 28 matches, still had to concede the title to Kent, the last great county side to emerge before the war snuffed out the Golden Age as surely as a candle burnt to the wick. The Kent side had an amateur gloss on a professional base of solid oak: Blythe, Fielder, Fairservice (has any professional cricketer been better named?), Seymour, Humphreys and Huish. Frank Woolley was also a professional but he played with all the carefree ease of the two outstanding amateurs around him, K.L. Hutchings and J.R. Mason. There was, said Neville Cardus, 'all summer in a stroke by Woolley.' If the war ended the Golden Age, the tall and elegant Woolley, who first played for Kent in 1906, carried at least some of the spirit of that age into a latter era.

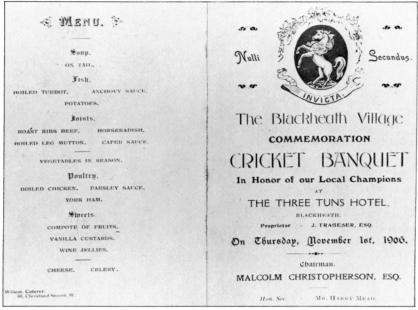

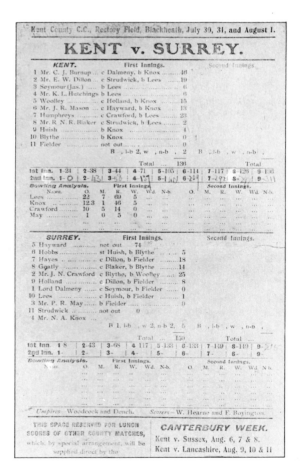

Above *Another dinner to the 1906 Kent XI. Five members of the Christopherson family had played for Kent in the 1880s and '90s.*

Left *J.R. Mason's autographed copy of the menu at one of many dinners given to the team during the months of celebration.*

Menu and toast list for the county club's own banquet.

Far left *A scorecard on the way to the title. Kent eventually won this game by one wicket, Colin Blythe taking 5 for 15 in Surrey's second innings.*

By the 1890s tours to Australia had become not only commonplace but also less of an adventure and social merry-go-round. Though there was much more socializing than on modern tours, and a much greater variety of matches, the cricket was the thing, and the Test cricket in particular.

The world of cricket was expanding. During the 1890s reputable, if not nationally representative, sides toured Ceylon, India, the West Indies, North America and South Africa. In some winters more than one English touring party went overseas. And not all the tours were treated with the same profound seriousness of those to Australia. Many were tours in the wider sense, providing a wonderful means for young amateur

The 1903–04 MCC side outside their hotel in Hobart, Tasmania before a sight-seeing tour to Mount Wellington.

cricketers to see the world.

One such was Pelham Warner, who described his first tour under Lord Hawke to the West Indies in 1897 as 'delightful, an experience and an education'. Later in the year, as soon, in fact, as the English cricket season had finished, he was off again, this time as captain, having raised a team and set sail for America 'all in the space of a fortnight'. The all-amateur side performed well with a notable exception against Philadelphia, to whom they lost by four wickets after being bowled out for 63 by J.B. King. In his autobiographical account of the tour, Warner has happier memories:

'We also played at Staten Island, New York and Baltimore, and on our arrival in Baltimore one of the papers wrote: "The hearts of Baltimore girls are going pit-a-pat!" Charming to a degree and very pretty they were, and shall any of us ever forget a delightful dinner

and dance, when a 'darkie' band played the most fascinating tunes? I stayed with the Lurmans. Our host had been wounded on the slopes of Gettysburg and much interesting talk did I have with him: and it was a delight to experience the comfort and atmosphere of an American country house.

'Our games in Philadelphia attracted great crowds, the country houses bringing large contingents; it reminded me of Eton v Harrow, with coaches crowded and all the ladies in their smartest frocks.'

Warner was affluent without being rich. The following winter he was asked by Lord Hawke to tour again, this time to South Africa, and he had to consider whether his legal career (after school at Rugby and university at Oxford he had qualified at the Bar) should come first:

'If I accepted it meant that I was not pursuing the law seriously, but when I looked round the Temple and saw the tremendous amount of brain-power which was massed there I came to the conclusion that I would in all likelihood never get into even the "fourth" or "fifth" eleven, and as the Baron emphasised the educational value of such a tour, after some hesitation I accepted.'

The strong team gathered by Hawke, seven amateurs and five professionals, went through the tour unbeaten, Warner making 132 not out in the Second Test at Johannesburg, for which he was rewarded with an engraved gold signet ring from the captain. Political troubles were brewing and the travelling was tiring on relatively unsophisticated railways. The team was involved in a train crash between Kimberley and Matjiesfontein. On another journey they left Kimberley early on a Friday morning and arrived at Bulawayo at four o'clock on the Sunday afternoon. The town was then in its infancy, as Warner recalled:

'Two or three years ago it had been the capital of a savage nation, whose life depended on the temper of the King, Lobengula. The ground on which we played had been the camp of Lobengula's army, but there was a fairly good batting wicket and a large, if rather rough, outfield. We were driven into the Matopos, and from a kopje saw the famous World's View. It is here that Cecil Rhodes lies.'

The English beat the Bulawayo XVIII and on the last evening sat down to a ten-course meal at the Bulawayo Club. Even in the wilds, such conventions were studiously observed. Warner does not relate whether the professionals were included in the meal. Knowing Lord Hawke's (and indeed Warner's) concern for their well-being, they probably were.

But various professional accounts of tours reveal that there were times when the distinctions were felt. In his diary of the 1897–98 tour of Australia, J.T.

Hearne considers it worthy of mention if the professionals stayed at the same hotel as the amateurs. At one point he claims that the Australian organizer of the tour is 'too little concerned about the pro's comfort', and there are frequent accounts of players being tormented by mosquitoes. But there were many pleasures too: Hearne found himself a girl-friend in Sydney, often went shooting or to the races, and thoroughly enjoyed the camaraderie of a team abroad. Generally the tours seemed as varied and educative for the Players as they were for the Gentlemen. And if the Australians were beaten, *everyone* celebrated!

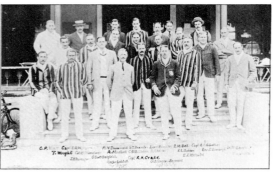

A 'Test Match' (strictly unofficial) in Cairo during MCC's first tour of Egypt in 1909.

At a 'Farewell to Melbourne' dinner for the 1907–08 tourists, given at the Grand Hotel, Melbourne. In the foreground the four central figures are, left to right: E.G. Hayes, S.F. Barnes, A. Fielder, C. Blythe.

Country-house cricket was both a product and a survivor of the Golden Age. Not much survived the Great War unchanged but the idea of inviting parties to a great country house for a week's or a weekend's entertainment with cricket as the raison d'être lasted remarkably far into the period between the wars. Then the cost of keeping big estates, maintaining a suitable cricket ground and entertaining large numbers of guests simply grew too great for all but the very few people who to this day maintain private grounds. While it lasted, country-house cricket was without doubt the supremely enjoyable and most civilized form of cricket ever played, and its heyday was the Edwardian era when, whatever hardships existed for the urban working class, those lucky enough to be born with wealth or with talent lived a life of ease and elegance.

The Great War is always, rightly no doubt, seen as the watershed which separated that carefree age from the assiduous realism of life thereafter, yet if H.G.D. 'Shrimp' Leveson-Gower is to be believed, times were already changing and country-house cricket was already on the wane well before the end of the century. Writing in 1903, he felt there was too much first-class cricket and not enough of the country-house variety, with 'gentlemen taking up professions much earlier' because 'now he must work to earn a living wage in the struggle for life'; he also remarked on the 'insidious beguiling of Golf, which attracts many a man from Saturday cricket'. All these things were diverting young men, said Leveson-Gower, from the peerless pleasure of a week of cricket at a country house, but they did not prevent him from describing what he considered to be his own ideal week.

Firstly, those involved in the party should know one another reasonably well. The hostess should act as a mother to the team and the 'old host' preferably as an umpire. (But supposing the poor chap wanted to play?) An additional essential was 'a bevy of nice girls to keep us all happy; perhaps if a match was over early we would have a ladies' match?' (How modern female hackles must rise at the smug patronizing tone of these remarks.) There would be a dance one night, on others songs, games, practical jokes, and 'any amount of happy innocent nonsense, as well as perchance a flirtation as hot as it is hopeless'.

The cricket itself was to be of sufficient importance to interest everybody but (and this was a Test player speaking) it was 'not to be allowed to develop into an infatuation, and therefore into a nuisance to the fair sex'. The ground should be good but not too good, for 'a perfect pitch breaks the hearts of the bowlers'. (Another England amateur, A.G. Steel, once remarked that all the four totals in a country-house match should be over 100 and under 200.) 'Shrimp' drew the line, however, at over-indulgence of a gastronomic kind, especially at lunch. The lunches should be good but served with only modest amounts of champagne, for 'men do not play good cricket on Perrier Jouet, followed by crème de menthe with two big cigars topping a rich and succulent menu'. (There were limits.)

Relaxed cricket was essential, but one may read between the lines even of Leveson-Gower to appreciate that it was serious enough whilst it was being played. Country-house cricket was especially popular with some of the best amateur batsmen because it gave them a chance to bowl as well, something that, with a few exceptions such as W.G. and A.G. Steel, was in the major first-class matches the general prerogative of the professionals.

The late Victorian and Edwardian eras saw the founding of most of the great wandering cricket clubs, many of which survive today. Amongst the most popular visiting sides at country-house weeks were the I Zingari, Free Foresters, Incogniti, the various public school Old Boys teams or those associated with Oxford and Cambridge–Harlequins, Authentics, Quidnuncs and Crusaders.

The literature of the time often uses country-house cricket as a setting for the events described, notably that of E.W. Hornung, whose gentleman crook Raffles, a Test player, often got up to his mischief on these occasions. Hornung himself was a keen country-house cricketer. An album which recently came to light describing matches played at Chiswick House in 1906 mentions Hornung making a duck against St George's Hospital (for Chiswick House) but a useful 20 against the Royal Gardens of Kew. Other visitors to Chiswick that summer included MCC (Gilbert Jessop made 53 and took five wickets), the Bushrangers, Aldwych Theatre and the Working Men's Club (whose players appear in the scorebook minus their initials).

For those who did not play in, or aspire to, first-class cricket, one of the great attractions of these matches must have been to play with or against some of the great names of the day. In another year at Chiswick no fewer than four South African Test players represented the MCC side, R.O. Schwarz taking seven for 39 with his leg-breaks and googlies and P.W. Sherwell scoring 65.

Despite Leveson-Gower's pessimism, the tradition of country-house cricket was to be maintained between the wars, albeit by a diminishing band. Indeed the 1920s and 1930s were to see the most famous country-house team of all, Sir Julien Cahn's XI (see Part Three).

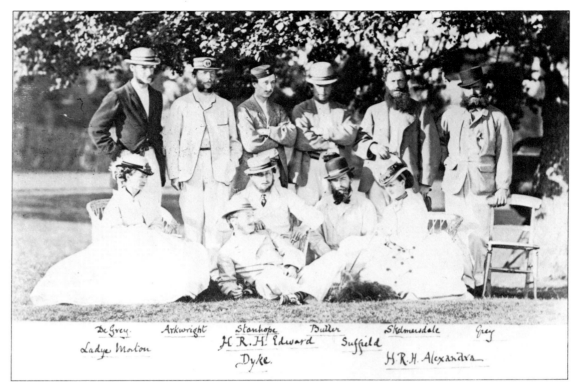

High society cricket.
The I Zingari team at
Sandringham in July 1866;
the Prince of Wales made a
duck.

De Grey.   Arkwright   Stanhope   Buller   Skelmersdale   Grey

Ladye Morton   H.R.H. Edward   Suffield

Dyke.   H.R.H. Alexandra

The ladies at Althorp for the
IZ match in August 1867.
Althorp is the seat of the
Spencer family, whose
descendant, Diana, married
the present Prince of Wales.

IZ at Althorp

Lady Emily Villiers   Miss Boyle.

Lord Cowper   The Princess Mary.   Lady Spencer   Lady C Bruce

Prince Teck

International cricket was enlivened in the first decade of the twentieth century by the emergence of South Africa as a serious contender in Test matches against England and Australia. Advance notice of the country's improvement was given by the side which visited in 1904 under the captaincy of Frank Mitchell, who had stayed behind after the last of Lord Hawke's tours to the Union. Playing 26 matches, Mitchell's team lost only three, with Tancred, Hathorn and himself doing well with the bat, Kotze proving the fastest bowler in the world since Kortright and E.A. Halliwell probably the finest contemporary wicket-keeper. But the most significant success was enjoyed by R.O. Schwarz who, after school at St Paul's where his distinction lay in batting and as a seam bowler, had played for

Middlesex with the originator of the googly, Bosanquet, and had also been an Oxford contemporary. Schwarz himself did not get a blue.

Apparently without telling anyone, he began practising the googly quietly by himself. He mastered it (though he could never bowl the leg-break) and achieved such bounce and turn that on the 1904 tour he took 96 wickets at an average of 14. He spread the new gospel on his return to South Africa where he worked as secretary to the cricket-loving financier Sir Abe Bailey, and when Warner's side arrived in South Africa in 1905-06 they were confronted by a much more experienced team than England had previously encountered. Moreover South Africa were well balanced, keeping the same eleven throughout a series which they won triumphantly, by four Tests to one, starting with a nerve-jangling one-wicket victory at the Wanderers, Johannesburg.

The victorious South African eleven was led by a new wicket-keeper batsman, Percy Sherwell. A steady hand of batsmen was completed by Louis Tancred, William Shalders, Maitland Hathorn, Gordon White (a beautiful off-side player), the big-hitting Jimmy Sinclair, Aubrey Faulkner and the tigerishly determined left-hander, Dave Nourse. (It was his 93 not out which won the day in the thrilling First Test.) To support the googlies of Schwarz, who was even more dangerous on matting wickets in South Africa than he was in England, were three more back-of-the-hand bowlers in Faulkner, Vogler and White. The more orthodox bowler, the fast-medium S.J. 'Tip' Snooke, took 24 wickets in the series.

When South Africa returned to England in 1907 they were treated seriously for the first time, losing the series 2–0 but doing so with honour and impressing themselves on the English public as being, in the words of *Wisden*, a team which 'treated cricket as a game, not a business' and 'played it on all occasions in the best

South Africans in England, 1907.

Surrey v South Africans, June 1912. The picture, from The Illustrated Sporting and Dramatic News, *shows Strudwick caught and bowled by Nourse.*

South Africans at practice on a matting pitch at The Oval, Durban.

possible spirit'. The leg-spinners Vogler and Faulkner took 65 of the 85 England wickets in the three Tests and Vogler was described in print by R.E. Foster as the best bowler in the world. Did S.F. Barnes read that? If so, he exacted terrible revenge, taking no fewer than 87 wickets in seven Tests against South Africa in England in 1912 and in South Africa in 1913–14, at an average of 9.8. But before the war one more exceptional batsman, Herbie Taylor, had emerged for South Africa and the country had firmly established a position of honour in international cricket which it was to hold until disqualified by political opposition to its Government.

The South African cricketers in Australia, 1910–11. One of the visiting players is explaining the mysteries of the googly in front of the pavilion at Melbourne.

Newlands, Cape Town, 1909–10, with the famous backcloth of Table Mountian. Hobbs is setting off for a single off Nourse during the then record opening partnership of 221 with Wilfred Rhodes. On the same ground in the previous Test a few days earlier these two had managed only six runs between them in both innings, but their stand on this occasion helped retrieve English pride with a nine-wicket victory. South Africa, googly bowlers to the fore on the matting wicket, won the series 3–2.

Whether because of the struggling nature of their beginnings or the continuing harshness of their environment, it seems that Australians have more or less always played their cricket 'tough'. From the earliest days there were various umpiring disputes and a second representative match between Australia and Lord Harris's English team in 1878–79 was cancelled after a riot at Sydney in the match against New South Wales. It was caused by the protests of the crowd against a run-out decision

The first tour of Australia. The arrival of Stephenson's team at the Café de Paris, Bourke Street, in the centre of Melbourne on Christmas Eve, 1861.

given by Umpire Coulthard, who was travelling with the English team, and to whom the uncompromising Australian captain, Dave Gregory, had already objected. The summer before there had been complaints in the Australian press about English umpiring (complaints repeated by visiting teams and their reporters ever since in a multitude of countries and tours), and when W.G. first visited Australia he was very unhappy about some of the decisions given against his team. As for the conduct of his team no-one, of course, played it much tougher than 'The Champion' himself.

Australian crowds did not fail to notice this. More than one subsequent English touring team complained of what A.E. Stoddart referred to as 'loud-voiced satire and banter'. Meanwhile the various cricketing successes against England were doing much to concentrate Australian minds on their own identity, gradually burying the rivalries between Victorians and New South Welshmen. In 1898 *The Bulletin* wrote: 'This ruthless rout of English cricket will do–and has done–more to enhance the cause of Australian nationality than could ever be achieved by miles of erudite essays and impassioned appeal.'

A year later in the magazine *Cricket*, the Australian manager said that one of the reasons for the success of his touring team was their more democratic view of captaincy and their rejection of the idea that some cricketers were gentlemen and others players. The English view of Australians at the time was not universally charitable. They were seen as ruthless on the field, often rough-mannered and, for so-called amateurs, over-commercial. One of the main reasons, in fact, for the stand taken by five English professionals in 1896, when at first they refused to play unless their fee for the match at The Oval was doubled, was their belief that the Australian players were making far more money than they were as full-time professionals. As *The Australian* expressed it in 1881: 'English professionals were irritated when they saw the Australians feted and lionised, and made much of, and treated as gentlemen, while he, poor devil, has to touch his hat to "my lord" or a "gentleman player".' The Australians themselves, however, were not without their discontented players at several times in the first generation of international cricketers. An Australian Cricket Council had attempted to override the early differences over tours to and from England, but as the great South Australian all-rounder G. Giffen wrote in his book *Bat and Ball*:
'The Cricket Council resolved in 1896 to take the matter [of a manager for the touring team] into its own hands…I, in common with many other cricketers, cannot see what the Council really has to do with the matter. If it financed the tours the position would be entirely different, but it did not take on its shoulders one iota of the financial responsibility; as in former years the players had to bear the whole of what risk there was.'

Giffen believed that six leading players should comprise the selection committee, adding that the 'outside' selection of the 1896 team caused 'no end of heartburning'. In 1904 there was an abortive attempt to form a national Board of Control. This was opposed by New South Wales because they felt that the Victorian Association was 'a mere cypher', dominated entirely by the Melbourne Cricket Club. Nevertheless the Board came into being the following year,

THE MATCH BETWEEN THE ALL-ENGLAND ELEVEN AND TWENTY-TWO OF THE NEW SOUTH WALES CRICKETERS, PLAYED IN THE DOMAIN AT SYDNEY.—SEE NEXT PAGE.

The English touring team of 1861 playing XXII of New South Wales at Sydney. They won this match by 49 runs, Mortlock making 76 and Sewell taking 9 for 28.

The old Albert ground in Redfern, Sydney, photographed during a single-wicket game in 1874. It has since been replaced by another Albert ground.

The Second Test match at Melbourne, 1907–08, where England beat Australia by 1 wicket. Spectator accommodation has always tended to be grander than that in England. Note the two huge and informative scoreboards.

The new Adelaide scoreboard, erected in 1911. MCC won this match against South Australia by an innings and 194 runs, their total of 563 including an innings of 151 by Plum Warner.

Illustrated London News sketch of the Melbourne Cricket Ground, depicting the opening match of the 1853–54 tour in which Parr's team drew with XXII of Victoria, R.C. Tinley taking 11 wickets in the first innings and 8 in the second.

CRICKET-MATCH AT MELBOURNE BETWEEN THE ALL-ENGLAND ELEVEN AND TWENTY-TWO OF VICTORIA.

including in its constitution a clause empowering the players to appoint their own manager. The new Board took control of the 1909 tour to England and there was trouble at once with a dispute over finances mainly involving Frank Laver, one of the team and the player's choice as manager, and Peter McAlister, the Board's appointee as vice-captain and treasurer.

Early in 1912 McAlister and Clem Hill, two of the three selectors, had a stand-up fight during a meeting in Sydney. Hill promptly resigned and five other men chosen to tour England the following summer refused the terms they were offered and were replaced. The Board won their battle with the players at the expense of an unsuccessful tour by an inexperienced team. As Johnny Moyes wrote: 'There were tough, unrelenting men on both sides, fighting for a principle in which they believed.'

Tough, unrelenting men have been at the heart of Australian cricket, on the field and off it, ever since. It is why they have been so hard to beat.

For the readers back home: an account in The Illustrated Sporting and Dramatic News *of the Second Test in Melbourne in 1901–02, which Australia won by 229 runs.*

Even during the Champagne Years, cricket could have its periods of austerity and sterility. A.G. Steel, for example, writing in 1900, suggested that the game as it was played then was 'in danger of degenerating from the finest of summer games into an exhibition of dullness and weariness. Cricket, to maintain its hold on the national character, must be eager, quick and full of action. Today it is the reverse.' Such heresy is contrary to all received wisdom about the Golden Age but there was one form of first-class cricket of the period to which the words could not possibly have applied: the cricket weeks and festivals.

The father of them all is the Canterbury Week, born in 1842 with a dual purpose, cricket by day and theatrical entertainment at night by the Old Stagers, a tradition which, like the cricket, still flourishes. The early matches were played at the Beverley Club but moved in 1847 to the present home, St Lawrence CC, where every August the tradition continues. There are few nobler sights in cricket than that lovely sloping ground with its handsome trees, bathed in sunshine

and surrounded by creamy-white tents topped with the gaudy colours of clubs dating from the Victorian or Edwardian eras.

The most famous of the festival weeks is Scarborough's, dating from 1876. Here the cricket is strictly for fun, both from the viewpoints of the players and the large holiday crowds. Sixes and close finishes are the stuff of Scarborough, which is breezily placed beside the ocean and is traditionally the scene of the last match played by most of the touring teams. C.I. Thornton and H.D.G. Leveson-Gower were the earliest organizers of the Festival and few players refused an invitation to take part. Though the resort could not precisely match the amateur dramatics of Canterbury's Old Stagers, there was evening entertainment aplenty in the theatres and concert halls and a famous hotel, the Marine, to stay at.

The Southern answer to Scarborough might be Hastings, where the Festival dates back to 1887. The tight little oblong-shaped ground in the middle of the town has views of the historic castle as well as a tang of salty air, and its combination of short boundaries and

A tent for amateurs and friends watching Kent at play: the players in blazers are C.J. Burnup (in the hat) and J.R. Mason (cap), both Kent captains of the Golden Age.

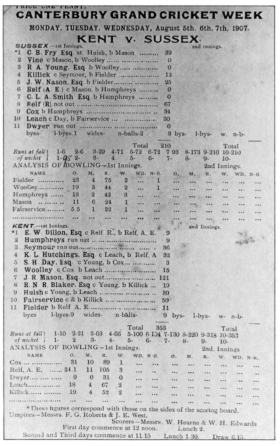

Right *Dress was important for cricket as it was for all sporting occasions. When Lord Harris once arrived at Royal Ascot in a smart brown suit, but minus the conventional topper and tails, the King greeted him caustically with: 'Oh, hello, Harris, been rattin?'*

Far right *The first of the two matches during Canterbury Cricket Week, 1907. This game was drawn, Relf scoring 210 in the second innings for Sussex.*

W.G. returning from the nets at the Hastings Festival match in 1898 between Mr Stoddart's Australian XI and Rest of England.

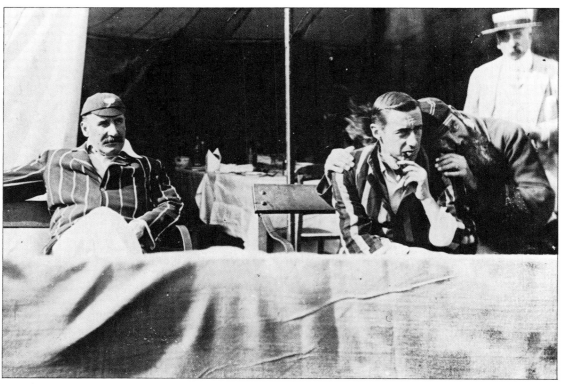

W.G. playing about at Hastings in 1901 with J.R. Mason (right) and Lord Hawke. They may have been watching the Gents v Players game which preceded the match between Yorkshire and an All England XI. (Grace and Mason, but not Hawke, were also playing for the Gentlemen.)

Scorecard of a Festival match at Scarborough in 1885 between I Zingari and Gentlemen of England.

GRAND CRICKET MATCH
I. ZINGARI v. GENTLEMEN OF ENGLAND.
Played on the Cricket Ground, Scarbro', Aug. 31st, and Sept. 1st and 2nd, 1885.

I. ZINGARI.	1st Innings.		2nd Innings.	
4 Mr. G. B. Studd	c Lucas b Rock	6	not out	55
5 Mr. J. G. Walker	st Wickham b Rock	111		
3 Mr. A. G. Steel	b Townsend	37	c Rock b Grace	0
1 Hon. A. Lyttelton	b Bastard		not out	47
2 Mr. H. Whitfeld	b Bastard	5	c Rock b Grace	23
Mr. A. J. Webbe	retired hurt	82		
6 Hon. M. B. Hawke	c Bainbridge b Townsend	21		
7 Mr. E. M. Hadow	b Bastard	11		
8 Mr. C. Wilson	b Grace	36		
9 Mr. A. H. Evans	st Wickham b Bastard	40		
10 Mr. G. H. Portal	c Wickham b Bastard	6		
11 Mr. S. Christopherson	not out	0		
	Wds bys 8 lb 11 nb	19	Wds bys lb 3 nb	3

Fall of the Wickets. Total .... 374 Total 132
1 2 3 4 5 6 7 8 9 10 1 2 3 4 5 6 7 8 9 10
12 79 80 96 229 274 290 352 367 374 49 49

ANALYSIS of the BOWLING.	1st Innings.				2nd Innings.			
	Overs.	Mdns.	Runs.	Wkts. Wd	Overs.	Mdns.	Runs.	Wkts.
Grace	26	12	37	1	..	..	..	0
Rock	39	16	77	2	..	..	..	0
Toppin	23	3	68		..	..	..	0
Bastard	49·1	15	86	5	..	..	..	0
Townsend	17	5	30	2	..	..	..	0
Page	10	1	32		..	..	..	0
Bainbridge	4	1	14		..	..	..	
Leadbeater	2	1	11		..	..	..	

GENT. OF ENGLAND.	1st Innings.		2nd Innings.	
Dr. W. G. Grace	b Steel	68		
Mr. C. I. Thornton	b Portal	4		
Mr. F. M. Lucas	b Wilson	31		
Mr. T. C. O'Brien	c Studd b Portal	45		
Mr. H. W. Bainbridge	c Portal b Studd	76		
Mr. F. Townsend	lbw b Steel	23		
Mr. C. W. Rock	c Whitfeld b Steel	1		
Mr. H. V. Page	c Studd b Steel	8		
Mr. H. Leadbeater	st Lyttelton b Steel	13		
Mr. C. Toppin	b Portal	8		
Rev. A. P. Wickham	c Lyttelton b Portal	5		
Mr. E. W. Bastard	not out	4		
	Wds bys 8 lb 4 nb	12	Wds bys lb nb	

Fall of the Wickets. Total .... 298 Total ....
1 2 3 4 5 6 7 8 9 10 1 2 3 4 5 6 7 8 9 10
30 96 124 174 222 224 236 281 289 289

ANALYSIS of the BOWLING.	1st Innings.				2nd Innings.			
	Overs	Mdns	Runs	Wkts Wd	Overs	Mdns	Runs	Wkts.
Steel	52	21	102	5	..	..	..	
Christopherson	14	6	37		..	..	..	
Portal	31	17	55	4	..	..	..	
Evans	14	5	35		..	..	..	
Wilson	8	2	23	1	..	..	..	
Hadow	10	3	14		..	..	..	
Studd	2	0	10	1	..	..	..	

Umpires:—Messrs. Anderson and King.

September 3, 4, and 5, GENTLEMEN v. PLAYERS.
September 7, 8, and 9, YORKSHIRE v. M.C.C.

At Festivals, cricket was only part of the entertainment. As at Canterbury, where the Old Stagers still perform in the evenings to this day, so at Scarborough the matches were often linked with theatrical performances.

seaside spirits has inspired many a display of dazzling hitting. It is a six-hitter's paradise.

A better cricket ground in some respects is The Saffrons at the rival Sussex resort of Eastbourne. A generously sized ground with a beautiful wicket, it was the scene of the famous defeat of the 1921 Australians by A.C. MacLaren's XI, who had been bowled out in the first innings for 43 by an apparently invincible Australian side. Such was their vulnerability to the delights of Festival cricket, however, that they were beaten again a few days later by C.I. Thornton's team at Scarborough.

Essex folk and Londoners on holiday have always enjoyed a splendid variety of cricket weeks at venues such as Westcliff, Clacton and Southend. It used to be called the 'Essex Circus', with tents, deckchairs and even a mobile scoreboard being transported for a week from Chelmsford to the seaside.

West Country cricket also has its associations with cricket weeks, notably the Cheltenham Festival, first staged in 1878. The cricket here, however, has less to do with holiday spirit than with sternly contested county matches, the spinners to the fore against the backcloth of the College's striking Gothic chapel. Bath, that best-preserved and least-spoilt of England's architectural city gems, is one of several Somerset grounds to have staged county weeks over the years. Set low and deep in a tree-lined valley, it looks up to numerous mellow stone buildings, the Abbey prominent amongst them, a source of consolation, no doubt, to many a batsman, for the wicket has often favoured the bowlers. Not so much, though, as at Weston-super-Mare, another ground ringed by tents for the major county games, where in the first cricket week of 1914 Alonzo Drake took all ten Somerset wickets in eight overs and five balls. Drake took 15 wickets in the match for 51 runs and also scored more runs in the game than anyone else, so he enjoyed himself. But it was hardly what was expected from cricket weeks and festivals. They were created for entertainment, with a capital E.

A porcelain figure of W. G., complete with MCC cap. The figure is nine inches in height and the bat is detachable. Probably made between 1870 and 1890. Certainly the face suggests a fairly youthful W. G. as does the relatively slim figure!

Right and centre left The bat with which W.G. scored 153 against Victoria at Melbourne in November 1891. Presented by Grace after the tour to Lord Sheffield, it appeared afterwards at various exhibitions.

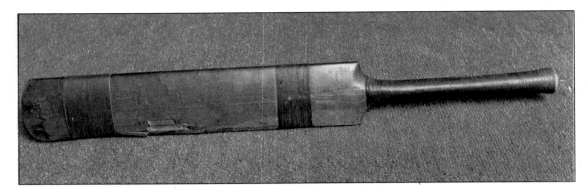

Centre right A medal struck to commemorate W.G.'s 50th birthday during the Gentlemen v Players match of 1898 and presented by the Doctor to each of his team in that game.

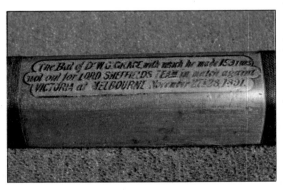

Below The menu of a dinner given by Gloucestershire CCC to celebrate W.G.'s hundredth hundred against Somerset in May 1895.

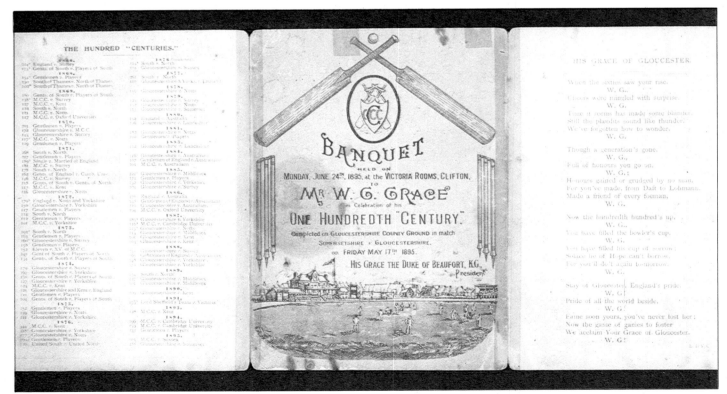

The passenger list for the voyage to Australia of the 1907-08 team. They travelled on the SS Ophir.

Below The date tells us that this was not the farewell dinner from Australia but a goodbye to the Grand Hotel, Melbourne after the Fourth Test.

Another farewell at the Grand Hotel, Melbourne! The team had not expected to return, but after the Fifth Test in Sydney they must have done so on their way to Adelaide to play South Australia.

Solid gold cuff-links, presented by the county to members of the Championship winning Kent side of 1906.

The improved lot of the professional cricketer towards the end of the nineteenth century was due in broad terms to an increased respect for those who made their living from a steadily more sophisticated and skilful game. More tangibly, they were aided by better education and the arrival of contracts, salaries and pensions.

Big differences remained between the Gentlemen and the Players. When the Old Trafford pavilion was built, for instance, three bathrooms were installed for amateurs, and only one for the professionals. But the successful players of the Golden Age were becoming prosperous as well as respectable, as any formal photograph of them dressed in smart three-piece suits avows. The biographer of Wilfred Rhodes, S. Rogerson, left this typical description of the great Yorkshire all-rounder sitting in a train in the early 1900s:

'He was wearing a well-cut grey flannel suit. His brown shoes shone with much polishing and his straw hat had the scarlet and yellow band of MCC, or else he was wearing an MCC tie, I forget which. With his deeply tanned face he looked, I remember thinking, almost exactly like the young captain in the 60th Rifles who used when on leave from India to attend the parish church at Pately Bridge.'

The main problem for all famous cricketers, whether they were amateur or professional, occurred after they had retired, or when younger players had forced them into the backwaters of the game. Some, like George Hirst at Eton, got excellent coaching jobs. For the amateurs there were jobs in the City or elsewhere. But the sun of public approval no longer shone on them. They were back in what has since become known as the rat-race, and many could not take either the relative boredom or the relative obscurity. For many professionals there was the additional problem of making ends meet; and for some the long-standing tradition of cricketers downing a few pints of ale at the end of the day became both a habit and a dangerous source of consolation. The careers of two successive Yorkshire and England slow left-arm bowlers, Ted Peate and Bobby Peel, were brought to an end because of over-indulgent drinking–in Peel's case, so the story goes, after he had relieved himself on the field of play in front of Lord Hawke, shortly before the start of a day's cricket.

The temptations of life at the top, and the disillusionment which often set in when careers had finished, led to many a tragic end. One of the first of the famous players to take his own life was Arthur Shrewsbury, the greatest professional batsman of his day, who shot himself in 1903, partly because he could

not believe that the illness from which he was suffering was curable and partly because, in the words of his *Wisden* obituary, 'the knowledge that his career on the cricket field was over had quite unhinged his mind'.

One would have thought cricket a good training for facing the burdens of life. In no game does heady glory turn so swiftly to downright miserable despair. In a game of golf or football there may be the memory of at least something done well to provide consolation, after a bad round or a heavy defeat; but in cricket a duck is a duck and nothing can relieve the gloom which surrounds it. Such experience, however, does not always breed resilience. Two of the most brilliant cricketers of their time, the Australian Albert Trott and Andrew Stoddart, his old England adversary and Middlesex team-mate, shot themselves within a few months of one another at their homes in London. Neither was in good health. Stoddart was at least affluent, with a good job as Secretary of Queen's Club. But for neither did life hold anything to compare with their days as sporting heroes.

C.D. Buxton, F.G. Bull, G.A. Faulkner and W.H. Scotton were amongst other cricketers of the time believed to have committed suicide for similar or allied reasons, but of all the many cricketers who died during the Great War, no-one's death was more poignant than that of the Somerset all-rounder F.P. Hardy who, on 9 March 1916, was found dead on the floor of a lavatory at King's Cross Station with his throat cut and a razor by his side. The thought of returning to the front, perhaps, had been too much to bear.

If suicides were far from rare amongst ex-cricketers, it would be unfair to give the impression that such melancholy endings were typical. Of the Kent team which played against the Australians in 1884, for instance, the first two to die were G.C. Hearne and Lord Harris, within a month of one another in 1932. Hearne was 76, Harris was 80.

Left *Arthur Shrewsbury: never at home unless batting in a cap. For W. G. he was the most dependable batsman of his day, but his end was tragic.*

Far left *Albert Trott: immortal for his six over the Lord's pavilion, but frail as all flesh.*

There is no doubt that in the twenty years before the Great War, cricket enjoyed its greatest period. The game was blissfully free of any serious controversies, widely played and watched, unrivalled by any other summer sport and adorned by some of the most brilliant players of all time, both from England and Australia.

It was the age of the English amateur. Stylish batsmen, carefully coached on superb pitches, poured out of the public schools, often via Oxford or Cambridge, to enrich county, Test and country-house cricket with their skill and spirit of attack. There was the Indian Prince, Ranjitsinhji, a marvel of supple movement and wristy grace, who in 1896 scored ten hundreds, the equal of W.G.'s most prolific season in 1871, and 2,870 runs, mainly for a Sussex side finishing bottom of the table. Equally legendary was his partner of so many huge stands at Hove, the supreme all-rounder C.B. Fry, academic genius, classical batsman and brilliant athlete. There was A.C. MacLaren, a batsman of lordly command and a haughty autocrat as a captain. Amongst his contemporaries was the more rounded hero of Cambridge and Yorkshire, F.S. Jackson, who enjoyed in 1905 a season of unending success as player and captain and rose to high political office later in life; R.E. Foster, one of the small host of Malvernian Test cricketers and one of seven brothers who played for Worcestershire, a dashing batsman and outstanding all-round games player; the elegant stylists Reggie Spooner and L.C.H. Palairet, who caressed the ball to the boundaries; and the mighty hitters C.I. Thornton and, especially, Gilbert Jessop, the Hercules who hit sixes harder than a cannon, scored his fifty-three centuries at the rate of over eighty an hour, and fielded at cover with athletic brilliance.

There were amateur bowlers of note, too, including F.R. Foster, waspish left-arm, who with S.F. Barnes won England a rubber in Australia, the hostile fast bowlers Walter Brearley and Neville Knox, and the great original B.J.T. Bosanquet, inventor of the googly, a weapon ironically destined to be used over the years with far greater success against England by bowlers overseas than ever English bowlers themselves achieved.

For all this galaxy–and many more–the Gentlemen were beaten by the professionals more often than not during the Golden Age. They possessed in S.F. Barnes a bowler who defied classification, being able to bowl almost anything at above or below medium pace with a command and venom that no-one has equalled. He played in only two full Championship seasons, for Lancashire, preferring to play in League cricket on his own terms. No League club for whom he played failed to win their competition, and if his 1,441 wickets for Staffordshire at 8.15 each may be denigrated as being earned in only minor county cricket, his 189 wickets in 27 Test matches at 16.43 remain an undying testament to his greatness.

Also from the professional ranks came the game's two premier all-rounders, Wilfred Rhodes, destined to take more wickets with his orthodox left-arm spin than any man in history and to thrust his way up the county and Test batting order from last to first, and George Hirst, who in 1906 performed the prodigious double-double of 2,000 runs and 200 wickets.

By the end of the period Jack Hobbs was

County cricket in the Golden Age. K.S. Ranjitsinhji and C.B. Fry batting for Sussex against Kent, for whom Alec Hearne is bowling – in his cap. The venue was the Angel ground at Tonbridge, once a fruitful nursery of Kent cricketers, now a leisure centre and car park.

developing into the finest batsman since W.G. (his mentor, Tom Hayward, had migrated from Cambridge to Surrey and he followed 'The Champion' to a hundred hundreds). There were other brilliant professional batsmen in Johnny Tyldesley, George Gunn and the emerging Frank Woolley. Dick Lilley was the best wicket-keeper of his day and there was high-class leg-spin from Len Braund (also a punishing batsman) and the artistic left-arm slow bowler Colin Blythe of Kent who between 1899 and 1914 took 2,506 wickets at 16.81.

With such an array of talent to choose from it might be thought that England would have dominated in the frequent Tests against Australia. But it was not so. Though Australia (not unnaturally with a much smaller population) had far fewer players of high class, they had quite enough to hold their own. Amongst their batsmen in the Golden Age, the tall, commanding and universally liked Victor Trumper was

Towards the end of an era. The MCC dinner on 1 May 1912 for the team returning victorious from a 4–1 win in Australia. Held at the Hotel Cecil, the dinner was attended by most of the notable cricketing characters of the time.

pre-eminent, with the left-handed Clem Hill and assiduous scorers such as Joe Darling and Warren Bardsley not far behind. The first great Australian all-rounder, George Giffen, had been followed by Warwick Armstrong, Monty Noble and Charlie Macartney. Amongst the fast bowlers to flourish were Ernie Jones and 'Tibby' Cotter and both the off-spinner Hughie Trumble and the leg-spin and googly expert, Dr H.V. Hordern, enjoyed great success against the old enemy.

So good were both teams, and so evenly matched, that luck was often the deciding factor during some epic series. In 1902, for instance, rain rescued Australia at Edgbaston after they had been bowled out for 36 by Hirst and Rhodes; they went on to win at Sheffield and by three runs at Old Trafford after Trumper's century before lunch on the first day when the wicket was at its best. With those victories in hand, England's famous triumph at The Oval thanks to Jessop's wonderful century in 75 minutes (after England had been 48 for 5) came too late. But in Australia in 1903–04 England regained the Ashes under Plum Warner, with F.S. Jackson their most successful batsman; and when 'Jacker' took charge at home in 1905, the fact that he won all five tosses helped England to retain the urn.

The fourteen men chosen to tour Australia in 1903–04. This was the first England team to go out under the auspices of MCC. They brought home the Ashes. Pictures from The Illustrated Sporting and Dramatic News. *Top, left to right: P.F. Warner, J.T. Tyldesley, W. Rhodes, G.H. Hirst, L.C. Braund. Centre: R.E. Foster, E.G. Arnold, A.F. Lilley, A. Fielder. Bottom: B.J.T. Bosanquet, T. Hayward, H. Strudwick, A.E. Knight, A.E. Relf.*

On 27 August 1914, W.G. Grace wrote the following letter to the Editor of *The Sportsman*: 'Sir. There are many cricketers who are already doing their duty, but there are many more who do not seem to realise that in all probability they will have to serve either at home or abroad before the war is brought to a conclusion. The fighting on the Continent is very severe, and will probably be prolonged. I think the time has arrived when the county cricket season should be closed, for it is not fitting at a time like the present that able-bodied men should play day after day and pleasure-seekers look on. There are so many who are young and able, and yet are hanging back. I should like to see all first-class cricketers of suitable age, etc., set a good example and come to the help of their country without delay in its hour of need. Yours, etc.,
W.G. Grace'

That was it. Bats were put away and exchanged for guns. The flower of a whole generation went to its death.

Cricket took a full share of the ghastly wholesale slaughter. One of the first to fall was the legendary schoolboy hero, A.E.J. Collins, who in a house match at Clifton had scored 628. A young cricket follower still alive in 1984, J.C. Bray, remembers putting up the scores at the Gibraltar Barracks of the Royal Engineers in 'July or August' 1914. Collins, playing in an inter-company match, hit five fours and was out in the same over. Before the end of the year, he was killed in France. Another young record-maker, Eustace Crawley, who had scored hundreds both for Harrow against Eton and for Cambridge against Oxford, was an early victim of the conflict. In 1915 John Howell, brilliant as a schoolboy at Repton, followed them to a cruelly early grave, along with Arthur Jaques, who had taken 168 wickets in only two seasons for Hampshire.

The toll grew remorselessly in fame and volume. K.L. Hutchings of Kent, the personification of amateur brilliance, fell in 1916 along with Percy Jeeves of Warwickshire, Major Booth of Yorkshire, W.B. Burns of Worcestershire and many others. In the peak year of 1917 the great spin bowler Colin Blythe, and two of his recent adversaries from South Africa, Reggie Schwarz and Gordon White, were added to the mournful list. The 1916 *Wisden* is the rarest of all the Almanacks partly because so many stricken parents sought it as a last memento of the cricketing prowess of their sons. That edition contains no fewer than 82 pages of obituaries.

The champagne had gone flat.

K.L. Hutchings of Kent, killed in 1916.

THE YEARS OF ACHIEVEMENT 1919-1939

The years between the wars were, despite some low points, the halcyon years for county cricket. After one unsatisfactory post-war season in 1919, when an experiment with two-day Championship matches and longer playing hours was tried and found wanting, the County Championship settled down again as the framework round which all other matches, Tests included, were built. Nowadays it is rather the reverse.

No club was more powerful than Yorkshire. In the twenty-one seasons between the wars they won the title twelve times. Lancashire won it on five occasions, Nottinghamshire twice, Middlesex and

Yorkshire in 1938: one of seven Championship-winning Yorkshire sides in the Thirties. Bill Bowes is absent. Back, left to right: W. Barber, W. Ringrose (scorer), E.P. Robinson, T.F. Smailes, H.S. Hargreaves, H. Verity, L. Hutton, B. Heyhirst (masseur), C. Turner. Seated: A. Wood, H. Sutcliffe, A.B. Sellers, M. Leyland, A. Mitchell.

Derbyshire once each. Kent, so powerful and attractive before the war, managed to finish in the top five in seventeen of the twenty-one seasons without once taking the Championship. At the other end of the scale, Northamptonshire finished bottom seven times in the 1930s and Worcestershire, who could not afford to take part in 1919, propped up the rest for three years in succession in the 1920s. Glamorgan, too, struggled to establish themselves after becoming the last of the present counties to join the circle, in 1921.

Yorkshire enjoyed two main periods of dominance–and dominance was the word for no side in county history, with the possible exception of Surrey in the 1950s, has so believed in its almost divine right to win. They won the two-day Championship in 1919 and then took the title four years running between 1922 and 1925. The team was soundly based on the immaculate batting of Herbert Sutcliffe and his

cheerful partner Percy Holmes, also an England player. The sturdy left-hander Maurice Leyland and the skilful Edgar Oldroyd were the other main run-scorers, with help from the all-rounders Rhodes and the merry left-hander, Roy Kilner. The wicket-keeper was the reliable Arthur Dolphin, and to support the spin of Rhodes and Kilner there was medium pace from Emmott Robinson, the speed of Abe Waddington and the varied ability of George Macaulay, bowling either fast-medium or slower off-cutters, according to conditions.

The county won three Championships in the early Thirties and four in the last five years before the war under the tough captaincy of Brian Sellers. His stalwarts, apart from Sutcliffe and Leyland, were the young opening batsman Len Hutton who scored his 364 for England at The Oval in 1938, the reliable Wilf 'Tiddlypush' Barber, and another England batsman in Arthur Mitchell, so talkative that they called him 'Ticker' though his talk was generally dour and humourless. He didn't play cricket for fun. Arthur Wood was the wicket-keeper, Bill Bowes the tall, intelligent young fast bowler, Ellis Robinson the off-spinner and Hedley Verity the highly skilled slow left-arm spinner without which no Yorkshire side was ever complete. Together these men played with a purposefulness that bordered on ruthlessness. Their dedication was total. If they were not playing matches, they were either practising in the nets or talking cricket in the bar.

If Lancashire were not so all-conquering, or so well equipped for all conditions, they were a hard team to beat with an outstanding batsman in Ernest Tyldesley and dependable ones in Harry Makepeace, Charlie Hallows and his fellow left-hander Eddie Paynter, a glutton for runs and a highly successful Test batsman. Jack Iddon and Leslie Hopwood both got useful runs as well as bowling slow left-arm, and fast bowlers over the years included the graceful and speedy Australian Ted McDonald, who had made such an indelible impression upon English cricket in partnership with Jack Gregory in 1921. Two English fast bowlers, Dick Pollard and Eddie Phillipson, may both be said to have lost their best years to the Second World War. The most talented of the spinners was Cecil Parkin, who could also use the new ball, though the portly leg-break bowler Dick Tyldesley was also a reliable wicket-taker. Parkin, who had lost his England place after criticizing his captain, Arthur Gilligan, in 1924, left Lancashire abruptly in the middle of the 1926 season when the new captain of the club, Major Leonard Green, dropped him for inconsistent performances. It may also have been an attempt to bring the wayward Parkin, a comedian but also a rebel, to heel. It failed, Parkin disappearing at once back to

Lancashire County Ground

LANCASHIRE v. KENT,

SATURDAY, MONDAY, TUESDAY, June 28, 30 and July 1, 1930.

KENT

		FIRST INNINGS.		SECOND INNINGS.	
1	Hardinge	c Hallows b McDonald..16		c Hopwood b Tyld R ...47	
2	Ashdown	b McDonald ...16		c Farrimond b McDon ...6	
3	Todd	b Hodgson ...16		c Farrimond b McDon ...33	
4	Ames (wkt.-kpr.)	b Hodgson ...50		c Farrimond b McDon ...5	
5	J A Deed	c Tyld R b McDonald ...22		c Farrimond b McDon.. 28	
6	T A Crawford	b Tyldesley R ...1		c Farrimond b McDon ...0	
7	G B Legge (Capt.)	b Tyldesley R ...0		c Farrimond b Tyld R ...0	
8	Fairservice	lbw b Tyldesley R....10		st Farrimond b Tyld R ...0	
9	Freeman	c Hodgson b McDonald..2		c Sibbles b McDonald ...7	
10	Wright	not out ...34		c Sibbles b Tyldesley R..19	
11	Peach	b McDonald ...11		not out ...1	
		byes 1lbs wds nbs 1		bys 1lbs wds nbs 1	
		Total........194		Total........147	

FALL OF WICKETS.

FIRST INNINGS.

1	2	3	4	5	6	7	8	9	10
26	45	113	114	115	129	145	149	150	194

SECOND INNINGS.

1	2	3	4	5	6	7	8	9	10
22	74	80	112	113	116	120	124	145	147

BOWLING ANALYSIS.

	FIRST INNINGS.						SECOND INNINGS.					
	Overs	Mdns.	Runs	Wkts.	Wds.	Nbs.	Overs	Mdns.	Runs	Wkts.	Wds.	Nbs.
McDonald	21.1	0	77	5	..	..	20	1	83	6	..	..
Sibbles	5	0	21	0	..	..	2	0	9	0	..	..
Tyldesley (R.)	19	6	61	3	..	..	9.4	1	25	4	..	..
Hodgson	7	0	21	2	..	..	10	1	29	0	..	..
Hopwood	4	1	13	0	..	..						

LANCASHIRE.

		FIRST INNINGS.		SECOND INNINGS.
1	Hallows	lbw b Ashdown ...2		
2	Watson	c Hardinge b Freeman.134		
3	Tyldesley, E	c Wright b Ashdown ...117		
4	Hopwood	st Ames b Freeman ...4		
5	Iddon	c Ames b Hardinge ...10		
6	Sibbles	b Wright ...7		
7	P T Eckersley (Capt.)	b Hardinge ...5		
8	Tyldesley, R	b Freeman ...22		
9	Farrimond (Wkt-kpr)	not out ...46		
10	Hodgson	b Wright ...7		
11	McDonald	b Freeman ...28		
		5byes 3lbs wds nbs 8		bys lbs wds nbs
		Total........390		Total.........

FALL OF WICKETS.

FIRST INNINGS.

1	2	3	4	5	6	7	8	9	10
7	213	256	265	276	278	298	325	383	390

SECOND INNINGS.

1	2	3	4	5	6	7	8	9	10

BOWLING ANALYSIS.

	FIRST INNINGS.						SECOND INNINGS.					
	Overs	Mdns.	Runs	Wkts.	Wds.	Nbs.	Overs	Mdns.	Runs	Wkts.	Wds.	Nbs.
Wright	20	3	60	2	..	..						
Ashdown	10	5	48	2	..	..						
Freeman	55	9	129	4	..	..						
Hardinge	12	4	70	2	..	..						
Peach	18	1	51	0	..	..						
Fairservice	5	1	24	0	..	..						

Umpires: DENTON and BEET

Times of Play—1st day 11-30 to 6-30; 2nd day 11-30 to 6-30; 3rd day 11-30 to 6-0 or 6-30. *Lunch* 1-30. *Tea Interval* 4-15 each day

Scorecard of the match in which Bill Farrimond, George Duckworth's deputy keeper, yet good enough to play for England, equalled the then record number of dismissals in an innings (seven). Note also Tich Freeman's 55-over stint, and the fact that Kent's bowling was opened by another leg-spinner, Doug Wright, even though the pitch was clearly not unsuited to Ted McDonald's fast bowling.

The
LANCASHIRE
COUNTY AND
MANCHESTER
CRICKET CLUB

COUNTY CHAMPIONSHIP 1930

DINNER

To Celebrate the winning of THE
COUNTY
CHAMPIONSHIP
1930

MIDLAND HOTEL
DECEMBER 15TH 1930
CHAIRMAN
SIR EDWIN STOCKTON
J.P.

More Championship celebrations, this time for Lancashire.

the League cricket from whence he had sprung, but Lancashire nevertheless went on to win the title.

This was a not untypical show of strength by the amateur establishment. At no period of cricket had the county clubs felt so financially secure as in this one and committees were often dictatorial, supporting their amateur captains on the whole, though they were not above ditching them fairly ruthlessly at the end of the season if they had failed to bring the club any success. Often the less competent amateurs were in any case gently controlled and advised by the wise old senior pros, and in 1928 Yorkshire actually offered the captaincy to Herbert Sutcliffe. When touring in South Africa Sutcliffe received the following letter from the Yorkshire Secretary, F.C. Toone:

'Dear Herbert,

At the committee meeting yesterday you were appointed captain for 1928 without your status being altered.

It is hoped that this will be agreeable to you and that you will accept the same and be happy and successful in your new and honoured position.'

Sutcliffe cabled back to the President, Lord Hawke:

'Official invitation received yesterday. Many thanks you and your committee. Great honour. Regret to

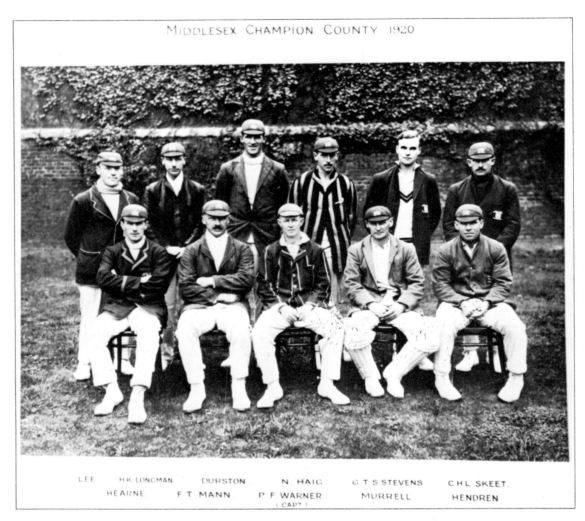

MIDDLESEX CHAMPION COUNTY 1920

LEE   H K LONGMAN   DURSTON   N. HAIG   G T S STEVENS   C H L SKEET.
HEARNE   F T MANN   P F WARNER   MURRELL   HENDREN
(CAPT)

Pelham Warner's Championship side of 1920. Middlesex also took the title the following year, under F. T. Mann.

decline. Willing to play under any captain elected.'

In a way it was odd that Sutcliffe should have declined because he later became a major in the Second World War and had deliberately cultivated his mien off the field, adopting an accent shorn of his native Yorkshire. Perhaps he was not ready to become an 'officer and a gentleman', or simply did not want the hassle of commanding his fellow professionals.

There was no question of a similar move being made in Middlesex. Their captains in the Championship-winning years of 1920 and 1921 were both establishment figures, the popular Plum Warner and the future England captain, F.T. Mann. Mainstay of their batting was Patsy Hendren and with the professional Jack Hearne augmented at various times by amateurs like Ian Peebles, Walter Robins and Greville Stevens, the county were seldom short of leg-spinners.

Nottinghamshire's strength remained in its professionals, led by the batsmen George Gunn, Walter Keeton, W.W. Whysall and Joe Hardstaff, and of course by the feared new-ball attack of Larwood and Voce, well supported by Fred Barratt, also capable of nasty pace, and the off-breaks of Sam Staples. They were led for many years by Arthur Carr, an amateur who himself fell out with the establishment after instructing Larwood and Voce to bowl leg-theory at Woodfull's 1934 Australians just when everyone was trying to be friendly in the wake of the bodyline explosion.

What Jack Crawford had found at Surrey in 1909, Arthur Carr discovered twenty-five years on: no-one could take on the committee of a county club and win, unless, of course, like Lord Harris or Lord Hawke, he was the committee.

Nottinghamshire, the 1929 champions. Back, left to right: W.R.D. Payton, H. Larwood, W. Walker, F. Barratt, W. Voce, B. Lilley, G.V. Gunn and J. Carlin (scorer). Seated: S.J. Staples, G. Gunn, A.W. Carr (capt.), W.W. Whysall, A. Staples.

Had television existed in the 1920s it is very doubtful whether Test cricket could have remained an attraction for long. Interest in matches between England and Australia was sustained because tours were not made every year and the players were not intimately known to large numbers of people. It was greatly to the good of cricket that when the cameras did arrive on the scene several more countries had joined the international fray.

The most important newcomers were undoubtedly the West Indies who showed their skill on a tour to England in 1923 and whose excellent record then earned them a full and official tour five years later. The game had taken a firm grip in the

The West Indies team, 1923. Standing, left to right: J.K. Holt, H. Wince, V. Pascall, J.A. Small, G.N. Francis, T.H. Mallett, G. John, R.L. Phillips. Seated: G. Challenor, G. Dewhurst, R.G. Austin, R.K. Nunes, P.H. Tarilton, C.R. Browne. Front: L.N. Constantine.

Caribbean islands long before, and the first English visit there had been as early as 1894–95. Not until they started to get overseas experience on a regular basis, however, was it gradually appreciated by everyone that the islands could produce the most natural cricketers in the world, including a succession of lissom fast bowlers and carefree, attacking batsmen.

The first of the great West Indian batsmen, George Challenor, was into his forties and past his best when West Indies played their first official Tests in England in 1928, but although England won the first series by three games to nil the West Indians still impressed shrewd judges as a team which needed only experience to mature their rich talents. There were three outstanding fast bowlers in George Francis,

Herman Griffith and the dazzling all-rounder Learie Constantine. Indeed, even then, West Indies could have picked a four-man fast attack if they had wanted to because another speedy bowler, George John, had been left behind. Like Challenor, John was past his best when official recognition came, but he had hustled a good many batsmen in England five years before.

When West Indies returned to England in 1933, they produced a batsman the equal of any in the world, save only Bradman and perhaps Hammond. Soon, indeed, he was to be dubbed 'the black Bradman'. He was George Headley, who on his first visit to England scored 2,230 runs at an average of 66, with seven hundreds including an innings of 169 not out at Old Trafford. Unfortunately, though, there was little batting support for Headley, and Francis and Constantine played in only one match each, since both were now engaged in the Lancashire League. Though this temporarily weakened the West Indian Test team it ultimately strengthened their cricket, for such was Constantine's reputation at Nelson that he blazed a trail followed by many future West Indians who not only enlivened the Lancashire Leagues but also gained valuable experience which they put to very good effect in future Tests.

The Old Trafford Test was notable also for the fact that England got a dose of their own medicine in the form of bodyline bowling by Constantine and Martindale. Neither, however, was quite as fast as Larwood and the pitch was slow, so Jardine's defiant century, admirable though it was as an expression of how to deal with this form of attack, was not a wholly valid rejoinder to those who claimed it to be unplayable.

The West Indies had their first victories against England at home in 1934–35. Headley made a double hundred at Kingston where the England captain, R.E.S. Wyatt, had his jaw broken by a ball from Martindale, a blow from which his side did not recover, despite a typically fine hundred from Leslie Ames. E.W. Swanton neatly summed up the status of West Indian cricket before the war when he said of this tour:

'Whatever the temperamental weaknesses from which the West Indies might suffer during a prolonged English tour, only the very best was good enough to oppose them on their own pitches and in front of their own enthusiastic crowds.'

New Zealand were next to join the circle of Test-playing countries. They had done well on a 'trial' tour of 1927 and in 1931 acquitted themselves very well in three Tests, their captain Tom Lowry having the luxury of being able to declare in the inaugural Test at Lord's to set England a target in the fourth innings

Members of the 1928 West Indies side. Left to right: J.A. Small, C.V. Wight, R.K. Nunes (capt.), L.N. Constantine, W.St. Hill. (Learie Constantine, feeling the cold, is in an overcoat!) Standing behind the seated group is M.P. Fernandes.

The Oval Test of 1939. George Headley lofts Doug Wright over the boundary to reach his 50 watched by the wicket-keeper Arthur Wood and Wally Hammond at slip. He was run out for 65 but West Indies still totalled 498 and three days were quite insufficient in which to achieve a positive result.

Above *The first New Zealand team arrives at Southampton in 1927, to be met by the Mayor, seen shaking hands with T.C. Lowry, the team captain. The ship is the* Majestic.

Right *This menu records the visit of Melbourne CC and the departure of the first NZ team to England. The Melbourne signatures include those of H.L. Hendry, H.I. Ebeling, Hugh Trumble, W.W. Armstrong and V.S. Ransford.*

LUNCHEON

GIVEN BY THE

New Zealand Cricket Council

on the occasion of the Visit of the

Melbourne Cricket Club Team

and to mark the departure of the First
New Zealand Cricket Team
to England.

Winter Garden,
Christchurch, N.Z.,
17th March, 1927.

WINE LIST

Hock
Claret
Whisky
Ale
Lemonade
Dry Ginger
Soda

which they came nowhere near attaining. If the bowling had been up to the standard of the batting they would have done even better because no fewer than six of the 1931 team reached 1,000 runs on the tour–Lowry, Dempster, Blunt, Mills, Vivian and Weir. In 1937 the bowling was bolstered by a well built fast-medium bowler of quality in Jack Cowie, 'The Bull', and the batting was enriched by a young left-hander named Martin Donnelly. For him the glory lay ahead.

As England settled into a pattern of Test matches every summer, India became the third country to add spice to the passing seasons. They too did well on their first visit, under the captaincy of the Maharajah of Porbandar, who owed his position to his birth not his ability. Nevertheless he presided over eight victories before the only Test of the tour, at Lord's. Ironically for a country whose lack of fast bowlers was often to put them at a disadvantage in future years, they had two of high quality in this match in Mahomed Nissar and Amar Singh, the latter a supple, graceful fast bowler who moved the ball late. Only Douglas Jardine's resolution in an uneven England batting display, and the inexperience of the Indian batting, avoided an embarrassing upset.

C.K. Nayudu proved himself an outstanding batsman on the tour, and when India played Jardine's strong England touring team at home in 1933–34 another high-class cricketer emerged in Lala Amarnath who, sadly, was to fall out with his captain, the Maharajah of Vizianagram, on the next tour to England in 1936, from which he was prematurely sent home. In his absence Mushtaq Ali and Vijay Merchant emerged as an opening pair of high quality. On their own pitches they had many prolific days ahead of them still. But the MCC team picked to tour the sub-continent in 1939–40 never arrived.

C.K. Nayudu. A revered figure in Indian cricket, now preserved at Indore, central India, in stone, though not, alas, in a pose that does full credit to his powers as a batsman.

Left *Portrait of Ranji, dressed as the Jam Sahib of Nawanagar, which hangs in his bedroom at the old palace in Jamnagar.*

Below *The All-India team of 1911, seen here at Hove v Sussex in August 1911. The captains are Dr H.D. Kanga (India, seated fourth left) and Mr H.P. Chaplin (Sussex, seated fifth left). Sussex gained a narrow and fortunate victory by 10 runs.*

One of the consequences of better prepared and more fully covered pitches in the years between the wars was an excess of drawn matches. The immediate post-war experiment of two-day County Championship matches with longer hours was quickly abandoned with far too many matches ending without a positive result, and in the early 1930s there was another period when a series of wet summers conspired with a Championship points system which gave too much reward for avoiding defeat and too little for outright victory to produce another spate of draws. Crowds started to decline because of this and also from a certain public disapproval of the furore caused by the bodyline controversy. But the mood soon passed and the game was flourishing again in England in the last years before the Second World War, not to

mention in several other countries who were spreading the boundaries of international cricket. By doing so they ended the day when an English summer could go by without any Test matches, when spectators were perfectly content with a diet of county matches, relieved by the regular struggles between the Gents and the Players.

Crowds for Tests, especially against Australia and particularly in the hot summer of 1921, remained high throughout the period, and all the traditional occasions remained very well supported. Though the Bank Holiday Roses matches, for instance, were often the epitome of dull attrition, the faithful supporters of Lancashire and Yorkshire filled Old Trafford or Headingley year after year. They were almost *expected* to be dull. Flamboyance of any kind was firmly disapproved of. Arthur Mitchell, who never praised

Crowds were always large for the big Test and county matches in the 1930s. This one filled Trent Bridge to the brim in 1934.

anyone, once growled at Ellis Robinson after he had dived to take a brilliant one-handed catch inches from the ground: 'Gettup, tha's makin' a bluddy exhibition of thisself.'

At the other end of the scale the Eton and Harrow match at Lord's still attracted crowds of some 30,000 to Lord's every year (it was, to most of them, more a social occasion than a cricket match). But, for every English boy, whatever the social standing of his school, cricket remained an essential part of his education, not yet challenged by other summer sports, and in those days before television and overseas holidays and mass travel by car, a holiday visit to a big cricket match was still one of the most popular forms of entertainment. The crowds were, however, predominantly male, and in fair weather or foul everyone carried a hat as well as his sandwiches.

Although England, having suffered far more casualties than Australia in the war, were so heavily outgunned by their old adversaries in 1921, their rapid improvement in the next few years allied to the better quality of the pitches meant that three days were insufficient to allow a finish in a Test match even though bowlers got through far more overs in a day than they do now. After four draws in 1926, the Fifth Test was played to a finish, ending on the fourth day in an England win; four-day Tests against Australia were accepted as necessary for the rest of the inter-war period.

Twice that number of days was not enough for a finish to the last Test played by England before war again broke out with Germany. The 'Timeless Test' at Durban was still an incredible run-glutted stalemate when England were forced to leave for home or miss the boat.

Massive turnout at Lord's in 1921 for the Test v Australia, recorded by The Illustrated London News.

The inter-war years, and the 1930s in particular, were batsmen's years. Wickets, both in England and Australia, were made for the run-scorers, with marl in England and bulli-mud in Australia being rolled so deep below clean-shaven surfaces that only wrist spinners got much use out of them. Original minds turned to expedients such as leg-theory of the kind used by Fred Root (fast inswingers to a leg-side field) and bodyline (short-pitched balls aimed at the chest with close leg-side men placed to catch the ball defensively fended off). Administrators turned instead to the laws: in 1927 the ball was made smaller; in 1931 the stumps were increased in height and breadth and in 1937, after two years of experiment, the lbw law was changed to include possible dismissals for balls pitched outside the off-stump. None of this prevented Don Bradman from averaging 108 in the 1938 series, nor England from running up 903 for 7 at The Oval.

Bradman, of course, was the record-breaker *par excellence*, though he never sought records, merely total domination of bowlers in the interests of victory for his team. With Hobbs still around, Bradman and Hammond emerging, a thinning out of fine bowlers by the war and steadily improving batting conditions, it was not surprising that a great many of the batting records still listed each year in the record books were

created in the inter-war years when, in the words of J.B. Hobbs, 'there are very few outstanding bowlers of real class'. Compared with the years before the 1914–18 war, Hobbs mentioned the 'over preparation of wickets', the obsession of bowlers with the inswinger intead of the outswinger and the lack of bowlers who could flight the ball with the subtlety of, for example, Colin Blythe.

Wickets were now generally covered in advance of a match, and this was one of the main reasons for the domination of batsmen like Hobbs, Sutcliffe, Hammond and, above all, Bradman. It is no coincidence that of the seven first-class individual scores of 400 or more, all have been made either in the inter-war period (two by Bill Ponsford, one by Bradman and one by Archie MacLaren) or since 1945 in India and Pakistan where conditions tend to be equally loaded in the batsman's favour.

The six batsmen with the highest number of hundreds–Hobbs, Hendren, Hammond, Mead, Sutcliffe and Woolley–all played in the 1920s and '30s. The same six occupy six of the first seven places of those who have piled up the highest number of runs in a career. When Hobbs himself resumed his cricket at The Oval after the First World War he was thirty-six years old. Before the war he had already scored 65 first-class hundreds in 11 years; in the next 15 years he

Jack Hobbs making the run required to pass W. G. Grace's career record of 54,896 runs. Surrey v Middlesex at The Oval, August 1930.

Don Bradman posing with Maurice Leyland, one of Yorkshire and England's staunchest left-hand bats.

The world record score for an innings in first-class cricket, beating the 1059 scored, again by Victoria, v Tasmania in the 1922–23 season. The innings lasted ten and a half hours. The opening partnership of 375 took 3¾ hours, the second-wicket partnership of 219 took under two hours. Ryder hit six sixes and thirty-three fours, mainly drives, in his 295, scored out of 449 in just over four hours.

Melbourne Cricket Ground

SHEFFIELD SHIELD MATCH

VICTORIA v NEW SOUTH WALES

DECEMBER: 24, 27, 28 & 29, 1926

NEW SOUTH WALES.	1st Innings.		2nd Innings.	
N. E. Phillips	c Blackie, b Liddicut	52	l b w, b Hartkopf	36
J. G. Morgan	c Love, b Liddicut	13	c King, b Liddicut	26
T. J. E. Andrews	st Ellis, b Hartkopf	42	b Liddicut	0
A. F. Kippax (Capt.)	b Liddicut	36	b Hartkopf	26
A. A. Ratcliffe	c Ryder, b Liddicut	2	c Morton, b Hartkopf	44
A. Jackson	c Ellis, b Blackie	4	not out	59
J. E. P. Hogg	not out	40	c Hendry, b Liddicut	13
A. A. Mailey	b Ryder	20	c Morton, b Hartkopf	3
J. N. Campbell	l b w, b Blackie	0	c Ryder, b Hartkopf	8
R. L. A. McNamee	b Ryder	8	b Liddicut	7
H. V. McGuirk	b Ryder	0	b Hartkopf	0
Bye 1, Leg Bye 1, No-balls 2		4	Byes 2, Leg Byes 4, No-balls 2	8
		Total 221		**Total 230**

Fall of Wickets	1	2	3	4	5	6	7	8	9	10
1st Innings	25	96	122	133	152	152	207	208	217	221
2nd Innings	67	67	77	112	164	184	189	206	229	230

BOWLING ANALYSIS.

	1st Innings.					2nd Innings.			
	Overs (8 balls)	Maidens	Runs	Wickets		Overs (8 balls)	Maidens	Runs	Wickets
Morton	15	4	43	—	Morton	11	—	42	—
Liddicut	21	7	50	4	Liddicut	19	2	66	4
Ryder	9	1	32	3	Blackie	5	1	16	—
Blackie	16	3	34	2	Hartkopf	16.3	—	98	6
Hendry	3	2	1	—					
Hartkopf	17	1	57	1					

Morton bowled 2 no-balls. Morton bowled 2 no-balls.

VICTORIA.

W. M. Woodfull (Capt.)	c Ratcliffe, b Andrews	133
W. H. Ponsford	b Morgan	352
H. S. T. L. Hendry	c Morgan, b Mailey	100
J. Ryder	c Kippax, b Andrews	295
H. S. B. Love	st Ratcliffe, b Mailey	6
S. P. King	st Ratcliffe, b Mailey	7
A. E. V. Hartkopf	c McGuirk, b Mailey	61
A. E. Liddicut	b McGuirk	36
J. L. Ellis	run out	63
F. L. Morton	run out	0
D. D. J. Blackie	not out	27
Byes 17, Leg Byes 8, No-balls 2		27
	Total	**1107**

Fall of Wickets	1	2	3	4	5	6	7	8	9	10
	375	594	614	631	657	834	915	1043	1046	1107

BOWLING ANALYSIS.

	Overs (8 balls)	Maidens	Runs	Wickets		Overs (8 balls)	Maidens	Runs	Wickets
McNamee	24	2	124	—	Phillips	11.7	—	64	—
McGuirk	26	1	130	1	Morgan	26	—	137	1
Mailey	64	—	362	4	Andrews	21	2	148	2
Campbell	11	—	89	—	Kippax	7	—	26	—

McNamee and Mailey each bowled a no-ball.

Umpires: J. RICHARDS and J. STAFFORD. Scorers: E. HEALY and A. B. AUMONT.

RESULT—Victoria won by an innings and 656 runs. Victoria's score constitutes a world's record in first class cricket.

The scoreboard at the back of the Hill on the Sydney Cricket Ground, recording England's highest Test score in Australia.

Far left *England stalwarts, and highly revered characters too. Left to right: Sir Jack Hobbs, Patsy Hendren, Herbert Sutcliffe.*

Left *Dinner for the 'Shilling Fund', set up on the return of Herbert Sutcliffe from the tour to Australia of 1924–25 (under A.E.R. Gilligan) during which he scored four Test centuries. It was his first Australian tour.*

proceeded to add another 132.

In Test matches, bowling of outstanding quality still had its rewards. The Ashes were won by Australia in 1920–21 and the following season in England largely through the sheer pace of Gregory and McDonald and they were seized by Jardine's team in 1932–33 through the at least equal pace of Larwood, Voce and Allen. But such bowling triumphs were few. The more typical impression of the period between the wars is still one of control by the batsmen and by one little man in particular, the genius, Don Bradman. In 52 Tests, the majority played between his début in 1928 and the start of the war, he scored only four runs under 7,000 at an average a fraction under 100. He had been producing fantastic achievements from his teenage years in a country district of New South Wales and when he came to England for the first time in 1930 he began with a double hundred at Worcester, made 300 in a day in the Leeds Test and only just under 1,000

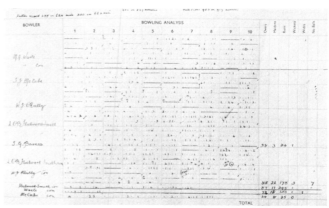

runs in the five Tests alone, at an average of 139.

Apart from the occasional bursts of success by fast bowlers (and, after Larwood, England had one of her fastest in Ken Farnes) it was patient spinners who reaped the biggest rewards. None was more successful than Tich Freeman, Kent's tireless five-foot two-inch leg-spin and googly bowler, who took 304 wickets in the 1928 season and during his career averaged no fewer than 188 wickets every summer.

Top and bottom The Oval scoreboard in 1938 at the fall of Hutton's wicket, and when England finally declared; they eventually beat Australia by an innings and 579 runs. Hutton's 364 surpassed the record 334 at Leeds by Bradman in 1930 – an innings which Hutton had

watched at the age of 14.

Centre The scoresheet of Hutton's historic innings. He batted 13 hours and 20 minutes, sharing two partnerships which improved on previous records: 382 with Leyland for the second wicket, and 215 with Hardstaff for the sixth.

Far left *Walter Reginald Hammond: 22 Test centuries, 167 in all. Perhaps he was England's greatest-ever all-rounder.*

Left *Phil Mead. Year in, year out, for a full generation, Phil Mead was the backbone of Hampshire's batting. He made more than 1,000 runs in 27 different seasons.*

Far left *Frank Woolley. 'There was all summer,' said Cardus, 'in a stroke by Woolley.' Languid left-hand batsman, fine slow left-arm bowler, he was a man who caught slip catches in his sleep.*

Left *Tich Freeman, the Kentish gnome whose leg-breaks and googlies dismissed 3,776 batsmen. And he looked so easy!*

The fact that so many young cricketers were lost during the Great War contributed greatly to the longevity of many of the inter-war stalwarts of the county game. The familiar faces appeared summer after summer, as perennial as the trees coming into leaf. Hampshire without Mead, Kent without Woolley, Yorkshire without Sutcliffe were like tea without milk.

Jack Hobbs was fifty-one when he retired in 1934; Wilfred Rhodes played until he was fifty-two, Woolley until he was fifty-one, Patsy Hendren until he was forty-nine, Percy Holmes until he was forty-six, and Willy Quaife until he was fifty-six, making a hundred in his last innings!

Every county, indeed, had its stalwarts. Yorkshire, perhaps, had rather more than their fair share, with Rhodes all wisdom and steadiness, and Emmott Robinson who thought of little else but Yorkshire cricket. Bill Bowes, something of a stalwart himself, told in his book *Express Deliveries* how these two sages would take the younger players up to a hotel bedroom and carefully place various articles such as shaving brushes, tooth and hair brushes, sponges, etc., on the eiderdown to represent fielders. A thorough post-mortem of the day would follow. Bowes recalls one day when he thought he was in for much criticism, having taken only 1 for 43, while Hedley Verity had taken 7 for 26. But it was to Verity that the first sharp question was put by 'Judge' Robinson at the evening inquest:

'Now then Hedley, what did you do today?'

Top *Harold Larwood and Bill Voce: in their prime in 1930.*
Above *Looking back: Larwood and Voce reunited at Trent Bridge in 1977.*

'Seven for 26, Emmott.'

Emmott smote the woodwork at the foot of his bed in disgust. 'Aye, seven for 26 and it owt to 'a been seven for 22. Ah never saw such bowlin'.'

For Rhodes and Robinson cricket was a lifetime's study, almost too serious for the kind of quip which George Macaulay, who played for sixteen seasons and was in a title-winning side in half of them, took pleasure in. He would bowl fast and then turn to off-spin if the pitch was favourable; when the wicket started to take spin, he would suddenly stiffen like a dog scenting a rabbit. Once when a possible catch bisected two fielders and neither moved, each leaving the ball to the other, he barked in exasperation: 'You two ought to be in Madame Tussauds.' And when three catches went down in quick succession on another day he called to the team in general: 'Alright, hands up anyone's who's playing.'

Sutcliffe, alone of the Yorkshire diehards in those all-conquering inter-war years, played through every season, impeccably turned-out, dedicated, polished, unfailing in his determination and concentration, and not without his own occasional wry remark. Ian Peebles told how one day, when he was completely nonplussed by a beauty from the Middlesex captain Nigel Haig, Sutcliffe got his own back by deflating the rejoicing bowler as he went past him on his way to the pavilion. Instead of 'Well bowled, Nigel', the remark was addressed to his partner Holmes. 'Sorry, Percy, careless shot.'

Other perennial figures of North-country cricket were the squarely-built, acrobatic Lancashire wicket-keeper, George Duckworth, the first about whom it was said: 'He makes more appeals than Doctor Barnardo'; Nottinghamshire's whimsical batting genius George Gunn; and Derbyshire's sound and reliable left-handed opening batsman Denis Smith, who played for twenty-six years.

Opening batsmen somehow seem to attract the word stalwart, perhaps because it is day-in, day-out reliability and a steadfast approach which enables them to last so long. Hampshire had the prime example in Phil Mead, the tall, idiosyncratic left-hander who never lost his appetite for runs, and Gloucestershire had a counterpart in Alf Dipper, Glamorgan in Dai Davies, Sussex in Ted Bowley, Worcestershire in H.H.I. Gibbons and Essex in A.C. Russell. Gloucestershire's perennial opener of the period, Charlie Barnett, whose career started in 1927, was rather too dashing a player to be aptly described as a stalwart: there were days when he could almost outshine Hammond himself.

For Middlesex Patsy Hendren lasted nearly as long as Sutcliffe, a squat little man with every stroke, capable of runs on every wicket and much loved by crowds for his penchant for visual comedy on the field. He went on until 1938, although like Jack Hobbs he had started before the 1914–18 war. Hobbs, 'The Master', scored 98 of his 197 hundreds after the age of forty, and his hundredth, at Taunton in August 1925, was a matter for national rejoicing. His opening partner Andy Sandham and the wicket-keeper Herbert Strudwick–Struddy to everyone–were other Oval favourites.

Kent possessed three professionals who gave more pleasure to spectators than any similar triumvirate: Frank Woolley with his willowy grace; Les Ames, ebullient wicket-keeper and very high-class batsman, and Tich Freeman who got so many of his wickets through stumpings by Ames and a fair few more through slip catches by Woolley! Nothing better exemplifies the huge gulf between inter-war county cricket and that of the present day than Freeman's career total of 3,776 wickets with leg-spinners at a cost of 18 each.

Long-serving bowlers of the faster variety were not so common, for obvious reasons, but there were some–men like Alec Kennedy of Hampshire, Nobby Clark of Northants, George Geary of Leicestershire and Fred Barratt of Nottinghamshire.

How hard they all laboured in the cause of their counties. Most would have agreed with Fred Root's final verdict on his own career: 'not very remunerative, but extremely happy'.

Herbert Sutcliffe and Percy Holmes, heirs to Brown and Tunnicliffe but undoubtedly Yorkshire's greatest opening pair. The match was at the Oval in 1933, and this was Holmes's last innings for Yorkshire.

Far left *'Struddy' – Herbert Strudwick, Surrey's wicket-keeper for thirty years and their scorer for another thirty! For many years he held the record for the most victims in a career – 1,241 catches and 54 stumpings.*

Left *Les Ames: the only wicket-keeper to have scored a hundred first-class hundreds.*

From the earliest days of Anglo-Australian cricket matches there had been an element of nationalistic fervour in the rivalry between the teams. It was sometimes evident amongst the players, and frequently so amongst spectators, occasionally stimulated by comments in the press. In Australia the riot during the game against New South Wales on Lord Harris's tour of 1878-79 had led to the abandonment of plans for a second Test match. In 1903 a Test at Sydney was held up when Umpire Crockett gave Clem Hill run out and a section of the crowd demonstrated violently. Warner was all for taking the England team off the field but his opposite number, Monty Noble, persuaded him not to.

Such incidents were isolated in matches that generally were fought toughly though chivalrously. Nevertheless there was a definite tendency for people to equate defeat on the cricket field with a denting of national pride. After all, cricket had been very much a part of the process of Empire-building, and the great game was one of the enduring legacies as the Empire

became a Commonwealth during the inter-war years with nations hitherto subservient to the Mother Country increasingly asserting their independence. Cricket had been a strong force in binding together the different Australian states, and as the nation began to grow up in world terms the glittering deeds of Bradman in England in 1930 were seen as a potent symbol of the apparent new confidence of Australia itself. Yet it was the brash confidence of adolescence, inclined to be quickly shattered and excessively self-conscious.

Outwardly English cricket took the mauling from Bradman squarely on the jaw, shaking hands at the end of the fight. But inwardly many were very concerned indeed with the question that if he could bat like this against them away from home, what humiliation might he not hand out on his own pitches? But there were hopeful signs in that Bradman had sometimes looked uneasy, despite scoring 232, against the pace of Larwood in the last Test of 1930, after being hit on the chest on a damp Oval wicket. Larwood's figures during this series were singularly

Warwick Armstrong – the Big Ship – leads out his near-invincible 1921 side at the start of the First Test at Trent Bridge. Jack Gregory, the player at the back of the group on the left, took 6 for 58, England were bowled out for 112, and the die was cast.

Harold Larwood bowling to Bill Woodfull during the Leeds Test of 1930. Don Bradman is the non-striker, A.P.F. Chapman is in the gully, and R.K. Tyldesley, the Falstaffian leg-spinner, is at silly mid-on, not exactly a picture of alertness.

Far left The close-of-play scorecard after the first day of the 1930 Leeds Test. Bradman scored 105 before lunch, 115 between lunch and tea, and 89 between tea and 'stumps'. He finished the series with 974 runs at an average of 139.14.

Left Tiger O'Reilly, a leg-break bowler with a fast bowler's temperament, a scourge of England and, in Bradman's words, 'the finest bowler I ever saw'.

Far left Tom Webster's perspicacious cartoon, drawn before the Old Trafford Test of 1930, from the Daily Mail, 25 July. In the event it was Bradman who did not like the wicket: Peebles dismissed him cheaply, and rain on the third and fourth days prevented a result.

Jack Gregory (far right) and Ted McDonald: the one 'towering, tanned and powerfully lithe', the other as graceful a fast bowler as there has ever been, though not in the same class as Gregory as a batsman.

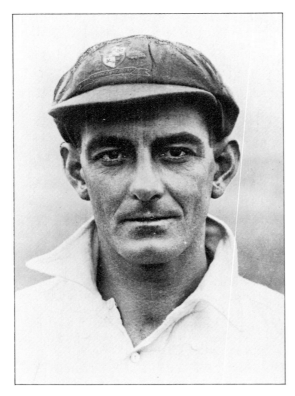

Far right 'Ponny' to Australians: Bill Ponsford, a murderer of indifferent bowling and a run machine upstaged only by Bradman. For a time he held the record for the world's highest score (429 against Tasmania) and for Victoria he scored nine double centuries.

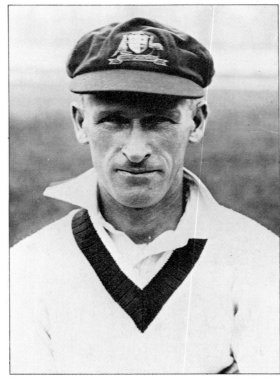

Right O'Reilly's most effective spinning partner, Clarrie Grimmett: an Australian Freeman but, unlike Freeman, a prolific wicket-taker at the highest level.

unimpressive, but he had bowled well in Australia in 1928–29 and the selectors were wise enough to appreciate that the bouncier wickets there would suit him again. They were wise enough too, or some would say unwise enough, to choose a captain who would use every means at his disposal to reduce the threat of Bradman.

Douglas Jardine, of Winchester, Oxford and Surrey, was, if not a cold fish, at least an aloof patrician figure. He was also a very determined man and as soon as he knew of his appointment he began planning the winter's campaign. With help from Arthur Carr, the Nottinghamshire captain, he evolved a scheme for making the most of the pace and accuracy of the two Notts bowlers Harold Larwood and Bill Voce. They were to bowl fast, short-of-a-length balls at the leg-stump to a packed leg-side field, forcing batsmen either to duck, hook dangerously, or fend the ball away off their chests in self-defence.

Many words have been spoken and written about how advanced the plan was before England arrived in Australia. The fact is that it worked well, from a cricketing viewpoint, helping England to regain the Ashes and win the series 4–1, and reducing the phenomenal Bradman to an average of only 56: riches for many, failure for him. Larwood took 33 wickets

with superbly accurate and very fast bowling. Voce took 15 and Allen, refusing to bowl to Jardine's plan, but nevertheless bowling fast and well, 21. The only serious injury occurred when Oldfield ducked into a shortish ball from Larwood at Adelaide and was hit on the head. Nowadays this is a commonplace sight in international cricket.

Bitterness at the tactics in Australia led to a cable from the Board of Control accusing England of unsportsmanlike conduct. MCC denied the charge from afar but offered to call the tour off if that was what the Australians wanted. They were forced to back-pedal but subsequent discussions reached, it is believed, Cabinet level and after some further instances of bodyline bowling in England, the tactic was outlawed by agreement rather than by law. In the then still fashionable phrase, it was not cricket. That the matter had indeed gone deeper than a mere cricketing argument is proved by a strongly worded editorial in the *Australian Cricketer* in February 1933:
'It [bodyline] prevents the batsman from even safely defending himself. To say otherwise is to brand Australian cricketers as cowards. That is at present being done only by people from safe distances of 10,000 miles. None of them would say it to our cricketers' faces. And everyone knows to whom

MCC aboard SS Orontes, *bound for Australia and the bitter series of 1932–33.*

The full leg-theory field. Woodfull ducks a Larwood bouncer.

It wasn't all one-way traffic, though Wally Hammond's injury – hit in the mouth trying to sweep Ironmonger – was hardly the fault of that medium-paced bowler. This was at Adelaide, in England's second innings, and Hammond made 85.

England would look if she was threatened in war again. Even the Germans have never pointed the finger of scorn at the Australians.'

The article praises Woodfull's refusal to attempt the same tactics in return and points out, with a prophetic eye towards the days of helmets and four fast bowlers a side:

'The only other alternative is the transformation of the game into a battle of armoured men, for keenness will undoubtedly force men to take full advantage of written laws and forget the unwritten laws…
Whatever Marylebone does for English cricket, the ruling authorities of Australian cricket will never allow their game to be marred by brutality, bitterness and viciousness.'

Gradually the ruffled feathers were smoothed down. Larwood never played for England again and, ironically, eventually settled in Australia. Jardine, though he led England the following winter in India, never played against Australia again. In time, goodwill was reasserted and cricket reverted, as assuredly it should have, to a game rather than a substitute for war. Violent tendencies only reappeared when in the late 1970s traditions of sportsmanship were again threatened, this time not by misplaced nationalism but by unchecked commercialism.

The Adelaide Test gave rise to the Australian cable of complaint to MCC. Here Woodfull loses his bat in fending the ball towards Larwood's leg trap.

Far left Douglas Jardine, clearly determined to get behind the line of Tim Wall's outswingers, leaves his leg-stump unguarded and is bowled at Adelaide. England, at one point 30 for 4 on the first day recovered to make 341 and eventually to win the match comfortably.

Left A symbol of courage. Eddie Paynter, ill from serious influenza, left his sickbed to make 83 at Brisbane.

Born in 1882, Sir Julien Cahn was the inheritor of a Nottingham furnishing business and a cricket fanatic. He developed the business into a small empire, establishing one of the first hire-purchase firms, and in addition to contributing to numerous charities and local activities, he indulged his passion for the game as no-one of similar ilk has ever done. He twice laid down sumptuous cricket grounds for his private use and from 1923 to 1941 his team played 621 matches, winning 299 of them and losing only 19.

Some of the best players of the era enjoyed his patronage, playing a peculiarly competitive brand of country-house cricket. Cahn himself was a modest performer, though intensely keen, an extremely slow bowler who had his days of success, usually through catches in the deep, and a very limited batsman who played in specially inflated pads, worn to protect unusually brittle bones.

Between 1929 and 1939 Sir Julien's XI made tours to Jamaica, Argentina, Denmark, North America, Ceylon and Malaya, and New Zealand. At home during these peak years of the Eleven some forty matches a season would be played. The side was built around a few stalwarts, some of whom were paid either by the match or by salary, sometimes in return for some vague managerial role in organizing the team or the ground. Others, like the South African D.P.B. Morkel, were set up in a local business, in Morkel's case a motoring enterprise in Nottingham. The regulars had to put up with the millionaire's occasional tendency to rudeness or eccentricity but they were rewarded with good, friendly but competitive cricket and off-the-field entertainment on the grand scale.

Spectators for the matches often ran to several thousands, especially for matches against visiting touring teams, but no entry charge was ever made. Any collections made were for local charities or benefits and for the major games scorecards would be available, sometimes printed on silk.

The team played on three home grounds. The first, the old YMCA ground, is the site of the present Nottingham County Hall. It was replaced in 1926 by Cahn's first private ground, at West Bridgford, close to Trent Bridge; this covered nine acres on a site adjacent to Loughborough Road. The outfield and square were

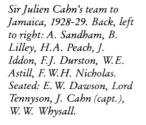

Sir Julien Cahn's team to Jamaica, 1928-29. Back, left to right: A. Sandham, B. Lilley, H.A. Peach, J. Iddon, F.J. Durston, W.E. Astill, F.W.H. Nicholas. Seated: E.W. Dawson, Lord Tennyson, J. Cahn (capt.), W.W. Whysall.

from the outset perfectly maintained and the pavilion was both spacious and grand. A new scorebox, large bathroom and dressing rooms, more than one dining room and a fine collection of old bats were amongst the main features, and the interior was large enough to be used as a tennis court. Neat flower beds bordered the pavilion, and on flags, ties and blazers the Cahn colours of black, pink and light blue were very much in evidence. The team wore caps of dark blue with the badge of a fox's head.

Only three years later, in 1929, Sir Julien and his team moved to still more grandiose surroundings, at the family's new home, Stanford Hall in Leicestershire. The magnificent house had been built in the eighteenth century and Cahn spent some £100,000 on the restoration of both the house and its large estate. When in 1930 Cahn bought the cricket collection of the historian and statistician F.S. Ashley-Cooper, the library at Stanford Hall became the repository of the greatest private collection of cricket books and pictures. Much of it is now at Lord's.

In 1937 a superb new theatre was built onto one wing of the house, and this is still in active use. Cahn himself used it to show films and produce conjuring shows, being himself an enthusiastic President of the Leicester Magic Circle. A Wurlitzer organ was brought from Paris. Above the new theatre was the 'Cricketers' Wing', providing accommodation for visiting teams. The estate also contained, apart from its proudest possession, the cricket ground, tennis courts, badminton and squash courts, a nine-hole golf course, a putting green, a pond for performing seals, a large lake stocked with trout, and a superb swimming pool, all the amenities being part of the great attraction of playing for or against the Eleven.

The cricket ground itself had been in existence before Cahn bought the estate but the square was at once re-laid and the outfield maintained to a much higher standard by two permanent groundsmen. The cricket played there, usually on Sundays before large crowds, ranged from good-class club cricket to genuine first-class. Amongst the 'star' players who appeared for the Eleven were the spinners I.A.R. Peebles, 'Tich' Richmond and Jack Walsh, the all-rounders R.W.V. Robins, G.F.H. Heane, D.P.B. Morkel and John Gunn, and two New Zealand Test batsmen,

Sir Julien Cahn's first private ground at West Bridgford, Nottingham.

Team list and itinerary of Sir Julien Cahn's tour to New Zealand, 1938–39, arranged and printed by the New Zealand Cricket Council.

Sir Julien Cahn's team to New Zealand, 1938–39. These were some of the notable players. Back: 2nd left, E.A. Watts; 4th left, J. Hardstaff Junior; 8th left, J.E. Walsh; 9th left, W.E. Astill. Seated: 1st left, C.S. Dempster; 5th left, J. Cahn; 6th left, G.F.H. Heane; 7th left, V.E. Jackson; 8th left, T.P.B. Smith.

NEW ZEALAND CRICKET COUNCIL

MEMBERS OF THE TEAM.

SIR JULIEN CAHN, Bart.

G. F. H. HEANE	Nottinghamshire
C. C. GOODWAY	Warwichshire
C. S. DEMPSTER	Leicestershire
V. E. JACKSON	New South Wales
J. G. LUSH	New South Wales
C. R. MAXWELL	Nottinghamshire
H. MUDGE	New South Wales
J. E. WALSH	Leicestershire
A. H. DYSON	Glamorgan
J. HARDSTAFF	Nottinghamshire
N. OLDFIELD	Lancashire
W. E. PHILLIPSON	Lancashire
T. P. B. SMITH	Essex
E. A. WATTS	Surrey
E. G. WOLFE	Manager
W. E. ASTILL	Baggage Man

Sir Julien Cahn's Team

NEW ZEALAND TOUR 1939

E. E. LUTTRELL, Hon. Secretary,
P.O. Box 958, Christchurch

W.&W. LTD.

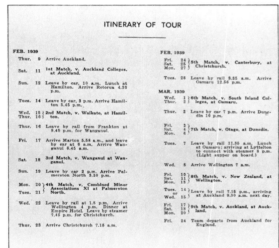

ITINERARY OF TOUR

FEB. 1939

Thur. 9 Arrive Auckland.

Sat. 11 1st Match, v. Auckland Colleges, at Auckland.

Sun. 12 Leave by car, 10 a.m. Lunch at Hamilton. Arrive Rotorua 4.30 p.m.

Tues. 14 Leave by car, 3 p.m. Arrive Hamilton 5.45 p.m.

Wed. 15 } 2nd Match, v. Waikato, at Hamilton.
Thur. 16 }

Thur. 16 Leave by rail from Frankton at 9.40 p.m. for Wanganui.

Fri. 17 Arrive Marton 5.58 a.m., and leave by car at 6 a.m. Arrive Wanganui 6.45 a.m.

Sat. 18 3rd Match, v. Wanganui at Wanganui.

Sun. 19 Leave by car 2 p.m. Arrive Palmerston North 3.30 p.m.

Mon. 20 } 4th Match, v. Combined Minor
Tues. 21 } Associations XI at Palmerston North.

Wed. 22 Leave by rail at 1.5 p.m. Arrive Wellington 4 p.m. Dinner at Empire Hotel. Leave by steamer 7.45 p.m. for Christchurch.

Thur. 23 Arrive Christchurch 7.15 a.m.

FEB. 1939

Fri. 24 } 5th Match, v. Canterbury, at
Sat. 25 } Christchurch.
Mon. 27 }

Tues. 28 Leave by rail 8.35 a.m. Arrive Oamaru 12.56 p.m.

MAR. 1939

Wed. 1 } 6th Match, v. South Island Col-
Thur. 2 } leges, at Oamaru.

Thur. 2 Leave by car 7 p.m. Arrive Dunedin 10 p.m.

Fri. 3 }
Sat. 4 } 7th Match, v. Otago, at Dunedin.
Mon. 6 }

Tues. 7 Leave by rail 11.35 a.m. Lunch at Oamaru; arriving at Lyttelton to connect with steamer 8 p.m. (Light supper on board.)

Wed. 8 Arrive Wellington 7 a.m.

Fri. 10 }
Sat. 11 } 8th Match, v. New Zealand, at
Mon. 13 } Wellington.

Tues. 14 } Leave by rail 7.15 p.m., arriving
or } at Auckland 9.30 a.m. next day.
Wed. 15 }

Fri. 17 }
Sat. 18 } 9th Match, v. Auckland, at Auck-
Mon. 20 } land.

Fri. 24 Team departs from Auckland for England.

C.S. Dempster and R.C. Blunt. The regular wicket-keeper, C.R.N. Maxwell, was an irregular county player and the two most prolific batsmen were F.C.W. Newman and G.F. Summers. Newman, Cahn's right-hand man almost from the outset of his cricketing adventures, played a few games for Surrey; Summers played only for Surrey's 2nd XI. Both amply proved by their performances (Newman over 14,000 runs at an average of 44 with 37 hundreds, Summers with over 13,000 at 42 with 30 hundreds) that they would have shone in regular first-class cricket. They preferred the delights of Stanford Hall, and not-infrequent tours overseas. And who can blame them?

The popularity and national significance of cricket between the wars were reflected in the knighthoods of some of the game's heroes. The first to be so honoured was Jack Hobbs, the most universally admired cricketer since Alfred Mynn. Despite the game's reputation for fair play, cricket has always been a game within which gossip has a warm breeding-ground, but about John Berry Hobbs no-one ever said an unkind word. There was nothing unkind, indeed, to say. His life off the field was a model of moderation, based on sound values of integrity and self-discipline learned early at his Cambridge home. On the field he was the most complete batsman the game had seen and a brilliant cover fielder in his pre-war days who ran out

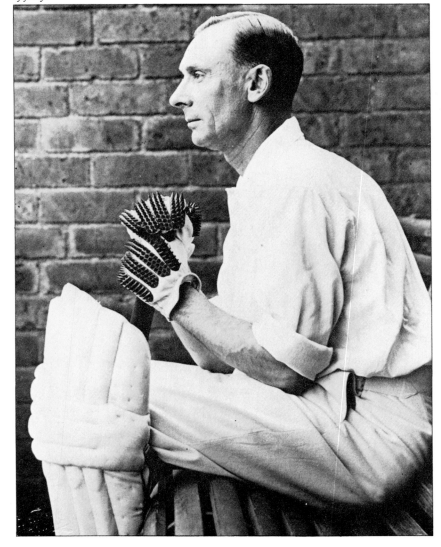

Sir John Berry Hobbs: to his contemporaries, just Jack Hobbs, impeccable gentleman, professional and master batsman. Ninety-eight of his first-class hundreds came after the age of forty.

fifteen batsmen on the MCC tour of Australia in 1911–12. Never by a word, a gesture or even a physical movement did he fall from grace.

Hobbs scored more first-class runs, 61,237, and hit more centuries, 197, than any other player, a record which must last for all time. No-one has, by sheer precept and example, had such a profound effect on the status of his profession. He was by no means a sycophant, quietly insisting, in 1924, on his right to take his wife on a tour of Australia. Because he was Hobbs, a player so essential to England and a character so respected, he was allowed to do so, though it was all against convention. When, in 1926, Arthur Carr became ill during the Old Trafford Test, it was Hobbs, not the amateur Greville Stevens, who was asked to take over as captain. His knighthood came in the Coronation year of 1953.

The elevation of Don Bradman to Sir Donald came sooner after his retirement from the game which he had dominated, to a greater or lesser extent, throughout his peerless career. Of him it would not be true to say that no unkind words were spoken. He was viewed by more than one of his Australian team-mates as selfish, though all the facts suggest that this was mere envy at the man's fantastic ability to steal every headline by the genius and ruthless concentration of his batting. Nor was he, in his younger days, the greatest story-teller in the bar. His dedication to cricket was total. Bradman would have been less than human if, as an amateur sportsman, he had not had to take decisions affecting his personal finances which sometimes offended people. The most famous and illustrious cricketer in the world, he was, after all, hot property. But he was as honest and level-headed in his business activities as he was in his approach to cricket, and almost equally successful.

As a captain of Australia, starting in 1936–37, he was as efficient and merciless as he was a batsman, and diplomatically he never put a foot wrong. No-one was more dignified in response to bodyline (he has maintained his silence on the matter into old age) and although he presided over another heavy defeat for England in the first Australian tour after the war, he was never more popular than in 1948. Who would have thought, after all he had done, that rather than being glad when he was out for nought in his last Test innings, many Englishmen should actually have found tears welling? If Bradman himself had a churning breast at the time, he did not show it, for he took his rare setbacks with a stoic dignity.

The third of the inter-war cricketers who came from the people to finish as a knight was Learie Constantine. His final title, in fact, was higher than that of a knight for he became a Life Peer, taking the

The Don, in the confident, indomitable prime of youth, and after dismissal in his last Test innings at Lord's, caught by Bill Edrich off Alec Bedser for 89.

title of Baron of Maraval and Nelson, where he had become one of the Lancashire League's favourite sons. His honours came more for his achievements as a Minister in the Trinidad Government and as his country's High Commissioner to England than for his achievements on the cricket field, though the second half of his career could not have happened without the first.

Constantine was a rapacious batsman, a fielder of cat-like reflexes and agility and a fast bowler with a bounding run and high, smooth action. He was never as consistent as the two post-war cricket knights from Barbados, Frank Worrell and the incomparable Gary Sobers, but he was a matchwinner, and he did the double on the 1928 tour of England. Indeed he had the whole country talking about him after his performance against Middlesex: going in at 79 for 5 in the first innings he hit 86 spectacular runs in less than an hour. Then he took 7 for 57 in the Middlesex second innings. The West Indians, left with 279 to win, were 121 for 5 when he came in to hit 103 out of the 133 scored in the next hour.

Constantine's fame as a cricketer and his intelligence and dignity as a man did much to raise the status of all West Indians in England, where he was revered almost as much as in the island where his father, foreman of a sugar plantation, had also been a first-class cricketer.

Learie Constantine plays a long-handled sweep during the West Indies tour of 1939. A vital, compelling cricketer, he was an entertainer rather than a consistent matchwinner, but, on his day, dazzlingly brilliant in any or all of the main departments of the game.

Successful cricket teams are invariably well led, though it is equally true that successful captains invariably have good teams. The period between the wars witnessed a great variety of approaches to captaincy–including the autocratic methods of Jardine, the 'lead-by-example' school of Douglas and Chapman, the sternly pragmatic attitudes of Armstrong, Bradman and Sellers and the original enterprise of Fender. Those who succeeded for longest shared two essential qualities: they put the needs of the team before those of themselves and they earned, in various ways, the respect of their men.

The role of the county captain had changed since before the First World War when some captains, notably Lord Hawke of Yorkshire, had taken on themselves not just the leadership of a team on the field, but also their moral welfare off it. Hawke presided over their financial affairs, kept strict limits on their drinking of ale, and insisted that each man should be well dressed and (apart from his moustache) clean-shaven. 'If I shave twice a day,' he commanded them, 'the least you can do is to shave once.'

English captains were usually men apart. They changed in different dressing-rooms from the professionals, sometimes even from the amateurs, and they expected obedient compliance with their decisions. This was the code which all players had been reared to accept. Nor was it unreasonable because a cricket field is a lonely place for captains, especially when two batsmen are in full flight, the bowlers are wilting and catches have been dropped.

Johnny Douglas, captain of Essex from 1901 to 1928, was no stranger to such situations. In that long span the highest the county ever finished in the Championship was sixth. As England captain in Australia in 1920–21 he suffered the misery of a 5–0 whitewash in the Test series, a very different story from the 4–1 success he had enjoyed ten years earlier as deputy for Pelham Warner, who was ill. But Douglas thrived on adversity: with his hair smoothed down and parted in the middle he would emerge from the pavilion to bat or open the bowling with a muscle-bristling determination appropriate to a man who had won the middleweight Olympic gold medal in 1908. On the whole he took his troops with him, although Cecil Parkin once caustically remarked: 'That's right, skipper. You bowl first and play them in, then put me on and I'll get them out.' Douglas had much moral courage and a fighting spirit which, in the words of Herbert Sutcliffe, was 'second only to Jardine's… He was brimful of the most sterling qualities.' Unfortunately, sensitivity was not one of them and he had little time for anyone who did not approach the game in the same wholehearted 'never-say-die' fashion

Below *An uncompromising captain and a highly enterprising one: Warwick Armstrong (left) with Percy Fender in 1921.*

Centre *Percy Chapman, a* Boy's Own Paper *hero in living substance, with his wife on the balcony of their home at Hythe, Kent.*

Right *Colonel J. W. H. T. Douglas, who presided over both triumphs and disasters in Australia, and led Essex with insatiable pugnacity.*

as he did. On the way to Australia in 1920 he told Percy Fender that there was no-one he would fancy bowling at more than Fender, no bowler he enjoyed batting against more. If it was intended as a jest or a spur, it was not successful, Fender being more inclined, no doubt, to view it as a sign that Douglas saw him as a rival for the England captaincy and did not propose to give him many chances. Nor, early on the tour, did he, though at one point the manager, Francis Toone, suggested to the out-of-form Douglas that Fender should replace him.

Fender himself had led Surrey for most of the previous season and was officially appointed to the job the following year, remaining as captain until 1931. He was altogether more thoughtful and resourceful and rather less dogmatic than the belligerent Douglas, and his captaincy of Surrey showed an enterprise and originality which endeared him both to his own team and to spectators. At a time when England's selectors were looking for the right captain, it was strange that they did not give him a chance, especially as more than one newspaper correspondent saw him in 1921 as the man to counter Warwick Armstrong's ruthless leadership of Australia. When Fender was picked for the Fourth Test of the summer, the *Morning Post* commented that it was 'a belated choice for perhaps the best captain among the counties'. Among Surrey's

players there was no questioning his popularity. Fender always insisted that he should lead all the team out together from the same gate, regarding the amateur/professional divide as outdated.

No English captain until Douglas Jardine was as uncompromising in his approach to winning cricket matches as Armstrong himself. He had been chosen by only one vote to lead his country, being someone who disliked cricket administrators almost as a matter of principle. In England in 1921, and indeed in Australia the previous winter, he let McDonald and Gregory bowl as much short stuff at England's rather timid batting as they wanted. No doubt their attack was relatively mild by the standards of the 1980s but memories in cricket are long and when Larwood and Voce were handing it out more than a decade later there were those who read it as revenge. One of the most famous images of Armstrong is of the huge man leaning against the boundary rails during the closing stages of the last Test at The Oval, a match ruined by rain, reading a paper and showing little interest in a game bound for a futile draw. Asked why, he later said: 'I wanted to see who we were playing against.'

In sharp contrast was the England captain chosen to succeed another hard man, Arthur Carr, for the last Test of the 1926 series. Percy Chapman, tall, strong, cherubic-faced, optimistic and full of flair, was

Below *Arthur Carr: more popular with his Nottinghamshire team than with the Establishment at Lord's.*

Centre *The Hon. Lionel Tennyson, the tough aristocrat who stood up better than most to Gregory and McDonald in 1921.*

Left *Frank Mann, mighty hitter and successful captain of Middlesex and England; both these posts were later held by his son, F.G.*

Below *R.E.S. Wyatt. A shrewd batsman and equally shrewd captain, his long first-class career began in 1923, and he captained Warwickshire before the war, and Worcestershire, with equal relish, after it.*

Right *Douglas Jardine in the Harlequin cap which challenged Australians like a red rag to a bull. Australian crowds disliked his apparent haughtiness so much that when he swatted away a fly in the field one day, a voice yelled: 'Keep yer hands off our flies, Jardine.'*

a fine, attacking left-handed batsman who led England with zest and a judgment which he did not often apply to his own batting. He, like Carr four years earlier, was unceremoniously ditched before the decisive Test of the 1930 series. R.E.S. Wyatt replaced him, but D.R. Jardine was the man chosen to lead in Australia two years later.

Had they been good enough players there would have been strong cases for making either Bev Lyon of Gloucestershire or Brian Sellers of Yorkshire the England captain in the 1930s. Lyon was a brilliantly inventive leader who seldom did the expected and looked for victory from the first ball of the match. Sellers was barely good enough for the Yorkshire eleven yet he led them with not a murmur of protest from 1933 until the war (and for two years after) winning six titles in all. Bill Bowes described him thus:

'Sentiment had no place in Sellers's make-up. A man could either do his stuff or he could not and if he could not then he must go... The side came first and in all cases of doubt the player was dropped... He was a dynamic captain, a keen student of the game and the rules and he would bring an umpire to order as easily as a player. At times he was a martinet but he loved the team as cricketers... He made fewer mistakes than most and would listen to advice... We shall always cherish the memory of that self-asserting, dominating figure whose personality made him the most colourful of captains.'

Cricketers have always, it seems, responded well to strong captains in the Lyon, Sellers, Armstrong or Jardine mould, and decisiveness has always been an essential quality for captains in a sport which demands much more from its leaders than any other.

THE POST WAR YEARS 1945-1963

Whereas during the First World War cricket had closed down almost completely as all attention was fixed on the grim and melancholy struggle in Europe, a different approach was taken between 1939 and 1945, even though the conflict was still more global in its nature than the first. A certain amount of cricket of more or less first-class standard was played, various matches at Lord's being seen as not only good for morale but also a very useful means of raising finance for the various wartime charities badly in need of funds. Sir Pelham Warner was the presiding genius.

England and Australia each won two matches with one drawn. Bill Edrich, Cyril Washbrook, Wally Hammond and Len Hutton all scored over 300 runs in the series but only Keith Miller did so for Australia, outscoring all batsmen on either side and hitting memorable hundreds at Lord's in the second and fourth games. It was a warning of what lay ahead from Miller, whose fast bowling partnership with Ray Lindwall had yet to be born. The carefree, cavalier approach of Miller was universally popular and so too was the whole approach of the Services captain, Lindsay Hassett, one of the greatest characters ever to wield a bat. A tiny, skilful batsman, he kept all amused with his mischievous sense of humour yet contrived to be one of the most effective diplomats his country ever had.

The best game of the whole season took place at Lord's late in August when a Dominions side defeated England by 45 runs at Lord's. The two sides scored 1,241 runs and wonderful hundreds were made by Martin Donnelly of New Zealand, Keith Miller and Wally Hammond, who got one in each innings. The bowling in the match was relatively weak and the bulk of it for England was done by two leg-spinners, Doug

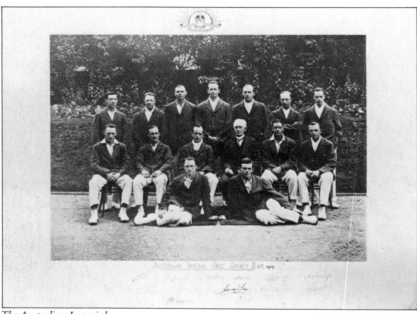

The Australian Imperial Forces team of 1919.

Remembering the hiding that England had taken at Australian hands in the years after the 1914–18 war, those with longer memories and cricket at heart may also have realized the importance of giving as many cricketers with the ability to play the game at the top level at least an occasional chance to keep their eye in. When peace at last came, no time was wasted.

An Australian Imperial Forces team had played twenty-eight matches in 1919, which helped to rehabilitate the game, and the AIF team of 1945 was even more popular and successful. Originally nothing like their programme of nearly fifty matches had been envisaged, but VE Day on 8 May sparked the hasty development of much more ambitious plans and in the end five 'Victory Tests' (counting in the record books as first-class matches but not as official Tests) were played, three at Lord's and one each at Bramall Lane and Old Trafford.

Hammond and Hassett tossing before the Fourth Victory Test at Lord's, 1945.

Wright and Eric Hollies. It must indeed have been a magnificently entertaining match to watch.

The shared experience of fighting a war had long ago restored a sense of proportion in the attitudes of Englishmen and Australians to mere cricket matches, but even closer bonds were forged during the summer of 1945 as the Forces team played its way round the United Kingdom. The team's manager, Keith Johnson, summed up the tour thus:

'There was something about the games of last season, something care-free and refreshing, which I hope has come to stay. I would liken it to a mixture of Lord's, Old Trafford, Trent Bridge, Bramall Lane and the village green; it was certainly a good mixture…we must take it in large doses.'

The sheer relief of living in an atmosphere free from the daily anxieties of war was, no doubt, the main reason for the spirit which prevailed. Gradually a sterner approach was to return to international cricket, but, in the terminology of the day, the 'Mother Country' was indebted again to her 'Colonial Cousin' for setting the noble game fully in motion again. Anyone who played in or watched the AIF matches looks back on them with a special pleasure.

Hammond batting in the Second Test at Sheffield in which he scored a superb 100 out of England's 286 on a tricky pitch.

The England team for the Fifth Victory Test, August 1945, with the Inter-Services Selection Committee. Back, left to right: H. Elliott (umpire), L.B. Fishlock, Sgt R. Pollard, Major F.A. Sloan, Pte G.H. Pope, Flt-Sgt W.E. Phillipson, Lieut J.D. Robertson, Lt-Col G.O. Allen. Seated: Flt-Sgt C. Washbrook, Sgt. L. Hutton, Maj-Gen T.F.N. Wilson, Flt-Lieut W.R. Hammond (capt.), W-Cdr W.H.N. Shakespeare, Lt-Col S.C. Griffith, Lieut D.V.P. Wright, Front: S-Ldr W.J. Edrich, Sgt W.B. Roberts.

The Australians were by no means the only popular team to tour England just after the war. The South Africans of 1947 played a full part in perhaps the most glorious summer of cricket ever played. More or less perfect weather was the prerequisite for many amazing deeds, none more so than those of Denis Compton and Bill Edrich, who both scored more than 3,500 runs in the greatest run spree by any pair of batsmen ever known. Never has there been such a summer for batsmen. Compton scored 18 first-class hundreds, Edrich and Jack Robertson 12 each, Len Hutton and Cyril Washbrook 11 each and Winston Place 10.

Compton and Edrich dominated in the five Tests against South Africa no less than in the County Championship and Edrich was also the second highest wicket-taker for England in a five-match series which England won 3–0. But South Africa, who in 1935 had won a rubber against England for the first time under H.F. Wade, had been as much debilitated by the war effort as England and had had rather less practice since.

They possessed an admirable captain in Alan Melville, a batsman of rare grace and charm, plus an assiduous accumulator of runs in Bruce Mitchell and a player of high class in Dudley Nourse. England also won the 1948–49 series in South Africa when, in the words of E.W. Swanton, 'sportsmanship and goodwill went hand in hand'.

Nourse was captain of the 1951 team to England, playing a leading role in every respect, but their record did not compare with that of Jack Cheetham's side in 1955, who came back from losing the first two Tests to win the next two at Old Trafford and Headingley; crowds of over 100,000 then saw Laker and Lock make winning use of their home pitch at The Oval. This, nonetheless, was a vintage South African side with an outstanding all-rounder in Trevor Goddard, left-handed opener of the batting and often of the bowling too. The batting was led by a skilful and determined opener in D.J. 'Jackie' McGlew and a dashing number five in Roy McLean. There was also an outstanding wicket-keeper batsman in John Waite

The 1947 South Africans in England. Back, left to right: T.A. Harris, C.McP. Overstone, D.W. Begbie, V.I. Smith, L. Tuckett, J.B. Plimsoll, L.W. Payn, J.D. Lindsay, G.M. Fullerton. Seated: O.C. Dawson, D.V. Dyer, B. Mitchell, A. Melville, A.S. Frames (manager), A.D. Nourse, K.G. Viljoen, N.F.B. Mann, A.M.B. Rowan.

Alan Melville, a graceful batsman and popular captain of both Sussex and South Africa, watched by Godfrey Evans and Bill Edrich during the Trent Bridge Test of 1947, the game in which he became the first South African to score a hundred in each innings of a Test.

(and another in reserve in Russell Endean, though he was usually played for his batting alone), a world-class off-spinner in Hugh Tayfield and a pair of genuinely quick bowlers in Peter Heine and Neil Adcock. The high point of a memorable tour was the Old Trafford Test when, in glorious weather, England made only 284 in the first innings despite a marvellous 158 by Denis Compton (Heine, Adcock and Goddard taking three wickets each) and South Africa responded with 521 for 8 declared, with centuries from McGlew, Waite and Paul Winslow, a hard-driving batsman who never had a finer hour. England fought back with 381 in the second innings, Peter May scoring 117, Compton 71, Colin Cowdrey 50, and Godfrey Evans, going in number 11, a courageous 17 despite batting with a finger fractured in two places while wicket-keeping. South Africa scrambled home by only three wickets in the end with a few minutes of the fifth day left.

Something of the quality of the whole series may be gleaned from the fact that England used a mixture of Tyson, Trueman, Statham, Loader, Bailey and Bedser to do their fast to fast-medium bowling and Laker, Lock, Appleyard, Titmus and Wardle to spin the ball. With the possible exception of Loader, every one of these men was a bowler from the highest drawer.

South Africa's penultimate visit to England in 1960 was altogether less happy. The Nationalist Government had just declared itself a Republic independent of the Commonwealth and for the first time cricketers tasted the bitterness of anti-apartheid feelings. The demonstrators who followed them round England in a wet summer were firing only the opening salvoes in a long and as yet unfinished battle to disrupt South African sport in an attempt to shift the intransigent lawmakers in Pretoria.

But in 1965 the weather was kinder and the cricket of Peter van der Merwe's talented side succeeded in transcending politics. In particular, the fielding of Colin Bland, a panther of a cover point with a throw as unerring as a missile, captured public imagination and had English batsmen in a tizzy whenever he came near the ball.

A pre-Test reception given in 1955 by South African grape promoters enabled Jack Cheetham to discuss field placings with his men. The players are, back, left to right: Murray, Endean, Waite, Mansell, Goddard, McLean, Tayfield, McGlew, Smith, Duckworth. Front: Keith, Fuller, Heine, Cheetham.

First innings of the Second Test at Cape Town in 1955–57: P.B.H. May c Waite b Tayfield 8. Was this the arm ball? May had his only poor Test series on this tour.

Below left Colin Bland, batting against Australia. His clean hitting and superlative cover fielding delighted English crowds in 1965. Seldom has anyone so stolen the limelight by fielding alone.

Below Peter van der Merwe, a fine captain, leading his team off the field after South Africa had beaten England in the Second Test at Trent Bridge in 1965.

The early 1950s witnessed the greatest flowering of cricketers at Fenner's, the perfectly groomed home of Cambridge cricket, for many years. This tended to blur the memory of the relative strength of Oxford cricket just after the war.

It was Oxford who won the first post-war Varsity match, their polished, commanding left-hander Martin Donnelly crowning a prolific season for them with a worthy 142 at Lord's. The tall fast bowler Philip Whitcombe and two fleet-of-foot batsmen in Geoffrey Keighley of Yorkshire and Tony Pawson of Kent, were among the outstanding players in the early post-war years in the Parks. Pawson, the son of A.G., led Oxford to victory in the 1948 University match, as his father had done before him. The year before, he and Keighley had set tongues wagging by running four no fewer than eight times. A cricketer and personality of spirit, Pawson led a team unbeaten except by the all-conquering Australians. He had two strong players from overseas, the South African Clive Van Ryneveld, and the future captain of Pakistan, Abdul Hafeez Kardar.

Cambridge, however, were the University to supply England with Test players. The two Essex stalwarts, Trevor Bailey and Doug Insole, were the first to distinguish themselves. Then, in 1950, the first four in the Cambridge batting order were John Dewes, David Sheppard, Hubert Doggart and Peter May. In the most ideal batting conditions, all prospered. The first three played for England that season while the fourth, May, was to develop into the most complete and commanding English batsman of his generation. Calm and determined, with a method of pure orthodoxy, he used his height and growing strength to dominate the best bowling in all conditions during the 1950s. Sheppard also became England captain, having scored 3,545 runs for Cambridge, more than any man

Oxford University, 1952. Back, left to right: M.C. Cowdrey, A.J. Coxon, D.C.P.R. Jowett, W.G.A. Willey, J.E. Bush, I.D.F. Coutts. Seated: P.J. Whitcombe, A.L. Dowding, P.D.S. Blake (capt.), B. Boobyer, W.M. Mitchell.

has achieved in three years at the university.

Cambridge produced useful bowlers also in the flighty off-spinner, Robin Marlar, who took 12 wickets in the 1953 match, and a wholehearted fast bowler, John Warr, one of the game's humourists, who was discovered in romantic fashion when bowling on Parker's Piece, the huge area of playing fields in the city centre where Jack Hobbs had played much of his early cricket. The South African Cuan McCarthy was one of the fiercest fast bowlers either University has possessed.

Between 1952 and 1955 Oxford won not a single game despite having two more England captains in Colin Cowdrey and M.J.K. Smith, both prolific batsmen. Cowdrey had a touch and talent given to few men in the history of the game. He hit his fours as if he felt sorry not just for the bowler but for the ball. Smith, applying a shrewd brain to the game, was a

good enough all-round games player to play rugby for England as well, in an age when double internationals were far rarer than they had been. He made a hundred in the three successive University matches. He thus upstaged Dennis Silk of Cambridge, who had scored hundreds two years in a row and who, like Sheppard, the future Bishop of Liverpool, went on to a distinguished career outside the game, becoming the most respected public school headmaster of recent times.

Gamini Goonesena from Ceylon was a fine all-round cricketer and popular captain whose team beat Oxford by an innings in 1957 after a fine spell of swing bowling by O.S. Wheatley. The same Wheatley, later of Warwickshire and Glamorgan, took no fewer than 80 wickets the following season in the short University fixture-list while Ted Dexter, the most gifted England amateur since May, hit well over 1,000 runs. A batsman

Cambridge, 1952. Back, left to right: F.C.M. Alexander, R. Subba Row, C.N. McCarthy, G.G. Tordoff, C.J.M. Kenny, M.H. Bushby. Seated: P.B.H. May, R.G. Marlar, D.S. Sheppard, J.J. Warr, M.H. Stevenson. Though much the weaker side, Oxford achieved a creditable draw in the Varsity match.

of textbook technique and immense talent, he was a wonderful sight for any spectator when going well, and his lofty command earned him the press name of 'Lord Ted'.

In 1959 came the first Oxford victory at Lord's for eight years, a triumph for their captain, A.C. Smith, who had presided over five other wins that season, helped by the Indian Test player A.A. Baig and two excellent opening bowlers in Andrew Corran of

Nottinghamshire and David Sayer of Kent.

The 1960s began with some outstanding efforts from two more future Test captains, A.R. Lewis for Cambridge and the brilliantly gifted Nawab of Pataudi, who until losing the sight of an eye in a car accident was promising to be a better player even than his famous father. But the decade which saw the official ending of the distinction between amateurs and professionals was to be a much less prosperous one for

The crowd indulge in a gentlemanly – or is it scholarly? – invasion of the field during an interval in the 1956 University match. By the 1970s crowds for the fixture had fallen from thousands to hundreds.

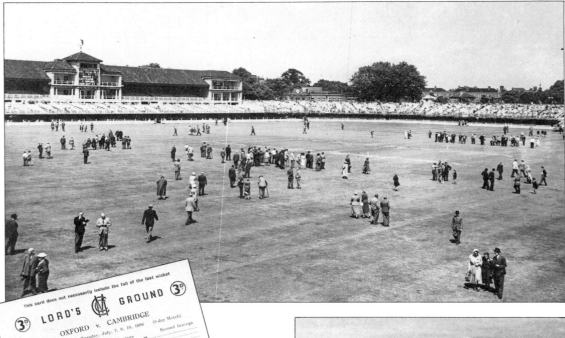

Right The scorecard after the first day's play in the 1956 match. The Oxford captain, Mike Smith, was to score his third successive Varsity match hundred.

Far right Ted Dexter, in Cambridge colours, bowling in the 1958 match under the sharp eye of Syd Buller.

the universities, due partly to greater concentration on the academic side of life (though two Cambridge stalwarts of these years, Mike Brearley and Eddie Craig, gained firsts) and partly to the ending of National Service which resulted in players just out of school being thrust into first-class cricket before most of them were ready for it.

The ending of National Service had an equally profound effect on the standard of Services cricket. At Lord's in 1949, for example, one P.B.H. May scored 162 not out and 58 not out when the Royal Navy played the RAF. In all, 26 Test players represented the Combined Services during their period of National Service, but although the standard of cricket produced by the Regulars thereafter was a little below first-class, there remained enough good cricketers to prove more than a match in most years for the best representative schools side in the annual match at Lord's.

The Combined Services, 1953. Back, left to right: F.A.G. Steer, M.D. Fenner, R. O'Brien, B.D. Wells, A.C.D. Ingleby-Mackenzie, M.J. Horton, D.J. Ward, A.C. Walton. Seated: R.G. Wilson, M.L.Y. Ainsworth, J.H.G. Deighton, A.H. Parnaby.

The Combined Services, 1955. Back, left to right: T.W. Cartwright, A.C.S. Leary, R.A. Goolf, R.G. Stevens, F.A.G. Steer, J.T. Murray, D. Heaton. Seated: A.L. Thackery, J.H.G. Deighton, M.L.Y. Ainsworth, A.C. Shirreff, P.E. Richardson.

ew touring teams have made such an impact as the 1950 West Indian team to England. Following three draws against New Zealand in the hot summer of 1949, the West Indians, under the captaincy of John Goddard, were given four five-day Tests. They won three of them.

The batting, already proven, was immensely strong, a dependable pair of openers in Stollmeyer and Rae being followed by three world-class batsmen in Walcott, Weekes and Worrell, the immortal 'Three Ws' from Barbados. On this tour Weekes averaged 79, scoring 2,310 runs, Worrell 68 and Walcott 55. Rae, Stollmeyer, Christiani, Gomez and Roy Marshall also made over 1,000 runs.

Despite this galaxy, at least as strong as any West Indian batting side since, the heroes of the tour, immortalized in a contemporary calypso, were 'those two little pals of mine', Ramadhin and Valentine. Both quite unknown before the tour, virtually so, indeed, even in the Caribbean, they bamboozled the English batting in the Second Test at Lord's and held the whip-hand thereafter. Valentine was an orthodox left-arm spinner who turned the ball sharply, Ramadhin a mysterious purveyor of mainly off-breaks spun with the wrist and what appeared to be a leg-spin action. His accuracy was far greater than that of the average orthodox leg-spinner. He took 135 wickets on the tour at 14 each, Valentine 123 at 17 each.

Although the West Indies subsequently produced the highest wicket-taker amongst all the spinners of Test cricket in Lance Gibbs, their great strength in the field was soon to be based not on slow bowlers but on a never-ending stream of fast ones.

Right *Alf Valentine (above) and Sonny Ramadhin, virtually unknown even in their own Caribbean before they burst to fame in 1950. Had Ramadhin been a quick bowler rather than a 'front of the hand wrist-spinner', the splayed left foot and apparently bent right arm would appear to have required closer scrutiny from umpires.*

Below *The immortal Three Ws from Barbados, during the 1957 tour: Worrell (left), Weekes and Walcott, with Ramadhin behind them.*

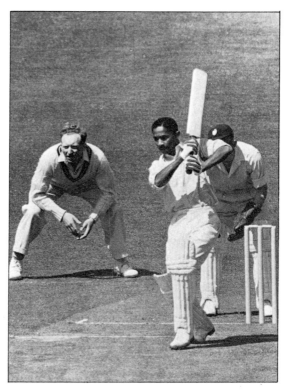

Above left *Frank Worrell: brilliant, classical batsman, valuable left-arm bowler, inspiring captain, batting against Surrey early in the 1950 tour watched by Stuart Surridge (slip) and Arthur McIntyre.*

Above *John Goddard: firm captain, fine left-handed batsman, brave fielder and useful bowler of medium-pace off-breaks, batting against England (Bailey and Evans look on) in 1950.*

Left *The West Indies at Lord's in 1950. Back, left to right: W. Ferguson (scorer), S. Ramadhin, K.B. Testrail, A.L. Valentine, L.R. Pierre, H.H.H. Johnson, C.L. Walcott, A.F. Rae, R.E. Marshall, E.A.V. Williams. Seated: R.J. Christiani, E. DeC. Weekes, G.E. Gomez, Rev R. Palmer-Barnes (manager), J.D.C. Goddard, J.B. Stollmeyer, P.E. Jones, F.M. Worrell.*

The 1950s witnessed the longest period of domination by one team in the history of the County Championship. Surrey won the title jointly in 1959 and then seven times running between 1952 and 1958. The essentials of their success were good leadership, 'sporting' pitches at The Oval which generally gave bowlers a chance to finish a match inside three days, a team spirit born, like Yorkshire's in the 1930s, on success and self-belief, and a thundering good side.

The first successful captain was Stuart Surridge, who took over in 1952 and never knew what it was like not to captain a title-winning team. A big, wholehearted, smiling man, he led by example in the field, being a brilliant close catcher, and made useful contributions with bat and ball, often at crucial times. In addition he used the immense playing resources at

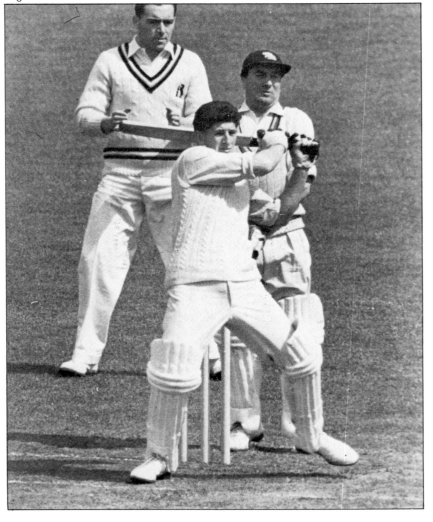

The young Ken Barrington, batting against MCC in 1953, watched by Alan Townsend and Godfrey Evans. A strokeplayer in his youth, Barrington developed into as solid and reliable a middle-order batsman as England has ever had.

his command with rare gusto and enterprise. Though the team was groaning with Test players, none were, or were allowed to become, prima donnas. They were all very much part of a team which sometimes worked with the efficiency of an expensive machine. Above all it possessed world-class bowlers. Alec Bedser and Peter Loader usually shared the new ball. Bedser was tireless, experienced and remorselessly accurate, a huge man relying mainly on inswingers but able also to make the ball leave the right-handed batsman late, often off the pitch with his lethal leg-cutter. Loader could be genuinely quick and was always hostile, never afraid to bowl the bouncer, unless it was at another fast bowler! Surridge's medium pace and Eric Bedser's off breaks were the supporting parts to the other leading roles, played by Jim Laker and Tony Lock, the best pair of spinners any county has ever had. Lock was also the most brilliant of a crop of superb close fielders in the Surrey team. Surridge and Mickey Stewart were almost as good.

The batting did not match the bowling, although the best batsman in the whole land, Peter May, who succeeded Surridge as captain and led the county to its last two titles, was frequently its backbone and its chief inspiraton. Round him were some good craftsmen, notably Tom Clark and his eventual partner Stewart, Bernie Constable and David Fletcher.

For a player of such outstanding success at the highest level, Ken Barrington took some time to establish himself. But the struggle he had to do so stood him in good stead. He became as reliable as the chimes of Big Ben after winning his cap in 1955, the year of his first caps for England, though his batting seldom revealed the spontaneous gaiety of his character.

Surrey's years of supremacy were played out against a number of changes to the character of county cricket. The 'sporting' wickets at The Oval were symptomatic of a general trend away from the slow, easy batting wickets of the inter-war years. Challenging and interesting though their cricket invariably was, crowds actually declined at The Oval during these all-conquering seasons. The reason was that crowds were being spoilt to some extent by an increasing coverage of Test cricket on television. Domestic cricket was already starting to be subordinated to international cricket and with the telly to watch at home or a car to take the family out to any number of different entertainments, sporting or otherwise, cricket was struggling to attract crowds other than for its big occasions.

During the Sixties the spin partnerships once so essential to any county's success–Laker and Lock,

Surrey's Championship-winning team in 1952. Back, left to right: D. G. W. Fletcher, G.A.R. Lock, J.W. McMahon, A.V. Bedser, J.C. Laker, G.J. Whittaker, B. Constable. Seated: E.A. Bedser, L.B. Fishlock, W.S. Surridge (capt.), J.F. Parker, A.J. McIntyre.

Peter May, a magisterial driver of a cricket ball, on his way to 88 against Derbyshire in 1952.

Alec Bedser, one of the key bowlers around whom Surrey's all-conquering side of the Fifties was built.

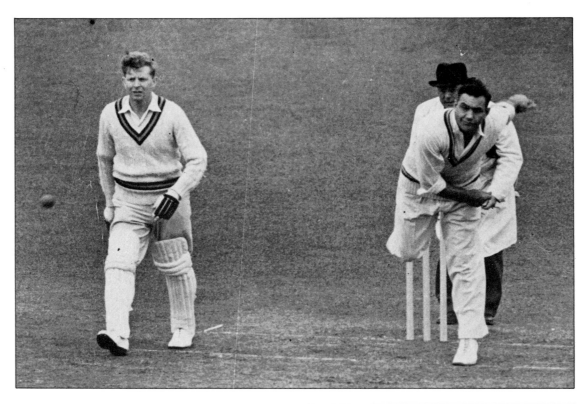

Surrey, Champions for a sixth successive year in 1957 – and there was one more title still to come! Back, left to right: H. Strudwick (scorer), D. Sydenham, M.D. Willett, G.A.R. Lock, B. Constable, R.C.E. Pratt, K.F. Barrington, M.J. Stewart, D. Gibson, T.H. Clark, P.J. Loader, D. Cox, A. Sandham (coach), J. Tait (masseur). Seated: D.G.W. Fletcher, J.C. Laker, Lord Tedder (president), P.B.H. May, A.V. Bedser, B.K. Castor (secretary), A.J. McIntyre, E.A. Bedser.

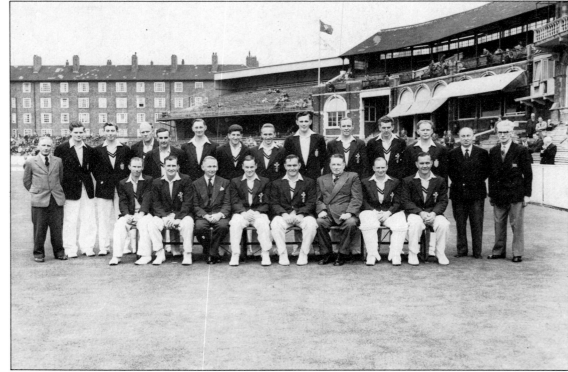

Surrey's other bowling mainstays were Jim Laker (left) and Tony Lock.

Appleyard and Wardle for Yorkshire, Hilton and Tattersall for Lancashire, Mortimore and Cook for Gloucestershire–gradually bowled fewer overs and took fewer wickets. New fertilizers led to lusher outfields that kept the shine on the ball longer, and swing bowlers became more useful to captains than spinners accustomed to 'buying' their wickets. And the arrival of one-day cricket led to a new emphasis on containing batsmen instead of trying anything to get them out.

When England regained the Ashes in the Coronation year of 1953, Australia had held them for nineteen years. They had emerged from the war far stronger, with Bradman deciding to play on for a few years as captain and possessing a devastating fast-bowling partnership in Ray Lindwall and Keith Miller, plus powerful batting not only from the Don himself but also from Sid Barnes, Arthur Morris, Lindsay Hassett and the brilliant left-hander, Neil Harvey.

The Australian team reached its post-war peak in 1948, Bradman's triumphant last tour and Harvey's first, when they went through England without a

Off duty, but on best behaviour, at Balmoral, where the King entertained the 1948 Australians to tea in September. Full-faced figures, left to right: Morris, Bradman, Loxton, Johnson, Hamence, Miller, Tallon, Saggers, Brown, McCool, Lindwall.

defeat. Not until the last game of the 1950–51 rubber did England win again after eleven defeats in the first fourteen post-war matches.

With Len Hutton and Denis Compton out of the very highest batting drawer (though Compton had a disastrous tour of Australia under Freddie Brown in 1950–51) England too were not without batting strength. Bill Edrich, Cyril Washbrook and Reg Simpson were also available, supported by a determined young all-rounder in Trevor Bailey. But good a bowler though Bailey was, and masterly a medium-pacer as was Alec Bedser–the best since, and the equal of, Maurice Tate–England fatally lacked the speed with which to counter the controlled fury of

Lindwall and Miller. Of them, as of one or two other fast-bowling combinations in the history of the Ashes, it may safely be said that, even against Bradman, England would have been on top if Lindwall and Miller had been playing for the other side.

As it was, England managed to win the only decisive match in the 1953 series without a settled fast-bowling pair, though both Trueman and Statham played in a series in which Bedser took 39 wickets but in which the great Surrey spin pair of Jim Laker and Tony Lock were the matchwinners in the deciding Test at The Oval.

In the next few years England had an embarrassment of riches. The retirement of their first professional captain, Len Hutton, after he had successfully defended the Ashes in Australia in 1954–55 was compensated for by the arrival of three superb middle-order batsmen, Peter May, Colin Cowdrey and Tom Graveney. For a few years in the middle Fifties England could also choose from, *inter alia*, Trueman, Statham, Tyson, Loader and Moss to bowl fast and Laker, Lock, the Yorkshire pair Appleyard and Wardle and the Lancashire pair Tattersall and Hilton to spin. Each was a tested off-spin/left-arm slow combination, Wardle having the additional skill of being able to bowl out of the back of his left-hand as well as orthodox finger spin, and Lock the additional advantage of being one of the finest close catchers of all time.

With a batsman of clinical power in May as the confident young captain, a now mature all-rounder in Bailey, and a wicket-keeper of dazzling ability in Godfrey Evans, England looked unbeatable when travelling to Australia again in 1958–59, having meanwhile whipped the old enemy at home in 1956, most notably at Old Trafford where Laker performed his feat of near perfection: 19 out of 20 wickets. But nothing went right for the team. The side's one weakness, the lack of an established pair of opening batsmen, was exploited by the astute new Australian captain Richie Benaud, whose pair of opening left-arm fast bowlers Alan Davidson and Ian Meckiff both enjoyed successful series. Neither, however, performed better than the captain himself, whose 31 wickets more than doubled the haul of Laker, England's most successful bowler. In addition the English side was disrupted by a succession of injuries and Tyson, the brutally fast conqueror of Australia under Hutton four years earlier, was not the same force, even when fit.

The controversies surrounding the actions of more than one of the Australian bowlers ('throw' and 'drag' are mentioned in another chapter) did not detract from the more positive and cohesive cricket of the Australians, whose top four in the batting order remained unchanged throughout the season: Colin

The Sphere's *tribute to the undefeated tourists of 1948.*

AUSTRALIANS WHO HAVE SHONE
Some Successes of the Now Completed Test Series

RAY LINDWALL WIELDS A STYLISH, AGGRESSIVE BAT : Australia's fast bowler in action at the wicket. He usually bats No. 8 and can be relied upon for good scores when they are most needed. His 1948 Test batting average is 31·83. Indeed he belongs to a team that really has no tail

THE PACE BOWLER WHO TAUGHT ENGLAND A LESSON : Ray Lindwall in action against England at the Oval. In the whole series he took 27 wickets, the same number as the great Macdonald took in the first series after the First World War In the first innings of this Fifth Test Lindwall took 6 wickets

THE GREATEST LEFT-HANDER SINCE BARDSLEY ? Morris (left) run-out after scoring a brilliant 196 in the last Test. Morris has never played with greater fluency than in this series, and he will now no doubt take on the mantle of Bradman as run-getter No. 1. He is also tipped for captaincy

THE MERRY MILLER FALLS TO THE WILES OF HOLLIES : Australia's No. 5, with his hair standing on end, falls full-length and is stumped by Godfrey Evans, England's agile keeper. Miller has had a great season over here, and has earned the reputation of being the brightest batsman in the Australian team

the balcony of the grandstand at the Kennington Oval cheers for Don Bradman, the Australian skipper. " This is crowd which gathered in front of the pavilion, " because definitely the last Test Match in which I shall ever play "

NEIL HARVEY WON HIS SPURS : The nineteen-year-old Victorian batsman hooking Hollies for four during his innings of 17. In the Fourth Test Harvey, coming in for injured Barnes, scored a brilliantly assured century when it was much needed, and, with ordinary luck, he is a certain choice for future tours. He has three brothers, and at least one of them is a star in the making

139

Godfrey Evans, off on a run after placing Miller past a typical Australian 'slips cordon' in 1953.

The Lord's Test of 1953. Morris, batting with Miller during their second-wicket partnership of 165, pulls Bedser for four. Note Evans, the supreme stylist among wicket-keepers, angled for a possible leg-side stumping.

Neil Harvey, caught Evans bowled Bedser for 122 in the Australian first innings at Old Trafford, 1953.

Benaud, Hole, Miller, Tallon and Hassett all look hopefully at the umpire but Len Hutton survived this lbw at Trent Bridge, 1953.

Tom Graveney seldom played at his cultured best against Australia, but at the end of the first day of the Leeds Test of 1953 he had held England together with 55 out of 142 for 7.

McDonald (520 runs at 65), Jim Burke, Harvey, and Norman O'Neill, the latter a complete batsman of powerful, athletic physique and a fine fielder in a side which seldom dropped a catch. Another of its strengths lay in a resilience due partly to the presence of three genuine all-rounders: Benaud himself, classical leg-spinner and dashing batsman, Davidson, left-handed in both batting and bowling, gifted and very strong, and Ken Mackay, a canny medium-paced bowler and a batsman who could outdo Bailey for obdurate adhesion to the crease.

The Australians held onto the Ashes through the Sixties, during which one of their best-ever opening partnerships emerged in the forms of Bobby Simpson, a compact, authoritative right-hander and a genius at slip, and Bill Lawry, the tall, angular left-hander who also liked to keep his best form for English opposition. The soundness of these two was well complemented by the menace at the other end of the team of Graham McKenzie, whose superb physique and exemplary fast bowler's action enabled him to take 100 Test wickets by the age of 23. He finished with 246 and unlike his even more successful successor from the same state of West Australia, Lillee, he played his cricket not with smirks and curses but with smiles and dignity.

Other notable Australians of the Sixties were the batsmen Brian Booth, Peter Burge, Bob Cowper, and the dashing and universally popular Doug Walters; the skilful wicket-keeper Wally Grout; sturdy fast-medium bowlers in Neil Hawke and Alan Connolly; and useful spinners in Tom Veivers, Ashley Mallett and the unorthodox right-armer, John Gleeson.

Luck, it must be said, did not always go England's way through the Sixties, when with batsmen of the class of Cowdrey, Graveney, Ted Dexter, Ken Barrington and Basil D'Oliveira to call on in the middle order, high-class openers in Bob Barber, Geoff Boycott and John Edrich, brilliant wicket-keepers in John Murray and his successor Alan Knott (and an adequate 'keeper and a fine batsman in Jim Parks), as well as a good variety of bowlers, the old country was usually at least a match for the Australians.

The breakthrough for England came under the uncompromising captaincy of Ray Illingworth in 1970–71 when Boycott had his most brilliant and prolific series, striking up an assertive, dominating partnership with Barber, and the fast bowling of John Snow was fiercer and more accurate than anything produced by the home team. For support Snow had a willing workhorse in Peter Lever and two crafty spin bowlers, Illingworth himself and the unique Derek Underwood, an orthodox left-arm spinner of medium pace and uncanny accuracy.

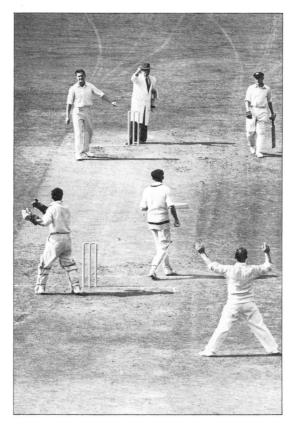

The Oval, 1953. Graeme Hole is lbw to Jim Laker in the second innings. Umpire, Dai Davies, non-striker, Morris, 'keeper, Evans, slip, Edrich.

The England twelve at The Oval in 1953 before, at last, The Ashes were retrieved. Back, left to right: T.E. Bailey, P.B.H. May, T.W. Graveney, J.C. Laker, G.A.R. Lock, J.H. Wardle, F.S. Trueman. Seated: W.J. Edrich, A.V. Bedser, L. Hutton, D.C.S. Compton, T.G. Evans.

Frank Tyson. Like Lindwall (below and on page 158), he was a 'dragger' of the back foot. Witnesses say that no one can have bowled faster than he did down-wind at Sydney in 1954–55.

Far right *F.S. Trueman: the model fast bowler's action.*

Right *Ray Lindwall: 228 wickets in 61 Tests.*

England's superiority was shortlived. In the middle 1970s Australia regrouped under a ruthless young captain in Ian Chappell, whose own batting was outstanding and paled only by comparison with that of his younger brother Greg, the complete, classical batsman. Walters and doughty fighters in Ian Redpath and Ross Edwards ensured that Australia got enough runs in 1974–75, but the rubber was mainly won for Australia by the devastating opening bowling partnership of Dennis Lillee and Jeff Thomson. Lillee went on to become the highest of all Test wicket-takers, with his frowning hostility, ideal action, immense strength, increasing command of all the fast-bowling skills, and not least the courage to bowl on through aches and pains. As for Thomson, who also had a long career but who was never quite so good after suffering a serious shoulder injury, for a two-year period he was as fast as Tyson, or Larwood, or...the wind. Hurling the ball down with the power of a charging bull, he could make it rise to head height off a length. With a third bowler, only fast-medium perhaps, but menacing nonetheless, in the strapping, cheerful Max Walker, Australia that season made batting a miserable business for opponents. The following year it was the West Indian batsmen who suffered the same unrelenting *Blitzkrieg*, only to form an even more total policy of bombardment themselves which has more or less dominated Test cricket ever since.

John Augustine Snow: wiry strength, smooth rhythm and, in Australia in 1970–71, calculating hostility.

Ian Chappell (left) with Jeff Thomson and Dennis Lillee after they had demolished England in 1974–75.

Another of the changes to the way of life of leading cricketers was the exchanging of the voyage by sea for a long-distance journey by air. M.J.K. Smith's team in 1965–66 was the first MCC team to fly all the way to Australia by air but it was already some time since the entire trip had been made by sea. Leisurely acclimatization became, with air travel, a sudden switch from winter to summer.

Air travel made it possible to shorten tours, to fly out replacements when players were injured or fell ill, and to stage far more tours than had taken place before. It also deprived touring teams of the chance to forge a team spirit and to ease themselves gently into their preparations for the mental and physical task ahead. Sir Neville Cardus left a vivid impression of a touring side at sea en route for the Antipodes in his book *Australian Summer*.

'The Red Sea is at its hottest, its stickiest, its cruellest… The other evening, a quarter of an hour before dinner, I met Captain Howard on the staircase; the manager of the MCC team had only ten minutes

ago changed into his dinner jacket. His collar was already a rag; Mr Gladstone, after four hours or so of eloquence, never more drastically reduced stiff linen into this state of shapeless wetness. From the foreheads of all of us waterfalls have descended, splashing and dashing like the cascades of Southey's poem. (Was it Southey–it is still too hot to think here, though at last we are emerging from the Red Sea and a breeze is stirring, giving us a sense of resurrection of all the world from the dead.)

'The team went quietly about their pleasures. Verity read *Seven Pillars of Wisdom* from beginning to end; Hammond won at all games, from chess to deck quoits. Maurice Leyland smoked his pipe, and Duckworth danced each evening with a nice understanding of what, socially, he was doing. Wyatt took many photographs and developed them himself. Fry, armed with a most complicated camera, also took many photographs, and none of them could be developed. When we reached Fremantle it was seven in the morning. We had to be up and about early. Many times on the voyage I had wakened in the dawn and

By 1953 they were travelling by air. Right to left are Len Hutton with three other Yorkshiremen – Johnny Wardle, Fred Trueman and Willie Watson – about to leave London Airport for the West Indies.

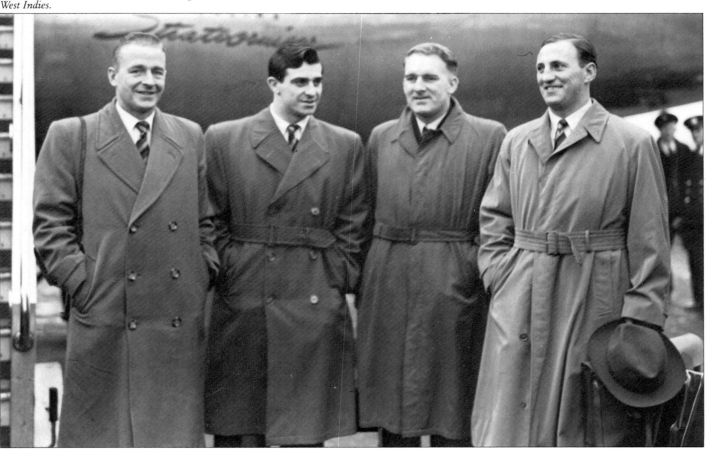

looked through my porthole. There is magic in a ship's porthole; it becomes a magic mirror. I saw the sunrise on the Indian Ocean through my porthole and felt ashamed to be prying into an act of beauty so secret and removed from human interference. Through my porthole I saw Australia for the first time.'

How different a story it became from the 1960s for the modern cricket traveller. One airport runway or one airport terminal is much like another. Nowadays even the hotels are much the same wherever a team travels. Lahore and Melbourne themselves seem remarkably similar when viewed from the Hilton Hotel.

Air travel has also changed the nature of cricket tours once a team arrives. A match against an Australian country eleven was once a major social event for the lucky country town concerned, a major outing for the visiting team and a major moment in a local cricketer's life, perhaps the high point of his whole career. But when it became possible to hop a few hundred miles by air after an early breakfast for a country match, and hop back again after the match,

the events lost their greatest value, namely of showing sophisticated touring countries something of the real Australia and putting those friendly, closely-knit country folk in close touch with household names from the Mother Country. To some of the cricketers they may have seemed boring events at times. But they were part of the variety of the tour, often amongst the highlights when viewed in retrospect. Nowadays touring teams do not bother with country matches at all.

Once again cricket has proved a faithful mirror of the life around it. The fact that air travel has made it possible to do everything faster has many advantages. For cricket tourists it means less wasted time, fewer periods of long-drawn-out boredom. But it means also that everything now tends to be done in too much of a hurry, with no chance for reflection, or for savouring the good things that happen, on the field and off it. Cricketers are here today, and have gone again tomorrow. They have probably already forgotten where they were yesterday.

Back home. The MCC party – or part of it – arriving home from India in March 1964. Left to right: John Price, John Edrich, Jeff Jones, Brian Bolus, David Larter and Jimmy Binks, the Yorkshire 'keeper who found himself opening the batting in the Calcutta Test because of illnesses and injuries.

Colin Cowdrey's team leave for the West Indies in December 1967. Up the steps from the foot are: Les Ames (manager), Alan Knott, Cowdrey, Robin Hobbs, Fred Titmus (destined to lose two toes in a boating accident), John Edrich, Basil D'Oliveira, Tom Graveney, Jim Parks, Ken Barrington, Colin Milburn, David Brown, Geoff Boycott, Pat Pocock, John Snow, Ken Higgs, Jeff Jones.

The era of the sportsman being used as the medium for advertising arrived almost by accident. Two years after his *annus mirabilis*, Denis Compton was awarded a benefit by Middlesex. He was as hopeless an organizer of his own affairs as he was brilliant a batsman and he called on the help of an Irish chartered accountant

named Bagenal Harvey to sort out the accounts and answer the multitude of letters. It quickly became clear to Harvey that Compton, whose face was known to millions even in the era before televised cricket, was not making what he ought to have been out of his success and fame.

For a percentage 'cut' of the new business that he attracted on Compton's behalf, Harvey set to work to get one of the country's most popular sportsmen his pound of flesh. Instead of £5 for the use of Compton's photograph, advertising agents were now obliged to pay twenty times that amount. A lucrative contract was secured to promote Brylcreem, and once they had got their man Beecham's, the company whose product Brylcreem was, made the fullest use of him. The photograph of Compton on the Brylcreem advertisements became as famous as that of the Bisto Kids. Compton, in fact, became known as the 'Brylcreem Boy'.

The contract with Beechams was negotiated through Royds Advertising Agency, who remained Compton's main employers when he retired from cricket. Harvey, meanwhile, had moved on to handle the affairs of many other outstanding sportsmen. He spawned a small army of sporting 'agents' who see it as their job to make as much money for a successful sportsman or sportswoman (and for themselves!) as they are able to in the relatively short time their client is at the top of his or her profession.

Compton was careful, before signing the Brylcreem contract, to refer it to Middlesex and MCC for their approval, which was readily given. But such has been the explosion since of commercialism in cricket, the authorities in all the Test-playing countries have had a struggle to keep any degree of control over what their players sign in the way of personal endorsements of anything from bats to breakfast cereals. There is often a danger of some personal sponsorship clashing with the interests of companies with whom the Cricket Boards have done business on behalf of all the players under their authority.

Human nature is greedy and unpleasantness has often been revealed as bat manufacturers vie with one another for 'star' names. When India, for example, won the World Cup unexpectedly in England in 1983, their captain Kapil Dev used a Slazenger bat although he had only recently signed a contract with an Indian firm. Another of India's leading all-rounders, Mohinder Amarnath, was also claimed by the Indian company, yet used Gunn and Moore bats throughout the World Cup. This was unfortunate since he was actually contracted to a third firm, Stuart Surridge!

In some sports, notably golf, the sports agent has become even more powerful than the sports

Denis Compton during his annus mirabilis. Has any sportsman ever held the stage with such heroic charm? No wonder advertisers saw him as a man who could help sell products.

Not the Brylcreem Boy, but a pretty good substitute! Keith Miller who, like Denis, never ignored an attractive lady.

Men of the World all the World over

know clean grooming depends on
BRYLCREEM
- it's not messy! not greasy!

Use Brylcreem—it's *all* your hair needs for health and appearance. Available in tubs or handy tubes.

THE PERFECT HAIRDRESSING — FOR EVERY STYLE OF HAIR

administrator. The American Mark McCormack is in a position, it seems, to make or break some tournaments according to whether he allows players on his books to take part. For taking part in many tournaments the star players receive appearance money. A golfer or tennis player winning a major tournament in the 1980s becomes a millionaire overnight as the agents start immediately to negotiate huge endorsement contracts on his or her behalf. It has not happened to nearly the same extent in cricket, a team game, but the Packer Revolution of 1977 had as one of its unseen seeds the decision by Denis Compton to ask a chartered accountant to look after his benefit affairs.

Compton in his role as an Arsenal footballer – and public relations man for British sport.

Since the beginning of the nineteenth century, and especially since the career of W.G. Grace, the matches between Gentlemen and Players had been one of the most important and popular features of any English cricket season. Between 1806 and 1962, 137 meetings between the two took place at Lord's, the Players winning 68 to the amateurs' 41. Between 1857 and 1934 fixtures were also played at The Oval, where the Gentlemen managed 16 wins to the Players' 34. Five other grounds staged a handful of matches. Until the last few years they were very sternly fought games indeed, with a Test place often at stake for many of the contestants from the 1880s onwards.

The aboliton of amateur status after the 1962 season thus ended a great tradition. The decision was merely a reflection of the economic and social forces which have shaped cricket throughout its history.

Though the Second World War may not have been quite such a watershed as the First, nevertheless it paved the way for much radical change in people's way of life. The Labour Government voted in after the war coincided in cricket with the general acceptance of professional rather than amateur captains. England won the Ashes in 1953 under her first professional leader, Len Hutton, and although Hutton was never appointed Yorkshire captain, H.E. 'Tom' Dollery led Warwickshire from 1949 with dignity as well as enterprise, taking them to the Championship in 1951.

During the war, when 'men' became officers very quickly, one or two ex-professionals, such as Walter Hammond and Bill Edrich, decided to join the ranks of the Gentlemen, though neither gave up being paid for playing cricket. It was the general recognition that a great many of the 'amateurs' were in fact 'shamateurs' that persuaded the Advisory County

The Players side for the last fixture against the Gentlemen, in 1962. Back, left to right: John Edrich, Phil Sharpe, Norman Gifford, Peter Walker, Mickey Stewart, Peter Parfitt. Seated: Fred Titmus, Derek Shackleton, Fred Trueman (capt.), Tom Graveney, Keith Andrew.

David Sheppard cuts Trueman but Mickey Stewart, a brilliant close fielder, managed, as cricket writers might once have said, to 'arrest the progress of the ball from his position in the gully'.

The Gentlemen, 1962. Back, left to right: R.M. Prideaux, D.B. Pithey, O.S. Wheatley, A.R. Lewis, A.C. Smith, E.J. Craig. Seated: R.W. Barber, T.E. Bailey, E.R. Dexter, D.S. Sheppard, M.J.K. Smith.

Cricket Committee in 1962 to recognize that any preservation of the distinction was meaningless.

There were several ways in which amateur cricketers had been finding the resources to play cricket for five months or more each year. Some were simply paid 'in the boot of the car'. Others accepted jobs with various firms who were glad to be associated with a well-known cricketer in a more or less public relations role. A few men, amongst them the England cricketers Trevor Bailey and Charles Palmer, became secretaries of their county clubs.

The majority of counties continued for many years to be captained by former University or public school men. But the independence of means which had enabled them to stand back occasionally from the game they were playing in order to put it into proportion with other things in life, disappeared when

they began playing it for a living. Safety-first tactics came more naturally than the instincts of the gambler. Men's livelihoods were at stake. It is not only the former amateurs who tell you that the game at this stage in its long history lost something irrevocable.

In the Sixties one man, Colin Ingleby-Mackenzie, who led Hampshire to their first Championship in 1961, rose above the stereotyped, safety-first tactics of the time, bringing a gambler's instinct to the taxing task of captaining a county side. 'I always insist my men are in bed by ten o'clock,' he would claim. 'After all, play starts at half-past eleven.' There were no other double-barrelled Etonians currently in charge of first-class cricket sides, and even this one was obliged to exchange his flannels for a pin-stripe suit much younger than his forbears would have done.

Leg-spinners spell entertainment. A ball from Bob Barber has, left to right, Eddie Craig, Ossie Wheatley, Alan Smith and Fred Titmus on their toes.

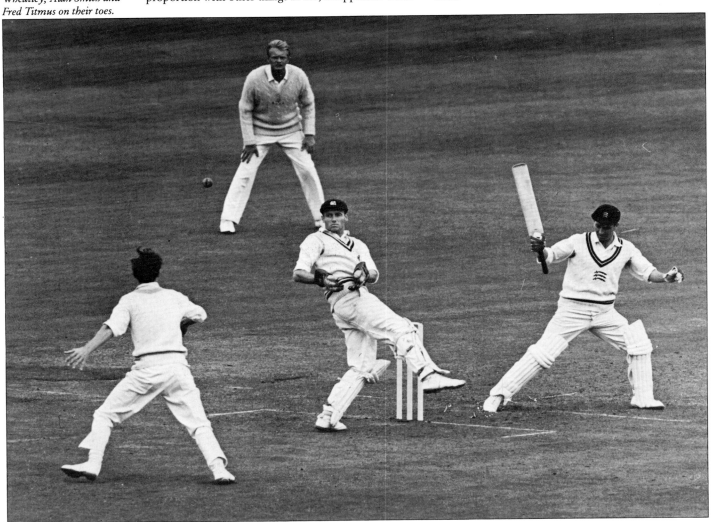

154

The very first cricket broadcast took place in Australia in 1922. Five years later Sir Pelham Warner made the first cricket commentary in England, on the match between Essex and the New Zealand touring team at Leyton. He was followed onto the airways by the Essex cricketer and clergyman, Rev. F.H. Gillingham, who was unfortunate enough to be faced by a break for rain during his first fifteen-minute stint and filled much of it by reading the various advertisements on the hoardings round The Oval. To advertise on the BBC was just about the ultimate broadcasting crime!

In 1930 a Test match was covered by brief commentary for the first time but it was the Australian Broadcasting Commission which first realized the mass appeal of such broadcasts. There was early competition for the rights to cover the Tests there involving commercial stations and the Australian Broadcasting Commission: shades of battles to come over television coverage in the 1970s.

Ironically it was a French commercial station which triggered the next advance. For the bodyline series of 1932–33 the Test cricketer Alan Fairfax was sent to Paris and, by means of detailed cables, he used great imagination and his close knowledge of the players to provide a graphic, yet unseen, account, of the Tests in the present tense. Those who heard the broadcasts in England found them compelling and the BBC responded in 1934 to the new demand.

Howard Marshall, whose mellifluous voice has become well known to later generations through the often-replayed recording of his description of Hutton's 364 in 1938, was the first well-known cricket commentator, with Michael Standing as his main aide and E.W. Swanton quickly establishing a reputation before the war. The commentary team for the memorable series against South Africa in 1947 was Swanton, Rex Alston, another stalwart, and two 'expert summarizers' in Arthur Gilligan and C.B. Fry. This was the year, too, in which John Arlott first made his mark on the cricket scene. He further established himself in 1948, overcoming what would at that time have been seen as the handicap of a regional accent by his genius for words, and developing into the finest descriptive commentator of them all. Far from being a handicap, indeed, his Hampshire drawl became his trademark, imitated wherever enthusiasts gathered round wirelesses to listen to the Tests. Since 1957 listeners have been able to follow every ball of Tests in England on the radio, and even in the modern era of skilled and sophisticated televised coverage of Test and international cricket, many people prefer to listen to the friendly ball-by-ball descriptions of play on Radio Three.

Televised cricket seemed a wonderful invention to any cricket-mad youngster when first it appeared, but one only has to see BBC archive material to realize the immense advances made since H.B.T. 'Teddy' Wakelam did the first commentary on a televised transmission of the 1938 Lord's Test. He was obliged to perform looking into the sun from a position in the Mound Stand, with no view of what the bowler was doing with the ball. Even in the early post-war years

Below left Howard Marshall, possessor of the first famous voice in BBC cricket broadcasting.

Below Rex Alston, one of the most lucid of cricket commentators, a talented athlete in his youth and a schoolmaster until he made a second career in sound broadcasting after the war. He is seen at The Oval, 1949.

wickets were often missed by the limited number of cameras. Nowadays it is rare for anything to happen on a cricket field which the cameras do not trap with their all-seeing eyes, be it a blinding catch in the gully, a skier in the deep or an old man going to sleep in the middle of a packed stand.

Televised cricket also had its early moments of embarrassment for the BBC, notably when a spectator, asked for his views on the cricket, stole his chance in front of the camera to tell the world about his revolutionary new calendar! It remains a debatable point whether the televising of Tests keeps spectators away from important matches. Sometimes, if the weather is cold and the cricket being played in a particular series has failed to ignite much public interest, there is no doubt that many settle for the comforts of watching at home. Yet televised matches are all the time selling the game afresh to a rising generation of potential players and spectators of the future. In any case, it has become Hobson's choice, for the administrators of first-class cricket in most Test-playing countries have come to rely on the fees they receive from the broadcasting companies.

Early television commentary at Lord's. E. W. Swanton, in characteristic mellifluous voice no doubt, with scorer Roy Webber perched on the top left of the Lord's pavilion, on a slim balcony over the visitors' dressing room. The old tavern is in the background. The match was the West Indies Test of 1957.

Right Arthur Wrigley, one of the small but devoted band of cricket scorers and statisticians who, over the years, have made life much easier for the commentators.

Far right John Arlott, commentating at Bristol with Ian Peebles by his side. The cigarette is nothing to do with any tobacco sponsorship of cricket – and St Bruno was supposed to be what he smoked!

The voice has become deeper, gruffer, but the descriptive brilliance remained at the Centenary Test. Arlott, late in his career, with Fred Trueman at his side.

When underarm bowling gave way to roundarm, and roundarm to overarm, there was much contemporary talk about what should and what should not constitute a fair delivery. During the late 1950s and early 1960s, when it was suggested that several well-known bowlers were throwing rather than bowling the ball, no-one questioned whether throwing should be illegal. The issues rather were about what exactly constituted a throw and which bowlers were transgressing the law. As Sir Donald Bradman observed at a time when the issue was one of the most pressing in the game: 'It is not a matter of fact, but of opinion and interpretation. It is so involved that two men of equal good will and sincerity could take opposite views.'

Amongst the Test bowlers to be called for

Drag, a testing problem for umpires. Ray Lindwall bowling in England in 1953, watched by Trevor Bailey. How could umpires look simultaneously at a bowler's back foot and his delivery arm? This, by the letter of the law, ought to have been a no-ball.

throwing during their careers in the Fifties and Sixties were Tony Lock of England, Ian Meckiff of Australia, Geoff Griffin of South Africa and Charlie Griffith of West Indies. Lock was a different case from the rest, partly because he was a slow bowler and partly because the kink in his action came not from any basic flaw but because he had spent much time practising at an indoor cricket school where the roof was too low for a full upward extension of his bowling arm. On seeing films of his action, he changed it halfway through his career and became, if anything, an even better bowler, though now deprived of his lethal 'faster ball'. A number of lesser slow bowlers also had suspect actions, notably the Australian Jim Burke, who seldom bowled seriously in first-class cricket and whose action was graphically described by Ian Peebles

as looking like 'a policeman bringing down his truncheon on a particularly short offender's head'.

The real trouble came with the fast bowlers because it is a fact that a ball thrown at a batsman takes fractionally longer for the eyes to 'pick up' than one bowled with a straight arm. Griffin, Meckiff and Griffith were all condemned by dramatic photographs showing not only a bent arm shortly before the delivery of the ball, but also two other tell-tale signs: a front foot splayed towards first slip and a chest opened up towards the batsman.

Both Griffin and Meckiff bowed out of Test cricket in circumstances of personal tragedy, although in Meckiff's case sympathy was tempered by the fact that he had taken 45 wickets with his fast left-arm deliveries in 17 Tests and had won the Second Test against England at Melbourne in 1958–59 with figures of 9 for 107. Bowling in his 18th Test against South Africa at Brisbane in 1963–64, he was called four times in his first over by the umpire, Colin Egar, and bowled no more. South Africans at least could sympathize, especially those who in 1960 had seen young Geoff Griffin, in his first Test appearance at Lord's, being called 11 times. In three previous matches on the tour he had been called 17 times and when Syd Buller again called him for throwing in an exhibition match played because of the early end to the Lord's Test, he was obliged to bowl underarm to finish an over. It was less Griffin's fault than that of the South African selectors, for choosing a man known to be under serious suspicion of 'chucking'.

The advent of the video camera has helped to prevent more than a very occasional instance of a bowler getting to the top of the cricket tree with a possibly unfair action, though in England barely a season passes without murmurings on the county circuit of some young fast bowler who 'chucks it'. The definition of a throw, as developed out of the traumatic events described above, is efficiently set down in the form of a note to Law 24 of the 1980 code, which says: 'A ball shall be deemed to have been thrown if, in the opinion of either umpire, the process of straightening the bowling arm, whether it be partial or complete, takes place during that part of the delivery swing which directly precedes the ball leaving the hand. This definition shall not debar a bowler from the use of the wrist in the delivery swing.'

'Drag' was a quite different problem which happened to come to the fore in the same MCC tour of Australia in 1958–59 which witnessed the first dramatic impact of Meckiff on the Test arena. One of his partners during the series was a tall fast bowler named Gordon Rorke of whom it was said that you had to be careful when batting against him that he did

Charlie Griffith of Barbados and West Indies, photographed from an incriminating angle. A good action for a javelin thrower, not so good for a bowler supposed to bowl with a straight arm.

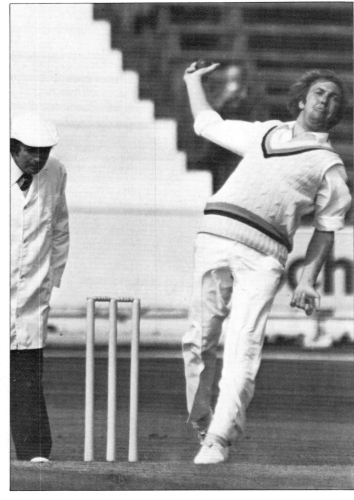

Above *Gary Bartlett of New Zealand, another who set batsmen murmuring and umpires frowning, here bowling against England in Dunedin in 1966.*

Right *When it comes to slow bowlers there must be some doubt whether a bent arm really matters. Geoff Cope of Yorkshire and England, bowling here against Warwickshire in 1978, was a slow off-spinner who spent hours in winter nets trying to iron out a kink in his right elbow. Eventually he had to leave first-class cricket.*

not tread on your toes as he followed through. The 'no-ball' law as it then stood enabled bowlers to drag their back foot as they took their long final stride. Often fast bowlers would drag the foot almost to the popping crease before actually releasing the ball, Ray Lindwall being a prime example. It was, of course, and is, impossible for an umpire to have his eyes simultaneously on a bowler's foot (be it his back foot or his front) and his bowling arm. The back foot was supposed to be behind the bowling crease at the moment of delivery, even if (after 1947) it was not actually grounded.

Since 1963 the popping crease has replaced the bowling crease as the key area. Some part of the bowler's front foot has to be behind the popping crease, whether it is grounded or raised, as the ball is delivered. For some reason there are still implacable opponents of the change to the no-ball law as it

affected the 'dragger', but a vast majority of umpires favour it and so do batsmen, for whom a yard stolen by a fast bowler can be crucial. The disadvantage from his point of view is that if a no-ball is called for a transgression by the front foot, he has little chance to adjust his stroke in time to take advantage of a 'free' hit.

From 1983 several countries began experimenting with a scoring system which counted no-balls and wides against the bowler's analysis, an excellent way of making bowlers pay proper heed to where their front feet were landing. Since mankind has grown so much taller since the length of the pitch was set at twenty-two yards, this author cannot understand why experiments have not also been made to lengthen the pitch by making bowlers land their front foot not behind the popping crease but behind the bowling crease instead.

West Indies v South Africa. Multi-racial crowds at one of the matches between the Springboks and the 'rebel' West Indians at Pretoria in February 1981: proof of a more liberal attitude by the Nationalist Government or merely useful propaganda? Or, more likely still, simply a successful attempt by wealthy cricket lovers to keep the game alive in the Republic.

It looks like whisky, not rum, but it makes little difference to the West Indies cricket fan who needs no stronger fuel than his inherited love for the game. Cricketers never go short of advice in the Caribbean either. This spectator was offering his views at Queen's Park Oval, Port of Spain during the Test against England in February 1981.

Eden Gardens, Calcutta; concrete and humanity in perfect harmony! No one knows exactly how many the ground holds, because Indian crowd numbers are not accurately calculated, but it certainly has the second largest capacity of any ground after Melbourne.

Below *The Maidaan at Bombay, scene of countless games of cricket every day during the season, some organized, many impromptu. All they need is a bat and a ball. A kettle helps too, for the Indians like their cup of tea even more than the British.*

Work on the roller by the ground staff at Bombay.

Far right *Another empty space, another game of cricket. A good looking shot by the batsman and a handsome 'pavilion'– a Hindu temple near Madras.*

Supporting the old country! An MCC member joins the locals at Queen's Park Oval, Port of Spain, 1981.

Below *One theory about the continuous supply of talented, uninhibited cricketers from the West Indies is that they learn their cricket with a soft ball. Beach cricket like this is fun, but serious fun. There are even beach cricket leagues. The bowlers can let fly and the batsmen learn to hit the ball on the up without worrying about getting injured.*

Pitch marking at Colombo during Sri Lanka's first ever Test Match against England in 1982. Who said a woman's place is in the home?

Far left *Politics have intruded on cricket's scene all too often in recent times. The pitch required an armed guard when England's touring team played a match at Jammu, India in December 1981.*

Above *'Watching' county cricket at Dartford, May 1982. All sorts and conditions of men can be found at county games in all weathers and though most go for the cricket, some appreciate the longer licensing hours, others the chance for a quick nap.*

Top right *Arundel in June can be idyllic . . . but the best laid plans can be disrupted by Divine interference. This hailstorm brought a swift end to a World Cup 'warm-up' between Australia and New Zealand in 1983.*

Right *Umpire at Work. The shooting-stick was once almost de rigueur for umpires. This one revived the custom for a match between the Taverners of England and Australia in August 1980.*

Bottom right *Starting young. Ben Allsop, aged five, batting during an interval in the Derbyshire v Yorkshire match, August 1980. The grip is unorthodox but the ball has been firmly hit so perhaps the coaches should leave him alone!*

YEARS OF RAPID CHANGE FROM 1964

'With a view to promote county cricket, and to establish a new and interesting series of matches at Lord's ground, the committee, in the course of the winter, offered a challenge cup for competition. Regulations were drawn up and sent to the counties. Five acceptances were received in the first instance, ties were drawn and the prospect of an interesting season was afforded ...'

The above is taken from the minutes of the MCC Annual General Meeting of 1873. In the event, the club's far-sighted ambition to establish a knockout competition for the county clubs faltered and only one such 'challenge' match was played, between Kent and Sussex in June 1873.

When Sussex next appeared in a knockout match at Lord's, ninety years had passed and a new competition was reaching a triumphant climax. The first 'Knockout Competition' of 1963 was an outstanding success, large crowds following the progress of Sussex and Worcestershire towards the final at Lord's which was a sellout. It has been so ever since.

The original competition was sponsored by the Gillette company for £6,500. The teams played 65 overs each, no bowler being allowed more than 15 overs and some wonderful cricket was the result. Gillette's patronage was so low-key that not until the second year did the competition become known as the Gillette Cup and it was some years after that before it was so called by all the newspapers. Yet when Gillette handed over their sponsorship to the National Westminster Bank after eighteen years, there was little doubt that this outstandingly popular competition had been well and truly established in the public mind.

The die was cast from the day Lord's staged that first ever one-day final and Ted Dexter raised the Gillette Cup, in the tradition of football captains at Wembley, before a full house. From this pioneering competition followed two more county one-day tournaments, the John Player Sunday League (foreshadowed by the success of the Rothmans 'Cavalier' matches which had packed in the crowds on Sundays in earlier years) and the Benson and Hedges. Fewer but similar competitions were introduced for first-class cricketers in other countries. Soon there were one-day internationals and a World Cup – and a worldwide acceptance of the idea that cricket could be commercially sponsored.

It soon became apparent that limited-overs cricket demanded a quite different strategy. When batting, the policy is a steady start, followed by a controlled acceleration and, if wickets are in hand, a general slog over the last ten overs. All sorts of technical improvisations and impurities crept into batsmen's techniques. Many a high-class player found himself unconsciously playing risky shots in Test matches which were the result of habits formed when trying to force the pace in limited-overs games. On the other hand some players, Glenn Turner of Worcestershire and New Zealand being perhaps the most obvious example, found a new freedom and a range of strokes they had not previously trusted themselves to use.

Wembley comes to Lord's – but, in the Sixties at least, with a certain dignity. Ted Dexter, captain of Sussex, holds the Gillette Cup aloft in 1964, after Sussex had retained the trophy they won in the inaugural year.

Ironically, in a game intended to place the emphasis on attack, the idea was not to get people out but to stop them scoring quickly. Slip fielders were dispensed with after a few overs or not used at all. Outright speed and flighty spin became less important than tying a batsman down by accuracy.

Fielding skills improved dramatically. Hitherto only a few enthusiasts like Tony Lock had considered it worth the dry-cleaning bill to dive for the ball. Now everyone in the team had to be an athlete and a gymnast. This in turn led to a greater emphasis on physical fitness and cricketers who spent as much time doing exercises in tracksuits as practising basic skills in the nets. Limited-overs cricket is now established as the most attractive form of the game as far as spectators are concerned. Crowds for one-day internationals have increased in the 1980s while those for Test matches, in general, have gone down. The same is true of domestic one-day cricket, in all countries, in relation to the traditional three- or four-day competitions. These competitions now depend for their survival on income received from crowds at one-day games and the sponsorship attracted by limited-overs tournaments. Yet without the skills attained in the two-innings matches, players would not be able to make limited-overs cricket a worthwhile attraction.

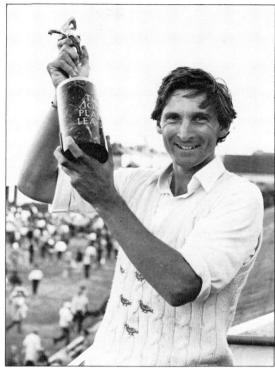

The forty-over John Player League has provided friendly family entertainment on Sunday afternoons, though purists naturally disapprove of the crude strokes and ultra-defensive fields and bowling tactics. Captains need to be flexible and quick-witted. John Barclay of Sussex is, and it was his team who won the trophy in 1982.

The Benson and Hedges Cup winners of 1979, Essex, who went on to win the Championship as well. One of the virtues of the one-day competitions was the chance they presented for hitherto unfashionable counties to share some laurels. Essex had won nothing before that season. Left to right: Allan Lilley, Ray East, John Lever, Keith Fletcher (with trophy), Keith Pont, Stuart Turner, Graham Gooch, Ken McEwan (partially obscured) and Mike Denness.

The 1983 Benson and Hedges Cup Final. It is rare to see two slips posted in a limited-overs match. Here Mike Gatting, the Middlesex captain, just fails to cling on to a flying snick, watched by two other English Test players, Phil Edmonds and wicket-keeper Paul Downton.

The dash for the pavilion at the end of one-day matches has become a necessity for the players as they try to avoid the invading hordes. This was the scene after the B & H final of 1980. Umpire Barry Meyer tries to save the stumps for another day, whilst David East and Norbert Phillip of the defeated Essex team head for home at the double. After the Prudential World Cup final of 1983, Michael Holding injured an ankle when trodden on in the rush.

Far left *The demise of Ian Botham in the last knockout cup final to be sponsored by Gillette, Somerset v Northants in 1979. One of the worst aspects of limited-overs cricket is the way it obliges good batsmen to indulge in eccentric shots to try to force the pace.*

Left *Somerset v Notts in the Benson and Hedges final, 1982. Somerset supporters predicting what Joel Garner, the 'Big Bird', will do to Notts captain Clive Rice. In fact he was out to the off-spin of Vic Marks and Somerset won easily.*

No county owes more to the advent of limited-overs cricket than Somerset. Brian Rose (right) was the captain through their most successful years but the outstanding individuals were Viv Richards, Joel Garner and Ian Botham. Here Garner is congratulated by Botham after dismissing Paul Todd in the 1982 B & H final.

Only the unrealistic would deny that there are things more important than cricket. Yet there have been times when this cherished game, subordinated though it may often have to be by political differences between nations, has proved the fruitless waste of international hostility. During the Boer Wars South Africa and England continued to play each other at cricket. And in 1970, when India and Pakistan were close to war, players from both countries cheerfully took the field together for a Rest of the World team in England.

At least other than at times of war, there is a case for regarding cricket as one of those occupations which should be considered free of politics in anything other than a totalitarian state. However many people may believe this, the fact remains that cricket has been peculiarly vulnerable to political interference of one kind or another in recent years. This has resulted in the abandonment of major matches in Pakistan (the Karachi Test of 1968–69, for example, ruined by student riots), the prolonged ostracizing of South Africa from international cricket circles, and the refusal by some Governments, notably that of Guyana, to allow their cricketers to play matches against teams containing anyone who has played in South Africa. That an unofficial 'apartheid' had existed in South Africa's complicatedly mixed society for years after the first arrival of the Dutch East India Company in 1652, is evident from the belated omission of a Malayan ('coloured' by modern South African designation) fast bowler named 'Krom' Hendricks in 1894 after he had been picked to tour England. Not, however, until the election of the Nationalist Government in South Africa in 1948 did the policy of 'separate development' of the different races become established in laws which condemned most black people to a life of subservience to the white minority.

By this time various racial groups had formed their own associations for organizing cricket, but in 1947 a new grouping of 'non-white' cricketers was formed under the label of the South African Cricket Board of Control. The white cricketers were represented on the Imperial Cricket Conference by the South African Cricket Association. In 1960, two years after Basil D'Oliveira, a Cape Coloured cricketer yet

Below *Spectator politics. A very poor-sized crowd attended the First Test between West Indies and England at Port of Spain in February 1981, partly because of a boycott of the game by Trinidadians protesting against the omission of their national captain, Deryck Murray.*

Right *On the same tour England declined to play the Test match in Georgetown after the Guyana Government had issued a deportation order on Robin Jackman, because he had played in South Africa.*

to make his name internationally known, had led a non-white touring team in East Africa, the SACA approached the Government for permission to play mixed cricket between the races. Throughout the 1960s, however, the Government refused to allow this, perhaps unaware of the growing force of political opposition outside South Africa to their policies. In 1968 Basil D'Oliveira, by now established as a Test cricketer in England, was picked (after originally being left out in controversial circumstances) for England's proposed tour of South Africa. The Prime Minister of the Republic, B.J. Vorster, refused to allow him to return and the tour was called off.

Opinions now hardened rapidly against South Africa. After intervention by the British Government, the South African tour of England scheduled for 1970 was called off, and the same fate awaited the South African tour to Australia which had been planned for 1971–72. South Africa, in fact, has not played a Test match of an official nature since, as the strongest team in the world, they soundly defeated Australia at home in 1969–70.

South Africa was told at the time by the United Kingdom's supreme cricketing body, the Cricket Council, that Tests between the two countries would not be resumed until cricket in South Africa was played, and teams selected, on a multi-racial basis. Since that time great efforts have been made by the cricketers in South Africa to do what they were asked to do and a breakthrough occurred in 1977 when, after prolonged diplomacy, a new administrative body, SACU, was set up to represent cricketers of all colours. Its first chairman was the Indian Rashid Varachia, who in 1947 had become the first secretary of the co-ordinated body representing non-whites, SACBOC.

Mixed cricket followed for all who wanted it, even between schools, although the majority of pupils went, and continue to go, to schools of one colour. At least black and white schools have played against each other since the late 1970s and there are several clubs where players of different races take the field together, notably the Avendale club at Cape Town where the all-rounder Omar Henry is one of many Cape Coloureds to have reached first-class standard. In addition, the SACU and the various Provincial associations spend much time and money on coaching African cricketers.

Left *John Emburey and Derek Underwood, England's best spinners, in Sri Lanka in 1982 a few days before departing in secrecy for South Africa.*

Far left *In 1978 several of the Pakistani Packer players suddenly flew to Karachi hoping to gain a propaganda coup by playing in a Test against England. England's reaction was to refuse to play the match if the Packer players were selected. Geoff Boycott had taken over the captaincy from the injured Mike Brearley and Ken Barrington, the England manager, was caught between his team's threatened strike and instructions from the TCCB that the team would be in breach of their contract if they did not play.*

Above *The English team which played a series against South Africa in March 1982: all were banned for three years from official Test cricket. Back, left to right: Wayne Larkins, Bob Woolmer, 'Tiger' Lance (manager), Les Taylor, Chris Old, Mike Hendrick, Peter Willey, John Lever. Seated: Geoff Humpage, Derek Underwood, Geoff Boycott, Graham Gooch (capt.), Peter Cooke (tour organizer), Dennis Amiss, Alan Knott.*

Above right *Scoreboard at Pretoria in February 1983.*

West Indian 'rebels' to South Africa, 1982-83. Back, left to right (players only): Richard Austin, Alvin Greenidge, Ray Wynter, Ezra Moseley, Herbert Chang, Everton Mattis, Franklyn Stephenson. Seated: Sylvester Clarke, Collis King, Derrick Parry, Alvin Kallicharran, Albert Padmore, Lawrence Rowe, Gregory Armstrong (manager), Colin Croft, Bernard Julien, Emerson Trotman, David Murray.

This has become for many a genuine mission rather than just an attempt to get back into favour with cricket authorities overseas, none of whom have shown much willingness themselves to help to develop the game in South Africa.

For various reasons, however, not all non-white cricketers joined the unified controlling body in 1977 and there has since been a rallying round the ranks of the rival South African Cricket Board (SACB) whose chairman, the politician Hassan Howa, has resolutely refused to co-operate with the white cricket authorities. His slogan 'No normal sport in an abnormal society' has become famous. In 1984 the SACB claimed to represent 10,000 non-white cricketers, mainly coloureds.

There is much sympathy outside South Africa for the cricketers of all hues there, but despite the efforts of various people to send unofficial touring parties, it has not led to any realistic hopes of a return to the International Cricket Conference by South Africa, who were excluded when the International body replaced the old Imperial Cricket Conference, of which South Africa had been a founder member. Consequently, when the ICC did nothing to implement the 1979 recommendation of their own 'fact-finding delegation' (not, unfortunately, fully representative) to send a multi-racial team to play against South Africa, SACU were pushed by private entrepreneurs to 'go it alone'.

With sponsorship from various large companies, an English team was invited out to play in March and April 1982. Rewards were substantial for the players,

led by the Test openers Graham Gooch and Geoff Boycott. Next season a Sri Lankan team visited South Africa, then a West Indian one which returned under the captaincy of Lawrence Rowe in 1983–84 to make a lengthy tour, followed with intense interest by people of various races in the Republic. It was a badly needed stimulus to the game in South Africa which had suffered in the years away from Test cricket. Nevertheless, during the first decade of isolation, the performances in English county cricket of Barry Richards, Mike Procter, Eddie Barlow, Ken McEwan, Clive Rice, Peter Kirsten and Vintcent Van der Bijl frequently showed followers of the game the strength of cricket in the Republic, and, all this time, Graeme Pollock, one of the finest batsmen in history, was producing outstanding performances in the Currie Cup.

But the possibility of a split between the black and white ICC-member countries helped to prevent any one national board of control from attempting to defy their own government policy by risking an official tour of South Africa. Instead an extremely hard line was taken against those who went as members of the specially invited international teams, several of England's leading Test players being banned for three years for their escapade in 1982 and those from Sri Lanka and West Indies being banned for life. One of the many ironies of the situation arose when the places of two of the Englishmen were taken by cricketers born and bred in South Africa who, knowing they would not be able to play for their own country, made use of British parents to qualify for England instead.

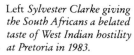

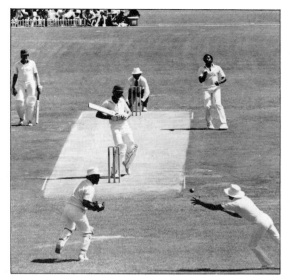

Left Sylvester Clarke giving the South Africans a belated taste of West Indian hostility at Pretoria in 1983.

Below left Joe Pamensky, President of the South African Cricket Association at a time when South Africa, tired of knocking politely at the closed door of the ICC, decided to force the issue by buying into the international market.

Centre Ali Bacher, South Africa's last Test captain who, as chairman of the

Transvaal Cricket Association, was the main organizer of the unofficial 'rebel' tours.

Above Hassan Howa, the long-serving chairman of the association for coloured cricketers, the South African Cricket Board.

South Africa's team for the unofficial Test at Durban, 1982–83. Back, left to right: Kenny Watson, Alan Kourie, Kevin McKenzie, Ken McEwan, Robbie Armitage, Steve Jefferies, Jimmy Cook, Garth Le Roux. Seated: Vintcent Van der Bijl, Barry Richards, Peter Kirsten, Graeme Pollock, Clive Rice, Ray Jennings.

From time to time during the history of cricket there have been attempts by leading players to increase their rewards from the game by withdrawing their 'service'. But such arguments as the Nottinghamshire players' strike of 1881 were shortlived, partly because the players had no alternative employment–or rather employers. In Australia in 1977, however, a revolution was made possible by the fact that it suited an immensely wealthy businessman named Kerry Packer to use the financial grievance of the leading players of the day against a complacent board of administrators for his own, and the players', mutual advantage. The result was a two-year disruption of international cricket, a big financial advance for the best players in all the Test countries (confirming an already established trend) and drastic changes in the conduct of the game

Mr Packer's World XI during their 'Grand Final' match against Australia at Sydney, 1979. Left to right: Dennis Amiss, Mike Denness (manager), Bruce Francis (ex-Australia, Packer employee, standing), Mike Procter, Bob Woolmer, Eddie Barlow, Barry Richards, Zaheer Abbas.

both administratively and on the field.

Cricket was booming in Australia in the 1970s. A talented home team under positive leadership by Ian Chappell and with one of history's fiercest fast-bowling partnerships in Dennis Lillee and Jeff Thomson defeated both England and West Indies in successive seasons in the middle years of the decade, by wide margins. Gates at the matches were enormous and commercial sponsors were showing a willingness to join the success. In 1975–76 the Australian Cricket Board made a huge profit during a season in which the revenue amounted to 1.9 million Australian dollars. The six Tests of that season accounted for just under a million dollars of which the Australian players–the chief *dramatis personae*–received 875 dollars a Test. This was in fact a better rate than the equivalent

payment to England players of £210 a Test, but it was clearly a somewhat mean share of quite a rich cake. The counter-argument was that the duty of any national cricket board was to plough profits back into the grass roots of the game in order to keep the cycle of production from schoolboy to Test player flowing as it must in any healthy sport.

Moreover, the fees to Australian Test players had already begun to increase in more ways than one before anyone came along to exploit their desire for more. The basic Test fee had doubled since 1974. In addition, the players initially had access to 30 per cent of the big sponsorship by the Benson and Hedges company of Australian first-class cricket which had first been negotiated in the 1974–75 season. By 1977–78 the initial B and H patronage of $A50,000 had risen to $A250,000, rising to $A350,000 the following year. In 1977–78, the first year of competition with a rival organization (Packer's), the Australian players received for the Tests against India $A1,852 if the match was lost and $A2,102 if the match was won. Nor was this all in response to a challenge, rather it was confirmation of an already established trend, as these words from a book by Greg Chappell, written just before the revolution, seem to prove:
'Cricketers' rewards have increased dramatically in a comparatively short time. In a matter of just two seasons the base Test payment doubled from $A200 to $A400. Sizeable bonuses have been handed out at the end of the past two series, provident fund money has been increased, cash endorsements are flowing as never before, and the Test team is now sponsored for three years.'

When Chappell wrote these words or, more likely in the dubious tradition of 'ghosted' players' books, these words were written for him, Kerry Packer's plans to bulldoze the cricket establishment of Australia into giving him a television contract were already formulated. In the middle of the highly popular Ashes series of 1974–75, Packer had approached the Board (some of whose members were golfing friends) about obtaining the television rights for cricket for his commercial network, Channel Nine. He was told in writing that he could indeed negotiate but when he actually came to do so he found that the Australian Broadcasting Commission, which had previously televised Australian first-class cricket (including the Sheffield Shield, for which Channel Nine were not apparently bidding), had already been granted rights for the next three years and that all that were negotiable were the commercial rights. After many subsequent legal battles in Australia, complicated by the fact that only the ABC's transmission can reach all the country areas as well as the cities, the Tests in the

The Packer message was carried everywhere by as many means as possible. The song 'C'mon, Aussie, C'mon!' became a top ten hit.

VFL Park, Melbourne, January 1979. Despite the publicity hype, World Series Cricket did not catch on until the second season when Packer won the right to use more of the traditional venues for cricket. The big brothers were watching, but not many spectators watched the big brothers!

1980s have been televised by both the ABC and the Channel Nine network. But at the early stages of the long dispute, Packer made it abundantly clear that he was interested only in 'exclusive rights' and offered $A500,000 for each of the next five years. The Board repeated that he could have commercial rights, but not exclusive ones, because of their prior commitment to the ABC.

During the last few months of 1976 work began on planning a series of matches the following season in Australia, to be promoted and televised by Channel Nine. Packer engaged two men, Austin Robertson and John Cornell, who ran a business promoting the affairs of sportsmen in Australia, to sign the top players for large sums–Lillee was paid a reported $A105,000. At this stage it was planned to hold a series of five-day and two-day matches between elevens chosen from a contracted squad of fifteen Australians and fifteen from the Rest of the World. When the plans came to fruition, a third side, of West Indians, was added.

However much they may have felt that they had a right to make what they could from their precarious livelihood as professional cricketers, many of those who signed did so with little thought for the game which had made them famous. In March 1977, for example, just before the Centenary Test between England and Australia, three members of the Australian Cricket Board met the five State cricket captains to discuss, amongst other matters designed to improve relations between players and administrators, the details of the latest Benson and Hedges sponsorship. During these discussions four of the five captains–Greg Chappell, Doug Walters, Richie Robinson and Rodney Marsh–had either signed contracts with the Packer group, or were shortly to do so. Yet they pledged to assist in the promotion of Benson and Hedges sponsorship and accepted the obligation not to enter into any agreements which might conflict. In the next few weeks, many leading players from several countries were cheerfully willing to sign contracts for beguiling sums regardless of the disruption the Packer matches were likely to cause to scheduled international cricket–the lifeblood of the game at all levels.

By the end of the Centenary Test, ten Australians had been signed and the England captain, the South African-born Tony Greig, was also signed both to captain the Rest of the World eleven and to act as a consultant and recruiter for other players. A few days later the former Australian captain Richie Benaud, who had in the past worked for the ACB as a public relations consultant, was also offered terms as a consultant. Benaud accepted on 6 April 1977 and gave Packer much valuable advice thereafter on how to handle the public relations–advising, for example, that he should make the most of a proposed coaching programme in New South Wales so that it could be seen that the Packer Group had the interests of grass-roots cricket at heart. With shrewd realism and foresight, Benaud predicted the hostile reaction of the ACB and the media.

In April a company was set up under the name of JP Sport Pty Ltd to administer what the press were to call 'Packer's Circus'. Mr Packer himself had a controlling interest through two personal shares and forty-nine owned by his company, Television Corporation Ltd. Within a fortnight of the company's formation, thirty-nine of the world's best players were contracted.

The signings had been carried out in total secrecy with all the signatories pledged to say nothing until the news of the big promotion was announced. In the event it leaked out to the press early in the 1977 Australian tour of England and the series for the Ashes which followed was played out against a dramatic background as the world's cricket authorities decided how to react. At the ICC meeting in June they decided to invite Mr Packer to discuss his plans with them, at the same time warning in a statement that a private promotion might 'seriously damage' international cricket.

On 23 June, Packer, Benaud and two colleagues met at Lord's with thirteen members of an emergency sub-committee set up by the ICC at their recent meeting. The meeting was at first cordial with Packer expressing his willingness to compromise if the ICC would do likewise. The chairman of the committee, that year's MCC President, 'Tadge' Webster, laid out five conditions which would have confined the proposed series of matches to six weeks so that they would not clash with important 'official' games. Packer agreed that each of the five conditions was open to discussion and then made two of his own, the first that the players he had signed should not be victimized and the second that Channel Nine should be guaranteed the exclusive television rights to Australian Test cricket after the current ABC contract had expired. He was happy to pay the market rate. The melodrama increased when, with cameras and journalists waiting outside the pavilion, Packer suggested that Richie Benaud should show him round Lord's whilst the ICC Committee discussed matters amongst themselves. Whilst Packer strolled in the sunshine round the ground whose foundations he had shaken, the two Australian delegates, Bob Parish and Ray Steele, said firmly that out of loyalty to the ABC they did not think they could make any guarantee about where the next contract should go just because Mr Packer was holding a pistol to their heads.

When Packer returned, and was told that he would have the right to negotiate on an equal basis with all the other TV companies, he made it plain that this was not what he had come for. Besieged by journalists outside (I was one) he said with little concealed venom: 'I am only in this area because of my conflict with the Australian Cricket Board. Had I got those rights I was prepared to withdraw from the scene and leave the running of cricket to the Board. I will now take no steps to help anyone. Everyman for himself and the devil take the hindmost.'

It was a declaration of open war and for two years the battle was fought on two fronts–on the cricket fields of Australia and in the courtrooms of both England and Australia. The official line of the Packer camp, that they had come into cricket to raise the salaries of the downtrodden players, was shown in that outburst to be nothing more than propaganda. He wanted the television rights and in time he was to get them, and a whole lot more besides.

Such success, however, did not come easily. The main grounds of Australia were made unavailable to the company which in July 1977 changed its name to World Series Cricket Pty Ltd. This meant finding other grounds not associated with cricket and the revolutionary preparation of pitches in concrete tubs inside greenhouses under the supervision of a young groundsman named John Maley, whom Packer had signed on because he had so improved the wicket at Brisbane's Test ground, the 'Gabba. Meanwhile there were rumours of many players having second thoughts especially when, on 26 July, the ICC announced that anyone playing in the Packer matches had until 1 October to withdraw, or they would be considered ineligible for Test matches. Moreover, they urged all the full member nations to follow the same policy of banning players from first-class cricket in their own countries. Their statement was couched in carefully thought-out legal terms. The ICC were already aware that the proposed bans might be challenged in the courts as being in restraint of trade.

The actions brought against the ICC and the TCCB by World Series Cricket and three of its new employees, Tony Greig, John Snow and Mike Procter, began in the High Court before Mr Justice Slade on 26 September 1977 and ended on 7 November. After weighing the evidence for 18 days, Mr Slade read a 221-page, five-and-a-half hour judgment which concluded that the proposed bans on the Packer players by the ICC (from Test cricket) and the TCCB (from English domestic cricket) were void and *ultra vires* because on the one hand they were an unreasonable restraint of trade and on the other they

amounted to an inducement to the players to break their contracts with WSC. Costs, amounting to about £200,000, were to be paid by the defendants. The only tiny crumbs of consolation for the defeated cricket authorities were the Judge's recognition that they had acted in what they believed to be the best interests of the game and, secondly, the distinction which he drew between retrospective action against those who had signed, and any future attempts to curb players from signing for a private promotion by warning that they might thus render themselves ineligible, at least for Test cricket.

The TCCB bore the brunt of the expenses of the case and the first season of WSC cricket went ahead in rivalry with an official Test series between India and what was no better than an Australian Second Eleven. It turned out, however, to be an

The drinks cart – one of many American-style adjuncts to the main business of the game itself.

enthralling series whereas the WSC matches were generally an expensive failure. Nevertheless, apart from the success of the artificially prepared turf pitches, which had been expertly lifted into slots in the middle of football pitches and which played excellently, there were other imaginative experiments which were to be exploited later in 'official' Australian cricket. The first regular floodlit cricket matches were played at VFL Park in Melbourne and the idea of a limited-overs game on a warm evening under floodlights with a white ball and black sightscreens proved instantly attractive to a mainly young Australian public.

The second year of WSC saw the end of some of the less happy gimmicks. Moreover, a new respectability attended the matches because further legal action and lobbying in important places had succeeded in acquiring for their use several traditional homes of Australian cricket, in particular the historic Sydney Cricket Ground.

In both years the matches were expensively and expansively promoted with all the razzmatazz associated with American baseball. The players wore coloured clothes and, with big money at stake, played with a genuine will to win, as well as a commitment to selling themselves as personalities. Many of the features of international cricket since, especially in Australia, were spawned by World Series Cricket. These included an emphasis on limited-overs internationals at the expense of Test matches (they were known in WSC language as 'SuperTests'); a large number of night matches; heavy advertising of cricket in the media, especially on television; coloured clothes; showmanship and aggro amongst the players, and a tactical reliance on fast bowlers, in particular on fast bowlers bowling short, resulting in the almost

'Marketing' was a key word in Packer cricket. Dennis Lillee and the other well-paid players had no qualms about acting as advertising boards.

universal use at high levels of protective helmets for batsmen.

The growing success of the WSC matches was underlined by disappointing crowds for the Ashes series between the young Australian side and England under the leadership of Mike Brearley. England's 5-1 victory in the series, though it was much less one-sided than it sounded, reduced the crowds and the ACB lost $A810,000 over the two years of WSC. The losses incurred by WSC were very much greater–at least four times–and with the Australian public, not to mention the rest of the cricket world, heartily sick of the civil war, there was a strong incentive for a compromise between the warring parties.

It came at the end of May 1979. Packer's company, PBL Sports Pty Ltd, was granted exclusive promotion rights to all matches arranged by the Board, including the sub-letting of the television rights, initially to Channel Nine though eventually the ABC successfully contested in the courts their right to co-televise the matches. The agreement with PBL was for ten years, and although the Board was officially in sole control henceforward of the conduct of the game in Australia, its leading members were obliged to accept many features of the WSC game, including an annual series of limited-overs internationals between at least three countries. In return for conceding what Mr Packer had originally fought for, the Board got a large guaranteed annual income.

WSC matches were not played again and the sixty-eight players in WSC employ were paid off, some of them rather disillusioned, others relieved to be back with a chance of playing officially sanctioned Test cricket again. The stigma attached to their association with WSC gradually faded but the wounds were not completely healed until the players concerned had retired; in Australia, it was not until 1984 that three of the leading 'rebels', Greg Chappell, Dennis Lillee and Rodney Marsh, left the game, taking with them one or two deep-seated divisions between themselves and other members of the Australian team who had not been a part of the Packer set-up. Moreover, WSC lived on visibly in the form of publicity material and invisibly in the whole approach to cricket in Australia. Henceforward every decision concerned with first-class cricket had commercial aspects to it.

The Packer Revolution will be remembered as the longest and most bitter dispute in the history of the game. It heralded an era of commercial ruthlessness both on the part of players and administrators. It established the right of players to be paid well for providing popular public entertainment; and it proved the power of television to influence the conduct of the game.

A bouncer from Wayne Daniel strikes Rodney Marsh on the head.

Ian Chappell bowled by Imran Khan in the Grand Final at Sydney, 1979.

From time to time since the earliest days of professional cricket, business interests as well as private patrons have invested money in the game. We have seen how the catering firm of Spiers and Pond underwrote, to their own considerable profit, the first England tour of Australia in the nineteenth century. Since 1963 the process has been greatly accelerated.

The Gillette Cup was the catalyst for a number of commercial sponsorships of English county cricket. In time sponsors were also found for Test cricket, and for the three-day County Championship, but the great attraction at first was the idea of limited-overs cricket which, with a result guaranteed in one day's cricket (given reasonable weather), has proved a great attraction to spectators.

Soon after Gillette came the tobacco manufacturers John Player to sponsor the new forty-

New ideas were not confined to Australia. An individual batting competition amongst most of the world's best players at The Oval in 1979 ended in victory for Clive Lloyd, but the sponsors evidently found it too expensive an idea to repeat.

over League, which comprised matches begun and finished in a single Sunday afternoon. This 'brand' of cricket had already been tested by another tobacco firm, Rothmans, whose 'Cavalier' matches had attracted big crowds. The John Player League also proved an extremely popular form of Sunday summer family entertainment. By 1975 the overall crowds for the competition had reached 300,000, though they started to fall away thereafter as the novelty began to wear off and other Sunday sporting entertainments proved even greater attractions.

John Player gave £35,000 to county cricket (through the parent body, the TCCB) in 1969 and when they renewed the contract in 1982 they raised their annual payment to £300,000, index-linked to defeat inflation in the following five years of their contract. Prize-money for the teams grew from £9,500 in 1969 to £56,000 in 1982. These were large sums, but

for a tobacco company whose advertising was restricted for health reasons by law it was an excellent means of keeping their brand names before the public.

Another tobacco firm, Benson and Hedges, sponsored the third county limited-overs competition, instituted in 1972. This was played on a league basis early in the season with eight counties qualifying for the final stages, played as a knockout cup. Each team in B and H cricket is allowed 55 overs, the amount that has become standard for other one-day competitions throughout the world. The fewer the overs in a limited-overs game, the greater the artificiality of the cricket. Only rarely has the Benson and Hedges competition aroused quite the same enthusiasm as the Gillette. If the number of overs played has been one reason, another is a general feeling that there are one too many competitions in county cricket. Once beyond its league stage, however, the knockout rounds of the Benson and Hedges take on a new interest, with the final at Lord's in July a spur to both spectators and players.

The Gillette company gave up their sponsorship of cricket throughout the world (similar knockout competitions under their patronage had been started in other countries too) in 1981 because, they claimed, people now associated the name Gillette with cricket rather than with razor blades. The message had been too successfully conveyed. Their mantle was eagerly taken on in England by the National Westminster Bank, whose first final proved one of the most thrilling of all limited-overs games, Derbyshire winning by virtue of a scrambled run off the last ball of the match. Sponsorship has not been confined to limited-overs cricket. Tests are also now played for commercially provided prize-money and with financial support lent to the governing body of cricket in the country concerned in return for association with the Test series and the national team. The Cornhill Insurance Company backed English Test cricket in this way for the first time in 1978 and a few years later the company's standing in the insurance world had risen dramatically as a result of their shrewd investment. Surveys showed that public awareness of the name Cornhill has risen from two per cent to seventeen per cent.

The effect on the players and their way of life was instantaneous. The Test fee to England cricketers went up from £210 to £1,000. For tours their basic salary was raised from £3,000 to £5,000. In addition the players had access to substantial prize-money and, apart from the Tests, limited-overs internationals became a regular part of the English season after 1972 and the most lucrative part of every Australian season after the treaty between the Packer organization and the Australian Cricket Board.

It was not just international cricket and the major domestic competitions that the sponsors were interested in. During the 1970s many a traditional club league found a local firm to sponsor it in a modest way, various new competitions sprang up for schools and even village cricketers found themselves given a chance to earn some extra money for club funds and an opportunity to play at Lord's. The national village competition was introduced in 1972 by *The Cricketer* magazine, who have organized it ever since. It was sponsored first by the whisky firm John Haig and then by the brewers, Samuel Whitbread. There was even a sponsored competition for primary school children–a tournament played with a soft ball and underwritten by the American chewing-gum firm, Wrigleys, who gave generous sums to youth cricket from 1969 when they formed the Wrigley Cricket Foundation.

Patronage at local level was in a way only an extension of what had always happened in amateur cricket with the local squire presenting a silver cup (or several silver cups) for local competition and perhaps digging into his pocket again if his own village side was short of capital. The difference, however, is that whereas the squire acted out of altruism or a sense of duty, the firms now engaged in sponsorship at local or national levels do so for sound commercial reasons: it is good for their image, it keeps their name in the minds of potential customers and it is a useful medium for entertaining their clients. Sponsors want their pound of flesh.

They do not always get it, however. One of the most interesting of the proliferating number of sponsorships in the 1970s was that by the car accessories firm, Holts Products, who offered substantial prize-money for matches between touring teams and English counties. Traditionally these had been amongst the major fixtures of any county's itinerary but both spectators and players had lost interest in them. Despite the sponsorship, touring teams continued to use the games as practice matches for getting their players into trim for Tests and one-day internationals, whilst counties merely continued to use the games to try out young players and rest experienced ones for what they considered to be more important matches in the various sponsored county competitions. On the one hand this suggested that there was now so much money in the game, the players had become somewhat blasé, on the other it showed that money was not considered to be all-important. They still had their priorities.

There was no sign by 1984 that cricket was losing its power to attract sponsors, though at first-class level most countries had become totally

dependent on this form of income and there was a worrying hiatus before the TCCB found another insurance company, Britannic Assurance, to take on the sponsorship of the County Championship after 1984. From 1977 it had been under the patronage of Schweppes, the soft drinks firm. In England it was estimated that the total cost of staging all first-class cricket was £8 million in 1984 and around £2 million of this was offset by direct income from the sponsors.

Below David Gower was the lucky recipient of this award in 1982–83, one of all sorts of perks for the modern international cricketer.

Bottom Play during a county indoor cricket competition at the start of the 1981 season, held in the Brighton Arena.

It is not just the first-class cricket grounds which have changed in appearance in the years since nations everywhere, but especially in England, began to recover from the austere years after the end of the Second World War. Even quite small village clubs began to find ways of raising money, often through loans from such organizations as The National Playing Fields Association, in order to build new pavilions or extend old ones. A bar became the first priority, a valuable source of continuous revenue for the clubs through the summer months at least, and such luxuries as showers, carpets and comfortable chairs became commonplace in the pavilions of village clubs which had once considered a rustic wooden structure with a couple of cramped dressing-rooms and a lavatory ample for the needs of 22 players before and after the game.

Where there's a will...
Cricket matches are all too often abandoned by umpires and players when some hard work and greater awareness of their duties as entertainers could make play possible. Despite this flood at The Oval in 1968, mopped up by spectators as well as by groundstaff, play resumed later in the day and Derek Underwood bowled England to victory.

Then it was off to the local pub, preferably within walking distance of the ground and often on the edge of the green itself. Many is the landlord of pubs called The Cricketers who has cursed the arrival of the new bar which club members have striven so hard for. Indeed at one club in Surrey new pavilions were twice burned down by the landlord's son! The modern club cricketer cannot enjoy quite the same cameraderie in his own bar that he used to at the local pub, however, and the change marks a break with tradition going as far back as the days of the Bat and Ball at Broad-Halfpenny Down.

When it comes to first-class cricket, the upkeep

of modern facilities has always been the biggest drain on the resources of any club. Big grounds, with spectators' accommodation open to the weather, and large, draughty pavilions housing offices as well as changing-rooms, will literally rot to pieces unless they are looked after. It costs over £175,000 a year to maintain the various buildings around Lord's–Pavilion, stands, squash courts, real tennis court, official MCC houses, etc.–and nearly £100,000 to cover such ground expenses as wages for the ground staff, repairs to covers and machinery, cost of fertilizers and other materials and equipment.

A few miles across London, Surrey's 1983 accounts revealed expenditure on cricket (mainly wages) the previous year to have been £341,000, plus £172,000 on marketing and £275,00 on finance and administration. These figures show that running a big cricket club is now a major business and clubs cannot afford to let their grounds become delapidated if they are to survive. The public has become more demanding since the early 1960s, when Alan Ross could write, with no fear of contradiction, that cricket 'is a sport without public relations, of monstrous discomfort and inadequate catering, of spartan conditions and no showmanship'.

Much has changed since then and many of the changes have had the customer in mind. Seating has become more modern and (slightly) more comfortable, the wooden benches of old gradually giving way to bright, plastic 'tip-up' bucket seats. Efforts have been made at many grounds to improve catering, so that, at Lord's for example, curries and other Oriental delicacies are always on sale if India or Pakistan are playing a Test there. (Inside the Pavilion there are still, for those who can afford them, smoked salmon and strawberries.) Members at Lord's now have a plush modern bar in their Pavilion as well as the incomparable (except perhaps at Melbourne) Long Room, and the more old-fashioned Writing Room.

On the field of play itself, the game has been relatively slow to make use of the new technology which began to invade all spheres of human activity in the 1970s. But by the end of 1984 the two premier grounds of Australia, at Sydney and Melbourne, not only had floodlights for night cricket but also huge electronic scoreboards on which almost any detail about the match could be displayed. In addition these giant boards could be turned instantaneously into enormous television screens, showing the crowd a replay of a shot played a few moments before or, more controversially, a batsman's dismissal and the players' reactions to it. At first it was decided not to show any dismissals involving an umpire's decision, for fear of violent crowd reaction, but the temptation to do so was sometimes too much. The obvious corollary to this was to use the technology to aid the umpires. Those who opposed the use of instant replays for split-second decisions (following appeals for stumpings and run-outs) which machines can make less fallibly than umpires, were probably only delaying the inevitable.

Out in the middle things have also changed. Fertilizers have made outfields, which once used to become deserts in dry weather, into permanent green pastures, thus keeping the shine on the ball and making life sweeter for seam and swing bowlers, and much less so for the spinners. Covering in wet weather has become more sophisticated and expansive. Experiments were made at Lord's, where the slope presents peculiar problems, with a hot-air cover. They

were not successful. But at Edgbaston a motorized cover was introduced in 1982 which protects virtually the whole playing area from rain, and can be rolled back to the edges of the ground, as soon as the weather relents, at the flick of a switch.

As the upkeep of good turf wickets has become increasingly expensive both in terms of wages to ground staff and equipment and materials, artificial cricket pitches made of tough green plastics have proliferated at club and school grounds wherever the game is played. The biggest variety of these pitches, and the biggest market for them, for reasons of climate, is in the United Kingdom. It seems only a matter of time before at least some cricket at the highest level is played on artificial surfaces.

Below left *Mopping up has become more sophisticated, and a big improvement was the huge cover at Edgbaston, introduced in 1982, which can cover almost the entire playing area.*

Below *Electronic information at Headingley, 1981.*

Bottom *The versatile board at Melbourne, first used in the 1982–83 season, which enabled spectators to see the instant replays which they had come to expect when watching at home.*

Many hands make light work, even with a heavy roller; photographed at the Jubilee Test in Bombay, 1980.

Calcutta, 1976–77. A final brushing for the Test wicket at Eden Gardens. India were bowled out cheaply twice by England on a pitch which had been prepared with a view to helping the home team's spinners. Increasingly in recent years the idea that all Test wickets should be hard and fast has been abandoned and home countries have tended instead to prepare pitches to suit their own bowling attacks.

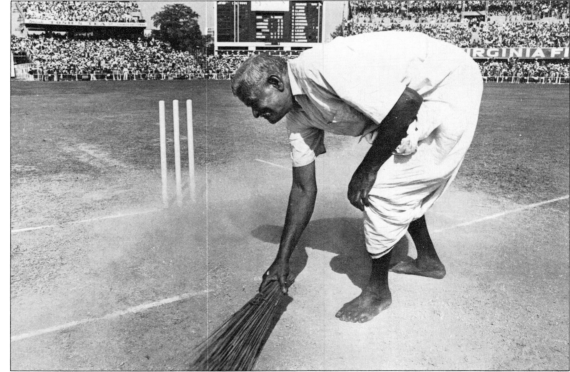

The 'Auto-Roller' may replace man-powered machines, but there is still a job for the old-fashioned broom.

Spiking and mopping: this looks more like a demonstration of agricultural machinery than a cricket scene.

Never has limited-overs cricket been seen in a better light than it was in the three World Cup tournaments held in England in 1975, 1979 and 1983. The geographical compactness of the country, multi-racial crowds ensuring strong local support for at least four of the competing nations, long summer days making it possible to stage 60-over matches, together with sound organization and low-key commercial overtones thanks to the sympathetic sponsoring company, Prudential Assurance, all added up to a recipe for success. Even the weather was kind.

When it snowed at Buxton on 2 June 1975, causing a day's play in a Championship match there to be abandoned, the worst fears of the organizers looked likely to be realized but in fact the competition was played throughout in sunny weather. Games were chivalrously and often excitingly conducted before enthusiastic and, for England, large crowds. In the space of a fortnight fifteen internationals were played, each of 60 overs a side, and the first World Cup Final was won at Lord's by the West Indies after a thrilling contest against Australia which did not finish until 8.45 pm. Lord's was full to the brim with 26,000 people and the match produced then record receipts of £66,000. The photograph of Prince Philip, Duke of Edinburgh, a happy choice as that year's President of MCC, presenting the Prudential Cup to Clive Lloyd has become one of the most familiar in cricket. Of the 563 runs produced during a tiring but enthralling day's cricket, West Indies scored only 17 more than Australia.

The contestants in the first World Cup were the six Test-playing countries, plus Sri Lanka (formerly Ceylon) and East Africa, who were reckoned to be the strongest of the 'associate member' countries of the ICC. Neither won a match, although Sri Lanka performed with considerable honour and when it was decided to hold a qualifying tournament for associate members three years later, Sri Lanka won it with some ease. This time their fellow-qualifiers were Canada. Sadly, an invitation to the politically ostracized cricketers of South Africa was not seriously considered.

England and New Zealand qualified for the 1975 semi-finals and they did so again four years later, with West Indies again getting through without a defeat. Australia, however, could defeat only Canada in their group of four and Pakistan qualified in their stead. In two excellent semi-finals West Indies defeated Pakistan at The Oval in a match producing 543 runs in brilliant sunshine before a 20,000 crowd, and on the same day England won the tensest of matches at Old Trafford against New Zealand, who fell a mere nine runs short of England's total of 221. Here the crowd was 22,000, the weather equally tropical and the mood euphoric.

The West Indies again emerged victorious at Lord's, Viv Richards supplying the matchwinning century that Lloyd had produced against Australia four years previously. Going in at 22 for 1, Richards hit 138 not out in a total of 286 for 9, stepping inside two 'unhittable' leg-stump yorkers in the last over from Hendrick and lofting them high over the square-leg boundary in a characteristic demonstration of his towering supremacy. Boycott and Brearley gave England a sound base on which to counter-attack, but in the post-tea phase of their opening stand of 129 they were unable to score nearly fast enough and the long-limbed Joel Garner proceeded to demolish England's talented middle-order batsmen–Randall, Gooch, Gower, Botham and Larkins–who were all obliged to

Scenes from the first Prudential World Cup in 1975, a feast of limited-overs cricket at its best. Here Dennis Amiss swings Abid Ali to the boundary on his way to a century against India; the wicket-keeper is Farokh Engineer. Amiss helped England to a huge total – and the Indians responded by playing for a draw!

Sri Lanka's batsmen came back bravely against a big Australian score at The Oval. This is Sidath Wettimuny, cutting Ashley Mallett for four.

Above *Immigrant West Indians had a wonderful time, cheering and dancing as the West Indies advanced to victory.*

Right *Alvin Kallicharran thrilled crowds with his neat, quick-footed batting, answering Dennis Lillee's bouncers with some crisp hooks. Against New Zealand, however, he missed this sweep and was no doubt amazed to see Ken Wadsworth scooping the ball up from his pads.*

Clive Lloyd took command of the final against Australia, scoring a superb 102. Few batsmen have hit the ball with such full-blooded gusto.

In the evening he received his just reward, and proudly holds the Prudential Cup, presented to him in near-darkness by Prince Philip, Duke of Edinburgh and the 1975 President of MCC, after a long and dramatic match.

try to run before they could walk.

By 1983, Sri Lanka had been accepted as a full, Test-playing member of ICC, so qualified for the finals as of right. Zimbabwe were by far the strongest of the other ambitious nations and added spice to another highly successful competition by defeating Australia and performing with credit in several other games. This time each country played the other three in their group twice during the qualifying rounds. This no doubt was a fairer test of the abilities of the competing teams and it did not have the same feeling of overkill as one gets from watching the annual Australian competitions when only three countries play each other over and over again at a limited number of venues. In England the extra games gave a chance to established county grounds like Bristol, Leicester and Taunton to stage matches. As a result the tournament was more interesting than ever and, with good weather generally prevailing again, West Indies, England, India and Pakistan qualified for the finals. The surprise team of the four were India, who had steadily been improving their performances in limited-overs cricket after starting the first World Cup with a humiliating defeat. Any suggestion that 'instant' cricket was foreign to the Indian temperament was exploded as a myth when India, playing well as a team under

charismatic leadership from their compelling all-rounder Kapil Dev, overcame England at Old Trafford and then, against all expectations, defeated West Indies in the Final at Lord's. Despite a narrow escape in 1975 against Pakistan, it was the first defeat for West Indies in any games in the three World Cups to date.

If the World Cup is to retain its rarity value and prestige, wherever it may in future be held, it is essential that it should only be staged every four years and that a way be found to force the players to hasten their over-rate to allow for 60-over matches even if the host country has shorter hours of daylight than England. The advantages of staging the tournament in India or Australia, where the grounds have much greater capacity, would be that the profits, amounting in 1983 to some £1 million, shared amongst all the ICC countries, would be potentially even greater. In 1983 a total of 228,000 people paid to watch the matches, producing gate receipts of £1,200,000. Sponsorship and broadcasting fees raised the total income by another £400,000 but overhead expenses reduced the profit by £600,000. This, however, was one modern competition in which, happily, money seemed less significant than the fact that the world's best cricketers were on parade together, playing the best of games in the best of spirits.

When in 1932–33 Douglas Jardine was pursuing ruthlessly his bodyline tactics in Australia, much to the indignation of the home team, their supporters and indeed most impartial observers, newspaper readers in England had only the reports of two of their countrymen to consider in trying to come to a judgment on the rights and wrongs of Jardine's strategy. One was Jack Hobbs, hamstrung by being recently retired and obliged to comment about his former county captain and in any case being 'ghosted' by Jack Ingham, a journalist who saw a good story in Australians 'squealing' about their defeats. The other was Bruce Harris of the *Evening Standard*, who was a tennis writer and apparently became a compliant apologist for Jardine's tactics.

Right *In tennis it would now be called 'abuse of the racquet'. Greg Chappell, furious at himself for playing an indiscreet shot at Perth in 1982–83.*

Above *The ABC radio commentary team at Perth in 1979–80 with the press box behind. Left to right: Bobby Simpson, the author, Alan McGilvray. It all looks a bit serious!*

The only other reports seen in England during the tour were by the former Australian captain Warwick Armstrong, whose own sportsmanship was in doubt after his leadership on the 1921 tour, and the Reuter correspondent Gilbert Mant, an Australian also, and under orders to report only the facts and the scores, without comment. It happened that both E.W. Swanton and S.J. Southerton, both knowledgeable and fearless cricket writers, narrowly missed going on the tour. But apart from the limited reports from those mentioned above, the occasional pictorial news report at the cinema was the only other contact between the Test series and its followers in England.

Fifty years on, the England team's tour of Australia under the captaincy of Bob Willis was played under an intense public gaze. Every ball of the main matches was recorded, albeit temporarily, on video tape. Every incident, on and off the field, was analyzed and discussed. The apparent over-weight of England's champion all-rounder, Ian Botham, was a talking point in bars up and down not just Australia, but England too. Instead of 'Did you see what Larwood did at Sydney last month? I saw it at the pictures on Wednesday,' it was 'Did you see what Botham did at Sydney last night? I saw it on the lunchtime news this morning. They replayed the incident four times. They'll no doubt be interviewing Botham on the telly this evening. In fact I hear a TCCB official has already left for Australia and will be talking to him about it tomorrow.'

International cricketers of the 1980s are obliged to live almost constantly in the public eye. It may or may not be fair to compare Ian Botham with Keith Miller, the Australian all-rounder who was in his prime straight after the Second World War, but whereas one emerged from a dashing career as a larger-than-life character who was widely admired for living life to the full off the field, Botham has found himself the not-entirely-guiltless victim of disapproving public scrutiny for treating life in much the same carefree way.

Test match players in the 1980s came under four different microscopes: there is ball-by-ball commentary on radio, copious coverage on television, a report and comment from the cricket correspondent of every national newspaper and, as often as not in the case of the tabloid papers, an additional report from an additional reporter, a 'newshound', whose job is to sniff out some particular incident and make the most of it to give his paper a good story. Often this may be a harmless and interesting analysis of a feature of the day's play–perhaps the background story of the hero of the day or

Left *The argument over Dennis Lillee's aluminium bat which raged for some ten minutes in the middle of the Perth Test of 1979–80. Umpires Weser and O'Connell eavesdrop on an animated debate between Lillee and Brearley.*

Below *This blade of grass looks a bit suspicious... Tony Greig analyzing everything from the bounce of the pitch to the 'degree of player comfort' before a day's play in the Brisbane Test of December 1982.*

an explanation of why so many catches were dropped–but sometimes these stories concern off-the-field incidents or activities. They can then become malicious.

It is always on tours that stories are printed which, sadly, bring cricket into disrepute. The clean sporting image of cricket in both England and Australia has taken some grievous blows in recent years as a result of the attentions of these newshounds. The media in both countries live in a highly competitive environment and cricketers are considered fair game if, like politicians, they sometimes slip from the high standards expected of people in public life. Moreover, the more famous the cricketer, the more careful he has to be. The Australian fast bowler Dennis Lillee could hardly have expected to escape censure for some of his exhibitionist performances on the field of play, notably kicking at an opposing player and

Left *Journalism on tours can be hard work, anxiously waiting for means of communication with offices at home. Journalists on the 1980–81 tour to the West Indies had to wait 12 hours at the Holiday Inn in Barbados to hear if the politicians would permit the tour to continue.*

Above *The Bangalore Test of 1981–82. The England captain Keith Fletcher, piqued at getting out – or being given out – taps the wicket with his bat in irritation as he makes for the pavilion. An official apology soon dispelled the rumpus but Fletcher lost the England captaincy after the tour.*

John Lever of Essex and England took the field during a Test in hot weather at Madras with vaselined strips which he hoped would stop the sweat from running down into his eyes. However, he was accused of using the vaseline to keep the shine on the ball. In fact India had already been undermined by Lever's swing bowling and a Cricket Council inquiry cleared the England team.

throwing his aluminium bat across a Test match field in a fury carefully cooked up to attract maximum public attention, but his colleague, Rodney Marsh, might have expected to have escaped the front pages when in the disappointed aftermath of a Test defeat he threw a punch at a spectator. Once upon a time such an incident would have been hushed up. Now it is trumpeted far and wide.

Botham's problems may be considered typical of those surrounding the relationship between cricketers and the media. When he first appeared for Somerset he was quickly spotted as a player of unusual qualities and the early publicity helped him to make the Test team sooner than he might otherwise have done. His sudden fame brought a steadily increasing flow of income from a number of sources, including a valuable contract to 'write' ghosted articles for *The Sun*. The fees he was able to command owed nothing to what he actually said or wrote, and everything to his being the most brilliant English all-round cricketer since W.G. But he could not come to terms with the fact that fame meant living his life responsibly. He hated the intrusions on his private life. And he resented the banner headlines when his many successes on the field were punctuated by almost equally dramatic failures.

Off the field he liked to live life dangerously, the same sometimes reckless spirit he brought to his cricket being evident in such incidents as twice overturning a brand new car at a motor-racing track, appearing in court accused of assault, severely cutting his hand on a plate-glass window in a pub, and playing football for Scunthorpe United shortly before an England cricket tour, despite having a suspect knee. Then, towards the end of a disappointing England tour of New Zealand and Pakistan in 1983–84, Botham, having started the tour as a hero with a century and a first innings haul of five wickets in the First Test, came home early with the sky once again falling round his ears. His left knee had swollen so badly that he needed an operation, and he was accused by a female New Zealand journalist of taking drugs in his hotel room, a story related with malevolent glee by one newspaper group in particular.

Great cricketers are not always great men and the close attentions of the modern media are bound to expose a talented player's faults and failings as openly as his glittering talents. Unfortunately the few players who sometimes set bad examples, either by their lapses from good behaviour on the field, or their lifestyle off it, are the ones who attract the publicity. This is bad for the game and bad for aspiring young cricketers. If the players themselves are to blame, so are those branches of the media who deliberately fan the flames of controversy.

The Indian crowd are slow to forgive – though they appear to like being photographed.

It was that most imaginative of cricket writers, Sir Neville Cardus, who wrote once of a 'white waterfall' to evoke the vision of cricketers coming down the steps of the Pavilion at Old Trafford at the start of a day's play. What would he have written of the players coming down the steps of the no-less-respectable Sydney Cricket Ground Pavilion for a night match of the 1980s? They look more like a shower of liquorice allsorts tumbling from a tin. Not only do they take the field quite differently –without the old steady, studied, dignified approach, now replaced by a sudden orgy of physical jerks as soon as each man's boots touch the turf–but of course they are dressed in coats of many colours.

Manning the defences. A batsman going out in a Test to face fast bowling often now wears a helmet, and chest and forearm protectors together with the gloves, pads, box and thigh pad or towel which club cricketers still find sufficient.

'Day–Night Internationals', pioneered by World Series Cricket in Australia and a proven success there as in other hot countries including the West Indies and South Africa, are 'marketed' as a 'new product' and the packaging has to be bright. Coloured clothes, as mentioned in an earlier chapter, were common in England in the eighteenth and nineteenth centuries and it was the touring elevens of the middle nineteenth century, in more than one way the forerunners of 'Kerry Packer's Circus', who first popularized the idea of teams playing together in the same coloured uniform, although when formally dressed the men of Hambledon had also had a uniform: sky-blue coats with buttons engraved 'CC'.

Nowadays, for internationals played in Australia and New Zealand, and also in domestic one-day (or night) cricket in Australia, the teams each have a two-tone 'suit' of matching shirt and trousers. Designed primarily for the attraction of the audience on colour television, the coloured clothes are a matter of taste. The West Indians certainly objected to the colour they were at first obliged to wear in Australia–shocking pink, a hue normally associated in the islands with male pansies! Generally speaking, it would be true to say that young spectators, and females, are attracted by coloured cricket clothes whereas those brought up in the tradition of white shirts, sweaters, flannels and pads, consider a coloured cap quite enough of a contrast. There is certainly something aesthetically pleasing about fifteen men in white on a green background on a sunny day. At first, coloured clothes on the greensward looked as odd as sea-gulls in the jungle.

Even when the occasion is more conventional, great changes have taken place in the clothes and equipment of the modern player. For the best part of a hundred years, the cap and, off field, the blazer, were the only signs of flamboyance. In first-class, though only very rarely in club cricket, the cap has now been replaced by a protective helmet like those worn by motor-cyclists. Shirts, traditionally always rolled up just above the elbow, are now often short-sleeved. The old-fashioned slightly creamy-coloured 'white' flannels have increasingly been replaced in the 1980s by track-suit style whites with elastic waists.

Batting gloves, for years white with green spiked rubber over the fingers, were replaced after the Second World War by gloves with padded 'sausage' fingers. Pads have become more bulky, for extra protection, though recently various lightweight leg-guards of artificial material have taken their place in some cricket bags. The bags themselves have also changed in shape and style. Boots have become much lighter, and only rarely now do they rise above the ankle, though once support for the ankle was considered essential, especially for a bowler. As for bats, they are still made of willow and, since an unsuccessful attempt by Dennis Lillee to introduce an aluminium bat (he used one in a Test match until ordered to change it by the umpires) the laws now specify that all bats used in a match must be made of wood. Their basic shape and size has hardly changed since the blade became straight in the eighteenth century, when its length and width was determined by law. But recently bats have generally become heavier, with the power and weight concentrated in the middle, a reflection of the growing strength of both batsmen and fast bowlers as men in 'developed countries' have become gradually taller and more richly fed.

Far left *Modern cricketers need large bags to carry all their gear and Viv Richards (Adelaide, 1980) looks as though he could do with two bags to hold all his equipment, plus his trophies!*

Left *Dennis Lillee caused a rumpus during the Perth Test of 1979–80 by using an aluminium bat which he was helping to market. England's captain Mike Brearley claimed it was damaging the ball and the umpires ordered Lillee to use a wooden bat. Here Greg Chappell, the Australian captain, takes the bat off the field after picking it up from the point where Lillee had hurled it angrily across the pitch.*

Jullundur in the Punjab, heart of the Indian sports manufacturing business. Workers are seen busily making the equipment sold in Britain under such famous trade names as Stuart Surridge and Duncan Fearnley.

Mike Brearley, ready for the fast bowlers before the Adelaide Test of 1978–79. Brearley was one of the first regularly to use the protective helmets which first became generally used in World Series Cricket when short-pitched bowling by fast bowlers was common, even against tail-end batsmen. The trend quickly spread to Test cricket.

Timber! One-day cricket has many advantages but encouraging orthodox technique is not one of them. Here an Essex batsman pays the penalty of hitting across the line against Joel Garner, Somerset v Essex, May 1983, Benson and Hedges Cup.

Same competition, similar shot, same result. Brian Hardie of Essex bowled by Sarfraz Nawaz of Northamptonshire in the final of the Benson and Hedges, 1980. The wicket-keeper is George Sharp.

History in the making. New Zealand take a large step towards their first Test win in England, at Leeds in 1983, as Howarth runs back to catch Botham from a top-edge sweep off Coney.

Silly point has become a fashionable position in modern Test cricket, but it can be a perilous one. David Gower leaps out of danger as Larry Gomes of West Indies forces off the back foot during a one-day international in St. Vincent. David Bairstow is the wicket-keeper. Gomes, a patient, orthodox left-hander was one of the unsung heroes of Clive Lloyd's all conquering West Indies team in the '70s and early '80s.

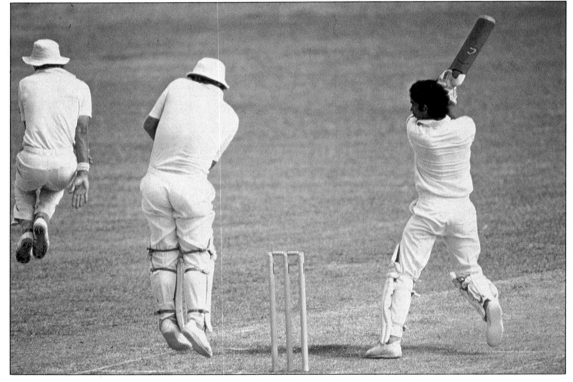

Moment of impact but not, alas, with the bat. Rick Darling, the Australian batsman, being hit on the temple by a ball from Kapil Dev in the sixth Test at Bombay, November 1979. Darling received several serious injuries during his short career from blows to head and body.

Bottom left *The bouncer has been more and more liberally used by an increasing number of fast bowlers. Here Mohinder Amarnath, wearing a solar topee (once belonging to his father Lala?) falls onto his stumps in trying to evade a bumper from Australia's Rodney Hogg, Bombay 1979.*

A good one for a Spot the Ball competition! Mohsin Khan appears to employ the back rather than the front of his bat whilst batting for Pakistan during the 1983 Prudential World Cup.

Below *A familiar dismissal in unfamiliar colours. Greg Chappell takes a typically brilliant catch off Dennis Lillee in a World Series match at Sydney in December 1978.*

A great bowler triumphant.
Derek Underwood, slow-
medium left-arm spinner,
kept on taking wickets even
after the era of fully covered
wickets denied him the wet
wickets on which he was so
lethal. The Kent stalwart
has just dismissed India's
Sandeep Patil in the first Test
of his last tour for England,
Bombay 1981. Botham,
Tavare and Taylor are the
other England players,
Swarup Kishen the umpire.

The brave new world.
Floodlit cricket before a full
house at Sydney, Australia v
England, January 1983.

Sri Lanka became the eighth Test-playing country when challenging England at Colombo in February 1982. Though the team performed with great credit, matching their far more experienced opponents for the first three days, it was clear that it would be some time before they won a Test match. The island was producing then, as it always had, a number of talented cricketers based on a tradition of schools cricket as strong as any on the globe, but the club cricket which followed was not of uniformly first-class standard. This is a problem Sri Lanka will have to solve if it is to hold its own in top international company but regular three-day cricket would mean setting up a professional infrastructure, something which will not easily be achieved in an economically poor country. Apart from the capital, only Kandy and Galle possess grounds suitable for Test cricket.

Soon after achieving Test status, following much patient diplomacy and many good performances against visiting teams from England and Australia, Sri Lanka's prospects were dimmed by the decision of several of their leading players to tour South Africa. Under Government pressure, the Sri Lankan Cricket Board felt constrained to ban the players from all cricket under their auspices for life. Since the tour to South Africa was in itself something of a non-event, the whole affair was disastrous for all parties.

Sri Lanka is a beautiful island and its people, be they Tamil or Cingalese–alas a sharp ethnic difference still exists and sometimes boils over into violence between the two–are charming and courteous. The weather is hot and humid all the year round, apart from in the monsoon season, and the pitches tend to favour spinners.

The first club on the island then called Ceylon was formed in Colombo in 1832. The annual schools match between St Thomas's College and Colombo Academy, later called Royal College, took place in 1879 and these days is such a feature of the season that it is televised. It was a master at Royal, Ashley Walker, who arranged the fixture and another Englishman, George Vanderpar, who was responsible for persuading some of the early English and Australian touring teams to break their journey by playing a match at Colombo. The first to do so was the Hon. Ivo Bligh's team of 1882, but the first MCC tour of any length did not take place until 1927.

Other countries were slow to encourage cricket in Ceylon and the first official visit of India came as late as 1945. Official visits from both West Indies and Pakistan followed four years later. In 1934 the gifted F.C. de Saram became the first to win a blue at Oxford. Although there were several more blues,

to follow, and individuals like Stanley Jayasinghe, Gamini Goonesena, Dan Piachaud and Clive Inman all made firm impacts upon first-class cricket in England, the modern era of competing on almost equal terms, at least on home soil, against the best teams of the world, did not really begin until the appointment of the talented batsman Michael Tissera as national captain in 1964. He was followed by a batsman of exceptional class in Anura Tennekoon who made a memorable hundred against Colin Cowdrey's MCC team in 1969 and scored 131 and 169 not out in successive unofficial Tests against India at home in 1974.

Further opportunities for Sri Lanka to gain experience abroad, and to press their case for full membership of the ICC, came with the World Cup competitions of 1975 and 1979 and through frequent exchanges of Under-19 tours between themselves and

Pakistan. Although Tennekoon had unfortunately retired when Test status arrived, Duleep Mendis, a dashing stroke-player, Roy Dias and Bandula Warnapura all proved themselves batsmen worthy of the highest company and two bowlers, the lively fast-medium Asantha de Mel and the experienced leg-spinner Somachandra de Silva also surprised anyone unwise enough to underestimate them. In addition, a young left-handed batsman, Arjuna Ranatunge, who was only 18 when making 50 in his first Test innings against England, showed immense promise.

Sri Lanka's first Test in England took place at Lord's in 1984, a proud occasion for many who had worked hard to establish their country amongst the elite of the game.

Sri Lanka took time, like all newcomers to Test cricket, to establish themselves in the international field but several talented players made an early mark. Here in action is Bandula Warnapura, Sri Lanka's first official Test captain.

It is not just modern first-class cricketers who come under more intense scrutiny than their predecessors. Umpires, without whom cricket could not be played, have lost the authority they once enjoyed as a never-to-be-questioned right. It has been stolen from them by television.

Every cricketer has been brought up to accept that the umpire's decision, made in good faith, should be accepted at all times. Unfortunately first-class cricketers soon learned that a television camera gave them an excellent chance, when they were looking for an excuse for their own failings or alternatively had a genuine grievance after a bad umpiring decision, to show by a look or a gesture that they had been the victim of injustice. Anyone who has ever played cricket knows the temptation to do this, with or without the

Firm and respected arbiters of the game. Umpires Syd Buller and Charlie Elliott, formerly of Worcestershire and Derbyshire, but better known in their role as Test umpires.

presence of a television camera. The television close-up, accompanied as it now is by electronic scoreboards in Australia, has underlined the desirability of players reacting to umpiring decisions with stoical calm. Inevitably they do not always do so.

If the TV camera has therefore made life harder for first-class cricketers it has done so to an even more marked degree for umpires. In the case of stumpings and run-outs, a slow-motion replay can categorically prove whether an umpire's decision was right or wrong. More often than not he is proved correct, but it is extremely embarrassing when the reverse is true: umpires are forgiven their mistakes much less easily than players.

There has recently been a growing chorus in favour of having 'neutral' umpires for Test matches, although so far the old tradition of the home country providing the match officials has prevailed. Neutral umpires would add to the expense of staging a Test series and would be no guarantee of better decisions. On the contrary, in England, where there are far more professional umpires, the vast majority of whom have played the game at first-class level, it would mean accepting inferior umpires simply to ensure that there would be no accusations of bias. Yet in other sports where internationals are umpired or refereed by neutral officials, one still hears criticisms that they have favoured the home side!

A suggestion which is more likely to be adopted is that in matches which are televised, umpires should have the right to call for the evidence of a slow-motion replay if they are doubtful about a run-out or stumping decision. This might be done by a third umpire off the field who would be able quickly to convey his opinion on the evidence of the camera. When it comes to lbw and caught-behind decisions, the umpire will always be on his own, obliged to make a quick decision on the basis of laws he knows inside out (if he is experienced enough to be standing in an important match) and a split-second view of the impact of ball on bat or pad. These are decisions which television cameras can never actually prove, but since the Channel Nine coverage of World Series Cricket, commentators in Australia have been all too ready to criticize umpires on the basis of such replays. In England their use has been restrained and sympathetic although once the watching public has got used to seeing replays, they expect and almost demand some analysis.

Apart from the extra pressure brought to bear on them by the all-seeing (yet not all-seeing) camera, the umpires have also in recent years been subjected to much dishonest appealing, especially in the case of catches by fielders close to the bat. The coming of protective helmets, not to mention boxes and shin-

The present fetish for playing spin bowlers with the bat behind the pad has made life even harder for umpires, especially when players tend to appeal for every 'catch' taken by close fielders. Umpire Bailhache would have been a brave man to have turned down this Australian demand for a bat-pad catch by Wood off Yardley at Perth in 1982–83. Randall was the victim.

Of all decisions, umpires in England least enjoy those concerning the fitness of the ground and bad light. The Centenary Test of 1980 at Lord's produced a particularly unhappy example. The occasion was far more important than the result of the match. But the captains, Ian Botham and Greg Chappell, and the umpires, Harold Bird and David Constant, failed to understand the harm they were doing to cricket's public image. On the Saturday of the match a full house saw virtually no cricket on a fine day after heavy overnight rain. Left to right: Jim Fairbrother (head groundsman), Botham, Lt-Col John Stephenson (MCC Assistant Secretary), Bird, Constant and Chappell.

Nowhere are umpires more in evidence than in India where interruptions in play are frequent. M. V. Gothoskar and Swarup Kishen (the heavy one) here try to sort out which replacement ball should be used during an India v England Test.

pads, has given fielders Dutch courage, but they often seem to crouch close to the wicket more to pressurize the batsman into a mistake than because there is the likelihood of a ball turning to take the edge of the bat. The bat-pad catch has become the main bane of umpires at international level, and the fact that matches are nowadays often played against an unremitting cacophony from the crowd must make it all the harder for umpires both to concentrate and to hear the tiny sound of a ball touching the edge of the bat.

Umpires are, at least, paid better than once they were for their very difficult jobs, demanding as they

Below Preparing to repulse invaders. Umpire Don Oslear seizes a stump with which to warn off invaders of the pitch during the England versus India World Cup semi-final match at Old Trafford in 1983.

Above left Bad light can cause dispute, even in Australia. Greg Chappell expresses his disapproval of the umpires' decision to offer the light to two struggling English batsmen, Gower and Fowler, at Brisbane in 1982–83.

are on both the mind and the body. The Test umpiring fee is in most countries now only a little below that of the players. In the age of television, moreover, some of the Test umpires have become minor celebrities themselves, notably perhaps 'Dickie' Bird, the former Yorkshire and Leicestershire cricketer, a loveable character with a rich Yorkshire accent and an intense love of his job. Such is his dedication that he was temporarily arrested at The Oval on the morning of his first county match in London for trying to clamber over the wall in the early hours of the morning, long before the gates had been opened!

Though it took them a long time to win a Test series in Australia, the West Indies established themselves in the second half of the twentieth century as the main producers of world-class cricketers. Before the Second World War only George Headley, a masterly player, had been recognized as a great batsman. After it, Walcott, Weekes, Worrell, Sobers, Kanhai, Hunte, Lloyd, Greenidge and Richards all established themselves as players of the highest calibre. They were backed up by a number of batsmen of only slightly less brilliance and, crucially, a seemingly unending supply of fast bowlers.

In the early 1960s the most feared pair of bowlers in the world were the Bajans Wesley Hall and Charlie Griffith. Hall, tall, broad and athletic, sprinting to the wicket off a long run with a gold crucifix glinting and bouncing on his chest, was as honest as he was fast. Griffith, powerfully built with an inswinging action sometimes considered suspect, had a lethal yorker and mean bouncer. West Indies had not at this stage conceived the idea of fielding more than two specialist fast bowlers regularly but they had another man of frightening speed available in the late 1950s in Roy Gilchrist and a dangerous new-ball bowler in Gary Sobers, who swung the ball late at speed from a perfect action, before turning to orthodox or unorthodox spin later in the innings.

For a time in the late 1960s Sobers carried the West Indians, with top-class bowling support only from Lance Gibbs, the long-fingered off-spinner with a looping flight and high bounce. Sobers was for most of his career the world's supreme all-rounder and crowds would go to watch him alone as once they had gone to see Grace or Bradman. He hit the ball exceptionally hard and with a pleasing grace, setting out always to take the initiative and following through fully with the bat whenever he played an attacking stroke. Amongst his feats were his six sixes off one over from Malcolm Nash of Glamorgan, a breath-taking 254 for the Rest of The World against Australia at Melbourne in 1971–72, the world record Test score of 365 not out against Pakistan at Kingston in 1958, and a marvellous all-round series as captain in England in 1966 when he took 20 wickets and scored 722 runs in five Tests at an average of 103. He also held 10 catches.

In 1975 the West Indies, now under Clive Lloyd, began a period of sustained excellence by winning the first World Cup. They were soundly thrashed the following season in Australia when Lillee and Thomson were both at their best but two outstanding young cricketers were blooded on that tour and emerged as world-beaters in England the following season. One was the Antiguan Viv Richards, built like a boxer and possessed of rare gifts of eye and timing; the other was Michael Holding, for a while the quickest and easily the most graceful bowler of his time. The team was seldom short of runs with Lloyd himself, an octopus on legs in the field and a commanding left-

Below Conrad Hunte was one of the best and perhaps most under-rated of West Indies opening batsmen. Batting here against Lock at Edgbaston, he scored hundreds in the first and last Tests of the 1963 series.

Right Some West Indians, on the other hand, can't bat! Lance Gibbs, the best off-spinner in the world in his time and the first spinner to take 300 Test wickets, was a genuine number eleven as this less-than-classic forward defensive stroke testifies. The match was the Edgbaston Test of 1963; Gibbs was bowled by Trueman, whose Test record he eventually broke, for a duck.

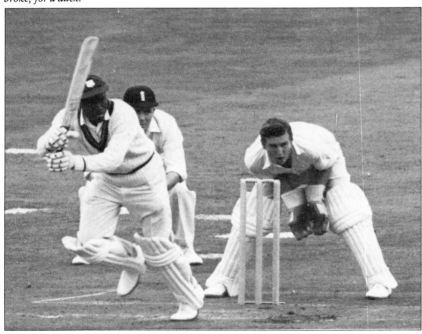

Left *Gary Sobers, who began his Test career primarily as a left-arm slow orthodox spinner. He could also bowl spin from the back of the hand and was a brilliant fielder anywhere, usually posted close to the bat. He was, for much of his career, the best batsman in the world. His opponents also feared greatly his ability to bowl fast left-arm, swinging the new ball at pace either way. Ted Dexter was here caught behind off the ball which left the right-hander in the Oval Test of 1963 (non-striker Phil Sharpe, umpire Syd Buller).*

Left and above left *Gibbs the bowler, on his way to eleven wickets against England at Old Trafford in 1963: Barrington was bowled for 8 and Close was caught by Sobers at slip.*

handed batsman who hit the ball with explosive power, supported by a brilliant pair of opening batsmen in Greenidge and Fredericks, later succeeded by another useful player in Haynes, and a batting craftsman of rare polish in Alvin Kallicharran, almost a left-handed Rohan Kanhai.

If Holding was the fastest of the bowlers, he was not necessarily the most hostile. Andy Roberts from Antigua, the first Test cap from that hitherto unfashionable cricket island, was very quick off a shortish run-up, and intelligent too. Bernard Julien, left-arm fast-medium, and Vanburn Holder, right-arm, honest and persistent, looked very good bowlers on their day, but bigger and better ones soon followed them off the Caribbean production-line: Colin Croft from Guyana; the man mountain, Joel 'Big Bird' Garner from Barbados (six feet eight inches tall and remorselessly accurate); the barrel-chested Sylvester Clarke; the whippy, athletic Malcolm Marshall, another Bajan; Winston Davis; Eldine Baptiste, and so on.

The great off-spinner, the lean and sinewy Lance Gibbs, had retired before the era of World Cups and one-day internationals had really got into its stride, but sadly it is questionable whether that matchwinning bowler, with his 309 wickets in Tests, would have been picked in the current West Indies team for limited-overs games. Perhaps he would even struggle for a place in the Test side. Three useful off-spinners, Albert Padmore, Derrick Parry and Roger Harper, have had little opportunity at the highest level because of the strategy of assault and battery, though by 1984 Harper appeared to have made himself an indispensable member of the team.

No holds barred: Croft giving the bouncer treatment to hapless Australians Kim Hughes (above) and Bruce Laird.

A quiet but significant influence on West Indies cricket during the period after retirement of Sir Frank Worrell was the wicket-keeper from Trinidad, Deryck Murray, a thoughtful man and undemonstrative character who first played Test cricket under Worrell in England in 1963 and continued to serve under Sobers and Lloyd. He was prominent in securing better financial terms for the team and in forming a West Indian Players' Association.

The big money available to Test cricketers from the late 1970s certainly helped to concentrate the minds of the top West Indian players. They became less mercurial, and under Lloyd's phlegmatic captaincy seemed capable, nine times out of ten, of rising to the challenge of major matches and proving their supremacy.

The poor West Indian record in Australia has been avenged in recent years by Clive Lloyd's powerful team. Lloyd holds the Frank Worrell Trophy in 1980 after victory at Adelaide. The trophy was presented by the Australian Cricket Board after the Worrell/Benaud series of 1960–61.

Professional on the field, happy-go-lucky off it. Desmond Haynes (centre) sums up the infectious West Indian joie de vivre *in the dressing-room at Adelaide in 1980.*

The great increase in the number of Test matches, and the growing tendency for players from overseas to spend their own close seasons in England, playing either in one of the leagues of the North country or in county cricket, led to a gradual evening of standards in international cricket during the 1970s, with notable improvements by New Zealand and the two countries from the Sub-Continent of India.

India and Pakistan had always been difficult to beat on their home pitches, especially when the matting wickets of old gave way to very slow pitches of assiduously rolled and deeply baked mud on which it was difficult to achieve a result. Overseas, however, the failure of these countries to produce a significant number of genuinely fast bowlers handicapped them in the field and their batsmen used to be undone either

Cricket relations between India and Pakistan were broken off for many years for political reasons but have since been resumed with frequent exchanges between the two. The majority of matches have been drawn. Here, in their first-ever Test, at Delhi in October 1952, Vinoo Mankad is bowled by Khan Mohammad for 11. India recovered to win the game by an innings.

by the extra movement afforded by greener wickets in England or by the extra bounce of the pitches in Australia and the West Indies.

Pakistan, in fact, did not take long to win a Test in England, the masterly medium-fast swing and cut bowling of Fazal Mahmood being mainly responsible for a surprise victory over an experimental England side at The Oval on their first tour in 1954. It took them twenty-eight years to record another win in England and such was the funereal pace of cricket in

their own country they had to wait another two years before registering their first home win against England, at Karachi in 1984. Yet in the years between they produced a whole series of world-class batsmen, most of whom played the game with marvellous flair and a combination of quick eyes, quick feet and steely wrists which has been as characteristic of the Pathans on the cricket fields as it has been on the squash courts.

Hanif Mohammad, the first of his country's great batsmen after the partition of India in 1947, was rather untypical of what was to follow. A tiny opening batsman, his judgment of length was masterly, and he could play all the shots if he wanted to, but the lasting memory is of a monumental patience which ground down the spirits of opposing bowlers and often bored spectators to distraction. Three of his brothers also played Test cricket-Wazir, Mushtaq and Sadiq, the best of them being Mushtaq who, in addition to his wristy brilliance as a batsman, was also a high-class leg-spin bowler.

The most prolific of the other outstanding Pakistan batsmen has been the bespectacled Zaheer Abbas, a stroke-player of silky smoothness who bats like an artist drawing a series of graceful curves on a green canvas. Such is the flexibility of his wrists that one often seems to see the bat bending in his hands, as if it is a pliable wand rather than a solid chunk of wood. Though he has never descended to the utilitarian, Zaheer has been quite ruthless in his command of opposing bowlers, quite prodigious in his appetite for runs. In his second Test match he hit 274 against England at Edgbaston and he has scored two hundreds in the same match on a record eight occasions. Another world record is his extraordinary feat of four times hitting a double hundred and a hundred in the same match.

Other world-class cricketers from Pakistan have included Asif Iqbal, Intikhab Alam, Javed Miandad and the princely looking Imran Khan, a magnificent all-round cricketer worshipped by female followers of the game for his proud good looks and fine physique and respected by all his opponents. It was his emergence as a fast bowler of searing pace in combination with Sarfraz Nawaz, a canny fast-medium bowler of great perseverence and engagingly eccentric character which, backed up by a genius leg-spin and googly bowler in Abdul Qadir, made Pakistan a match for anyone in the early 1980s.

Indian cricketers are generally less spectacular than their Moslem neighbours but they too have been able to compete with everyone on equal terms in all conditions in recent years because of the proliferation of Tests and one-day internationals. In Sunil Gavaskar from Bombay, the country has produced the most

Looking younger than his 19 years, the infant prodigy Hanif Mohammad clips a ball to fine leg early in the 1954 tour. Tiny of height and build, he was yet to prove the patient master of most of the fast bowlers who hurled the ball at him over the ensuing years, hitting 12 Test hundreds in 55 matches and scoring the highest individual innings in first-class cricket, 499.

An irresistible appeal. Abdul Qadir, by far the best leg-spinner in the world in the early 1980s, has Gower lbw in Pakistan in 1983–84.

The teams for the first official Test in England after the war, at Lord's in 1946. Back, left to right: Gul Mohamed, C. Washbrook, Abdul Hafeez, J. T. Ikin, Mr Ferguson. Standing: V. Mankad, D. C. S. Compton, C. S. Nayudu, T. F. Smailes, V. S. Hazare, A. V. Bedser, R. S. Modi, J. Hardstaff, S. G. Shinde, D. V. P. Wright. Seated: Mr P. Gupta (manager), L. Hutton, L. Armanath, Col Rait-Kerr, The Nawab of Pataudi (capt. of India), W. R. Hammond (capt. of England), V. Merchant, P. A. Gibb, D. D. Hindlekar, E. R. T. Holmes (a selector). Front: D. Brookes (reserve), S. W. Sohoni (reserve).

Right *India's unexpected but well merited World Cup triumph in 1983. Kapil Dev, the captain, had been an inspiration with his vigorous all-round cricket.*

Far right *Another captain, another cup, another place. Sunil Gavaskar holds aloft the Asian Cup, won by India against Sri Lanka and Pakistan in 1984 at the splendid stadium created out of virgin desert by the enthusiasm and patronage of a wealthy Arab cricket follower, Sheikh Abdul Rehman Bukhatir (left).*

prolific Test batsman since Sir Donald Bradman. Like Bradman a small man, Gavaskar has relied on a technique of pure orthodoxy and a happy combination of natural ability, courage and concentration. Unlike Bradman he seldom took control of an opposing attack, but once set he gives bowlers the same sinking feeling that they will never be able to get him out. Gavaskar became during the 1983–84 season the first batsman to score 30 Test centuries and the highest scorer in the game's history.

The batting of Gavaskar and the shrewd, quietly effective captaincy of Ajit Wadekar, a solid left-handed batsman from Bombay, enabled India to exploit during the 1970s as talented a bunch of spin bowlers as any one nation has ever produced. Three of them, Chandra, Bedi and Prasanna, were world-class, each totally different from the others; often two of them were put on after only a few token overs from the medium-paced opening bowlers (though three of these, Abid Ali, Solkar and Ghavri enjoyed their new-ball triumphs from time to time). The leg-spinner was Bhagwat Chandrasekhar, a Southern Indian who had polio as a child which left him with a withered right arm. Somehow he turned this into an advantage,

bringing it over his shoulder at great speed and bowling a mixture of leg-breaks, top spinners and (more often) googlies at varying speed, sometimes really fast. On his day he was an irresistible matchwinner, notably when bowling his country to their first success in England in 1971 and their first in Australia in 1977–78 (12 for 104 in the match). Chandra's most dangerous accomplice was Bishen Bedi, a left-arm spin bowler of liquid grace who seemed, despite being a heavily built Sikh, to move as if on ball bearings. All the slow bowler's arts were at his command and he loved bowling, flexing his fingers with relish as he waited his turn. In support of these two, India possessed a subtle, accurate off-spin bowler in Erapalli Prasanna and, should he be out of form or favour, another highly skilled slow off-break bowler in Srinivasaraghavan Venkataraghavan. For some reason cricketers preferred to call him just Venkat.

India faded briefly when these spinners disappeared gradually from the international scene but they then produced their finest all-rounder since Vinoo Mankad in Kapil Dev, from the hitherto unfashionable cricketing State of Haryana. Tall and wiry, Kapil plays cricket with supreme vigour, bowling fast with a

Sunil Gavaskar, India's record-breaking opening batsman, a brave and superbly accomplished player. No-one has scored more Test hundreds. Here he sweeps past Mike Gatting, watched by Keith Fletcher, during a typically prolific series against England in 1981–82.

beautiful action and hitting the ball vast distances with clean power. Though he had many good players around him–Mohinder Amarnath, Madan Lal, Ravi Shastri, Sandeep Patil and the sparkling wicket-keeper, Syed Kirmani–the World Cup triumph in England in 1983 was largely Kapil's.

No country took longer to overcome an unconscious feeling of inferiority every time they took the field in a Test match than New Zealand. But the nation which had taken 26 years and 45 Test matches to record her first win achieved no fewer than eight Test victories between 1980 and 1983–84 to underline her coming of age.

The first real high point in New Zealand Test cricket came in 1961–62 when under the captaincy of the country's first great all-rounder, the muscular John Reid, a series was squared for the first time thanks to two wins in South Africa–a South African side, moreover, containing such high-class players as McGlew, McLean, Waite, Barlow, Bland, Heine, Adcock and Peter Pollock. Apart from the prolific Reid, the fast-medium bowling of Dick Motz and Frank Cameron and some doughty innings by Graham Dowling were mainly responsible for this remarkably successful tour, all the more meritorious for the fact that it was made without the services of New Zealand's other leading batsman of the time, the left-handed Bert Sutcliffe.

Nothing to match this was achieved until two more Test victories were gained away from home, one

in India and one in Pakistan during a long tour of the Orient in 1969–70. But at this stage a success against Australia and England was considered highly unlikely and it was not until the season of 1973–74 that the real breakthrough came with a victory over Australia at Christchurch. It was appropriate that the New Zealand captain on this occasion should have been Bevan Congdon, who had come close to leading New Zealand to victory over England a few months earlier at Lord's in a match in which he himself made his second successive Test score of 170-plus. Even more significant was the fact that Glenn Turner, throughout his career one of the world's best batsmen and a player hardened by regular professional experience in England, scored hundreds in both innings of a relatively low-scoring match.

Two cricketers destined to play in a later New Zealand side for whom winning became much less of a novelty were Richard Hadlee, then a very fast bowler, who developed into a brilliant all-rounder who hit the ball hard and bowled at fast-medium with a control of swing and cut matched only in his era by Dennis Lillee, and a tall all-rounder of less natural ability, Jeremy Coney, who epitomized his country's determined but relatively unsophisticated approach to cricket. Other stalwarts of the Congdon era were Hadlee's elder brother Dayle (both are sons of the former New Zealand captain Walter Hadlee), another spirited all-rounder in Vic Pollard, two talented batsmen in Brian Hastings and Mark Burgess, and a left-arm slow

New Zealand in England in 1949. Back, left to right: V.J. Scott, T.B. Burtt, F.L.H. Mooney, C. Burke, G.O. Rabone, H.B. Cave, J.R. Reid, J.A. Hayes, F.B. Smith, G.F. Cresswell. Seated: M.P. Donnelly, W.M. Wallace, W.A. Hadlee, J. Cowie, B. Sutcliffe.

bowler of quality in Hedley Howarth.

Both Richard Hadlee and his opening partner Richard Collinge, a strapping left-arm fast bowler, shared in the country's next great triumph, the first win over England, in Wellington in 1977-78. So, too, did Howarth's younger brother Geoff, a professional with Surrey who presided over a succession of fine achievements by New Zealand in the post-Packer years, when the increased number of international matches so enhanced the prospects of the once 'minor' Test nations by giving them so much more practice at the highest level. In 1979-80 New Zealand at home actually defeated the mighty West Indians 1-0 in a three-match series, though Clive Lloyd's side were tired after a long tour of Australia and played without spirit or discipline. This result, however, proved to Howarth and an increasingly confident team that they could be a match for anyone and in the space of a few months in 1983-84, New Zealand achieved their first Test victory in England (at Headingley) and then their first win over England in a rubber, inflicting at Christchurch a drubbing the like of which the Mother Country had seldom had from anyone. Bowled out for fewer than 100 runs in both innings, England went down by an innings and 132 runs to add more fuel to the boom in cricket in New Zealand.

Turner had by now retired, having played in very few Tests in the later part of his career, but Richard Hadlee had become a bigger matchwinner than ever. He had useful seam-bowling support from the faithful Ewen Chatfield (who had so nearly died on the field after swallowing his tongue when hit by a bouncer) and the strapping Lance Cairns, a canny medium-paced bowler so strong that he could hit sixes with the apparent force of a man holing a downhill putt. Howarth also had batting of requisite Test class in the left-handed openers John Wright and Bruce Edgar, another left-hander, John Reid (no relation to the former captain), and another of the country's sets of brothers, the Crowes, Jeff and the richly gifted Martin. Spinners also played a part in the success from time to time, notably the left-arm slow man Stephen Boock and the tall off-spinner, John Bracewell, whose brother Brendan had briefly looked to be a fast bowler of real potential.

All these brothers were somehow typical of the family atmosphere which has hung happily around successive New Zealand teams. Though the ruthless nature of much of post-Packer international cricket has touched New Zealand as well as every other top country, what has been lost in carefree innocence has been compensated for by a new self-respect. Success has once again been proved a sure breeder of more success.

Christchurch, 1983–84: triumph for New Zealand, almost unprecedented humiliation for England. Tony Pigott, here lbw to Cairns, had cancelled his wedding when called up to play as a replacement but need not have done so because the game was over in 12 hours and 1 minute of cricket.

No more self-doubts. New Zealand, firmly established at last as a world power in cricket, celebrate their first win on English soil at Headingley in 1983. Lance Cairns, the bowling hero of the game, clearly has no appreciation of the cost of champagne.

Opinions vary, and always will, about the relative merits of cricketers of different eras. The greater number of Test matches has made nonsense of records, at least as a yardstick by which to compare cricketers ancient and modern. Moreover, the coming of limited-overs cricket has placed a different emphasis on the skills a player is required to develop. Nowadays everyone must be a good fielder, and a good

Two smiling champions: Ian Botham and Sir Garfield Sobers at The Oval in 1982 where the younger all-round genius dismissed the older one in a sponsored charity match.

all-rounder counts for more than a specialist batsman or bowler.

Perhaps this is why the early 1980s saw the flowering of four of the greatest all-round players the game has known: from England, Ian Botham; from Pakistan, Imran Khan; from India, Kapil Dev, and from New Zealand, Richard Hadlee. When it came to limited-overs cricket, two superb batsmen, the West Indian Viv Richards and the Australian Greg Chappell,

did enough bowling to be considered all-rounders too, but in Test cricket the performances of their national teams were often either successful or not according to what Botham, Imran, Kapil or Hadlee achieved.

The best batsman of the four was Botham, a heavily built, fearless son of North country parents who had moved to Somerset. By the time he returned home early from the 1983–84 tour of New Zealand and Pakistan, Botham had packed in 67 Tests since his début in 1977, hitting 13 hundreds and taking 286 wickets. For a few years he was a medium-fast bowler of world class, able to gain very late outswing from a fine action and to bowl unchanged for long periods in even the hottest weather. His bowling lost its venom, if not its spirit, but he remained a batsman who could turn any match upside down, as indeed he did at Headingley in 1981 when his amazing display of violent driving and hooking enabled England to come back from the dead against Australia and ultimately to win the Ashes. It was one of only two occasions when a side following on in a Test has won the match. Only Jessop amongst English Test cricketers has been able to hit high-class bowling for six as often as Botham.

Of the bowlers, Hadlee is the supreme artist. Dark, lean and muscular, he began life as a fierce fast bowler but was forced by the threat of injury to turn himself into a fast-medium bowler who could bowl the genuinely quick delivery as a surprise packet. No modern bowler, except the Australian champion Dennis Lillee, has moved the ball so much as Hadlee, who more than any contemporary fast bowler gives the impression of thinking about each ball he bowls and being able to do exactly what he wants with it each time.

Hadlee's left-handed batting, based on attack, has also turned many a Test-match tide back in New Zealand's favour, though it is doubtful whether his technique is sound enough for him to hold a place in his Test side on batting alone, as any one of the other three (especially Botham and Imran Khan) could certainly do if they were forced to give up bowling.

These four modern aspirants to the mantle won a century ago by W.G. were at once products and victims of the era of commercial cricket ushered in by the Packer Revolution. By the end of the 1983–84 season all were rich and famous; but only one, Hadlee, was actually fit to play cricket. Kapil Dev and Botham were both suffering serious knee injuries; Imran had been unable to bowl properly for a year because of a stress fracture of his left shin, caused by constant jarring of the front leg on hard wickets.

It was beginning to dawn on more and more players and administrators (it had long ago done so to more objective observers) that cricket was shortening

From the left: *Imran Khan, Ian Botham, Kapil Dev and Richard Hadlee – the finest all-rounders of their era, fit to rank with the best in any period of the game.*

Champions with the bat.

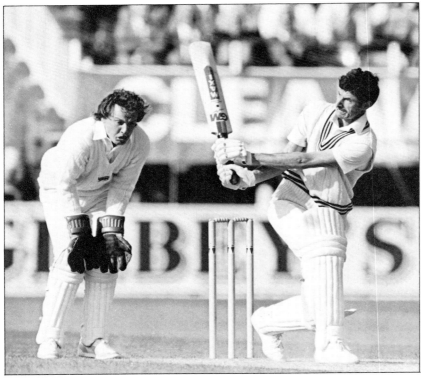

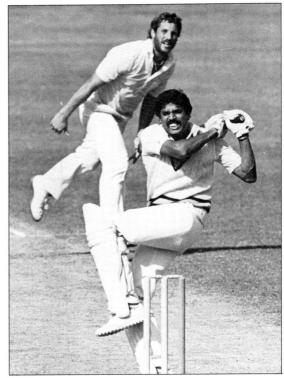

Masters with the ball.

the careers of its players and devaluing its major matches by holding far too many international contests. For financial reasons international cricket had by the 1980s subordinated all other first-class cricket. Many of the leading players actually played more internationals than they did domestic cricket in their own country. In the 1980s, quite apart from all the one-day internationals, the majority of them played in Australia, a regular Test cricketer could expect to play on average at least 12 Tests a year. England, to give one example, were scheduled to play no fewer than 26 Test matches between January 1984 and August 1985. Only a decade earlier it would have taken four or five years for a player to appear in so many.

Inevitably the sense of occasion for both players and spectators has decreased. Records have become telescoped and the increased exposure of the top players has removed the mystique they used to enjoy in the days before television when the nearest most people got to a close-up was through binoculars from the boundary's edge. Now every grin and every growl is as familiar as every square-cut and cover-drive. Unless the members of ICC voluntarily agree a maximum number of Tests and internationals each year–which will not be easy because they need the income to recoup the cost of running their own domestic game–the present overkill may be followed by general disillusionment.

ACKNOWLEDGMENTS

The publishers would like to acknowledge with thanks
the considerable help given by the Devonshire cricket
collector Roger Mann. Most of the illustrations for the
years to 1939 were selected from his extensive
collection of prints, old photographs, ephemera and
memorabilia. These illustrations were specially
reproduced for this book by Adrian Murrell who also
provided the majority of the contemporary
photographs.

The publishers would also like to thank the following
sources for their help in providing additional
illustrations. (Where there is more than one illustration
on a page, the credits start with the picture furthest to
the left and nearest the top of the page and work down
each column.)

BBC Copyright Photographs 155*b*, 156*a*
BBC Hulton Picture Library 156*c*
Central Press Agency 93*b*, 96, 98, 102*a*, 102*d*, 106,
  111*c*, 1117*c*, 125, 127*a*, 127*b*, 127*c*, 132*b*, 133*a*,
  133*c*, 135*b*, 136*b*, 138, 140*a*, 141*a*, 141*b*, 143*a*,
  143*b*, 144*b*, 146, 167*b*, 182, 186, 187, 188*a*, 188*b*,
  202, 206*a*, 206*b*, 207*a*, 207*b*, 207*c*, 214
The Cricketer 101*b*, 118*a*, 145*c*, 160*a*
Patrick Eagar 59*a*, 104*b*
Fox Photos 158
A.G. Goodchild 126
Illustrated London News 10, 48, 49, 68*b*, 69*a*, 69*c*,
  71*a*, 72*a*, 72*b*, 72*c*, 73, 82, 84-5, 97*b*, 111*a*, 1117*b*,
  139
Ken Kelly 160*b*
Keystone Press Agency 110*a*, 132*a*, 145*a*, 147, 148-9,
  189*b*, 210, 211*a*
MCC 8, 9*b*, 13*a*, 13*b*, 13*c*, 14, 15*b*, 18, 23, 24*a*, 25*a*,
  45, 51*c*, 52, 59*c*, 67*a*, 67*b*, 68*a*, 70, 71*b*, 81*a*, 81*b*,
  89*a*, 90, 102*b*, 102*d*, 110*a*, 122*a*
S & G Press Agency 117*a*, 122*b*, 123*a*, 123*b*, 124, 128,
  129, 130*a*, 130*c*, 131*a*, 131*b*, 132*b*, 133*b*, 134, 135*a*,
  136*a*, 137*a*, 137*b*, 140*b*, 142, 144*a*, 145*b*, 150*a*, .
  152, 153*a*, 153*b*, 154, 155*a*, 156*b*, 166, 189*a*, 212*a*
Syndication International 159
Bob Thomas 172*a*
Yorkshire Post 88

AY OF LIFE CRICKET-A WAY OF LIFE CRICKET-A WAY OF LIFE CRICKET-A WAY OF LIFE CRICKET-A WAY O
-A WAY OF LIFE CRICKET-A WAY OF LIFE CRICKET-A WAY OF LIFE CRICKET-A WAY OF LIFE CRICKET-A WA
ET-A WAY OF LIFE CRICKET-A WAY OF LIFE CRICKET-A WAY OF LIFE CRICKET-A WAY OF LIFE CRICKET-A
CKET-A WAY OF LIFE CRICKET-A WAY OF LIFE CRICKET-A WAY OF LIFE CRICKET-A WAY OF LIFE CRICKET
RICKET-A WAY OF LIFE CRICKET-A WAY OF LIFE CRICKET-A WAY OF LIFE CRICKET-A WAY OF LIFE CRICK
CRICKET-A WAY OF LIFE CRICKET-A WAY OF LIFE CRICKET-A WAY OF LIFE CRICKET-A WAY OF LIFE CR
FE CRICKET-A WAY OF LIFE CRICKET-A WAY OF LIFE CRICKET-A WAY OF LIFE CRICKET-A WAY OF LIFE
F LIFE CRICKET-A WAY OF LIFE CRICKET-A WAY OF LIFE CRICKET-A WAY OF LIFE CRICKET-A WAY OF LIF
Y OF LIFE CRICKET-A WAY OF LIFE CRICKET-A WAY OF LIFE CRICKET-A WAY OF LIFE CRICKET-A WAY OF
AY OF LIFE CRICKET-A WAY OF LIFE CRICKET-A WAY OF LIFE CRICKET-A WAY OF LIFE CRICKET-A WAY O
-A WAY OF LIFE CRICKET-A WAY OF LIFE CRICKET-A WAY OF LIFE CRICKET-A WAY OF LIFE CRICKET-A WA
ET-A WAY OF LIFE CRICKET-A WAY OF LIFE CRICKET-A WAY OF LIFE CRICKET-A WAY OF LIFE CRICKET-A
ICKET-A WAY OF LIFE CRICKET-A WAY OF LIFE CRICKET-A WAY OF LIFE CRICKET-A WAY OF LIFE CRICKE
CRICKET-A WAY OF LIFE CRICKET-A WAY OF LIFE CRICKET-A WAY OF LIFE CRICKET-A WAY OF LIFE CRIC
CRICKET-A WAY OF LIFE CRICKET-A WAY OF LIFE CRICKET-A WAY OF LIFE CRICKET-A WAY OF LIFE CI
IFE CRICKET-A WAY OF LIFE CRICKET-A WAY OF LIFE CRICKET-A WAY OF LIFE CRICKET-A WAY OF LIFE
F LIFE CRICKET-A WAY OF LIFE CRICKET-A WAY OF LIFE CRICKET-A WAY OF LIFE CRICKET-A WAY OF LIF
Y OF LIFE CRICKET-A WAY OF LIFE CRICKET-A WAY OF LIFE CRICKET-A WAY OF LIFE CRICKET-A WAY OF
WAY OF LIFE CRICKET-A WAY OF LIFE CRICKET-A WAY OF LIFE CRICKET-A WAY OF LIFE CRICKET-A WAY
-A WAY OF LIFE CRICKET-A WAY OF LIFE CRICKET-A WAY OF LIFE CRICKET-A WAY OF LIFE CRICKET-A W
KET-A WAY OF LIFE CRICKET-A WAY OF LIFE CRICKET-A WAY OF LIFE CRICKET-A WAY OF LIFE CRICKET-
RICKET-A WAY OF LIFE CRICKET-A WAY OF LIFE CRICKET-A WAY OF LIFE CRICKET-A WAY OF LIFE CRICK
CRICKET-A WAY OF LIFE CRICKET-A WAY OF LIFE CRICKET-A WAY OF LIFE CRICKET-A WAY OF LIFE CRIC
E CRICKET-A WAY OF LIFE CRICKET-A WAY OF LIFE CRICKET-A WAY OF LIFE CRICKET-A WAY OF LIFE C
LIFE CRICKET-A WAY OF LIFE CRICKET-A WAY OF LIFE CRICKET-A WAY OF LIFE CRICKET-A WAY OF LIFE
F LIFE CRICKET-A WAY OF LIFE CRICKET-A WAY OF LIFE CRICKET-A WAY OF LIFE CRICKET-A WAY OF LI
Y OF LIFE CRICKET-A WAY OF LIFE CRICKET-A WAY OF LIFE CRICKET-A WAY OF LIFE CRICKET-A WAY OF
WAY OF LIFE CRICKET-A WAY OF LIFE CRICKET-A WAY OF LIFE CRICKET-A WAY OF LIFE CRICKET-A WAY
T-A WAY OF LIFE CRICKET-A WAY OF LIFE CRICKET-A WAY OF LIFE CRICKET-A WAY OF LIFE CRICKET-A W
KET-A WAY OF LIFE CRICKET-A WAY OF LIFE CRICKET-A WAY OF LIFE CRICKET-A WAY OF LIFE CRICKET-
RICKET-A WAY OF LIFE CRICKET-A WAY OF LIFE CRICKET-A WAY OF LIFE CRICKET-A WAY OF LIFE CRICK
CRICKET-A WAY OF LIFE CRICKET-A WAY OF LIFE CRICKET-A WAY OF LIFE CRICKET-A WAY OF LIFE CRI
E CRICKET-A WAY OF LIFE CRICKET-A WAY OF LIFE CRICKET-A WAY OF LIFE CRICKET-A WAY OF LIFE
LIFE CRICKET-A WAY OF LIFE CRICKET-A WAY OF LIFE CRICKET-A WAY OF LIFE CRICKET-A WAY OF LIFE
F LIFE CRICKET-A WAY OF LIFE CRICKET-A WAY OF LIFE CRICKET-A WAY OF LIFE CRICKET-A WAY OF LI
Y OF LIFE CRICKET-A WAY OF LIFE CRICKET-A WAY OF LIFE CRICKET-A WAY OF LIFE CRICKET-A WAY OF
WAY OF LIFE CRICKET-A WAY OF LIFE CRICKET-A WAY OF LIFE CRICKET-A WAY OF LIFE CRICKET-A WAY
T-A WAY OF LIFE CRICKET-A WAY OF LIFE CRICKET-A WAY OF LIFE CRICKET-A WAY OF LIFE CRICKET-A W
KET-A WAY OF LIFE CRICKET-A WAY OF LIFE CRICKET-A WAY OF LIFE CRICKET-A WAY OF LIFE CRICKET-
ICKET-A WAY OF LIFE CRICKET-A WAY OF LIFE CRICKET-A WAY OF LIFE CRICKET-A WAY OF LIFE CRICK
CRICKET-A WAY OF LIFE CRICKET-A WAY OF LIFE CRICKET-A WAY OF LIFE CRICKET-A WAY OF LIFE CRI
E CRICKET-A WAY OF LIFE CRICKET-A WAY OF LIFE CRICKET-A WAY OF LIFE CRICKET-A WAY OF LIFE C
LIFE CRICKET-A WAY OF LIFE CRICKET-A WAY OF LIFE CRICKET-A WAY OF LIFE CRICKET-A WAY OF LIFE
F LIFE CRICKET-A WAY OF LIFE CRICKET-A WAY OF LIFE CRICKET-A WAY OF LIFE CRICKET-A WAY OF LIF
Y OF LIFE CRICKET-A WAY OF LIFE CRICKET-A WAY OF LIFE CRICKET-A WAY OF LIFE CRICKET-A WAY OF
WAY OF LIFE CRICKET-A WAY OF LIFE CRICKET-A WAY OF LIFE CRICKET-A WAY OF LIFE CRICKET-A WAY
T-A WAY OF LIFE CRICKET-A WAY OF LIFE CRICKET-A WAY OF LIFE CRICKET-A WAY OF LIFE CRICKET-A W